The Price of Life

Also by Jenny Kleeman

Sex Robots & Vegan Meat

The Price of Life

In Search of What We're Worth and Who Decides

JENNY KLEEMAN

PICADOR

First published 2024 by Picador
an imprint of Pan Macmillan
The Smithson, 6 Briset Street, London EC1M 5NR
EU representative: Macmillan Publishers Ireland Ltd, 1st Floor,
The Liffey Trust Centre, 117–126 Sheriff Street Upper,
Dublin 1, D01 YC43
Associated companies throughout the world
www.panmacmillan.com

ISBN 978-1-0350-0496-6 HB
ISBN 978-1-0350-0497-3 TPB

1 3 5 7 9 8 6 4 2

A CIP catalogue record for this book is available from the British Library.

Typeset in Warnock Pro by Palimpsest Book Production Ltd, Falkirk, Stirlingshire

Printed and bound by CPI Group (UK) Ltd, Croydon, CR0 4YY

For my parents, David and Manou

Contents

Preface

There are numbers on your head. They have been there since before you were born. They will change over the course of your life, depending on who you happen to be and what happens to you. You will die, but the numbers will remain, sometimes for years after you're gone. Your life will depend on them. They will determine what you are worth, and whether your life is worth saving.

We like to think that human beings can't be bought, but that doesn't mean no price can be put on a human life. The cost of saving a life, creating a life, taking a life or compensating for a life taken is routinely calculated and put into practice by philanthropists, judges, police chiefs, businesses, charities, actuaries, healthcare providers, policymakers and criminals. They each use their own formulae and come up with wildly different final numbers, but two things unite them: they are all prepared to use dispassionate logic to quantify what's supposed to be incalculable, and they generally want to keep their numbers quiet.

If you think you can't put a value on life – that it's priceless, and trying to work out what a person is worth is crass and gross – think again, because the people who, every day, set the price of your life don't have these misgivings. Our squeamishness only helps them to get on with their business unchallenged.

Isn't it better to know who these people are, what they think we're worth, and how they came up with the price tags?

The prices put on human lives today tend to be implicit, revealed in everyday decisions rather than bid out loud in public auctions like the slave markets of Ancient Rome. Every time a life-saving measure is judged to be too expensive – a piece of cutting-edge medical research, a product recall on a faulty car, or a new childproof cap on a bottle of bleach, putting more lifeboats on the *Titanic*, or keeping hard shoulders on our motorways instead of turning them into extra lanes – we reveal the limits of what we think a human life is worth. The deaths that subsequently occur have been factored in as acceptable when weighed against the cost of preventing them. The moment we stop being happy to pay to save a life is when we reveal the price that we're comfortable paying for one.

This kind of calculation may feel morally repellent, but in a world of finite resources, you've got to stop somewhere. If we were willing to spend unlimited sums to save one person's life, other people would die from lack of food or medicine as a result. If you truly value life, it can't be priceless. But how you determine where to stop, and therefore what the price is, is very much up for debate.

Economists, who specialize in cost–benefit analysis and uncomfortable trade-offs, have been putting a monetary value on lives for years. From the mid-twentieth century, technocratic approaches to government – where a scientific method is applied to social problems – began to dominate in the US and Europe, and analysis of costs and benefits became a fundamental part of making life-or-death decisions. If we apply rational, quantitative methods to ethical choices and policymaking, so the thinking goes, we can come up with something that is objectively right and best for everyone, rather than something clouded by emotion and politics. The right way can be found through numbers.

In the twenty-first century, quantities matter as much as qualities when it comes to measuring and comparing human experiences; sometimes they matter more. We increasingly look to data to provide us with objective answers to even the knottiest ethical questions. An ever-growing number of judgements are being left to formulae and algorithms, from which crimes to prosecute to which YouTube videos to ban to which needy people most deserve the money of the world's billionaires. Life now comes with a score. Your worth as a person can be reduced to likes, views and follows; your well-being to the number of steps you take a day and the hours your smartwatch tells you you've slept. Numbers require less effort to process and decode than feelings. Quantification makes for easy comparison, and also for monetization.

The quantification of everything has crept in without us noticing. Huge parts of our lives are being governed by philosophies and methodologies that a small number of people have developed and articulated, without us being aware of it, or having chosen it, or voted for it. While the number of metrics grows, gaps between them remain, the things we can't quantify – yet. What if the view count on your post comes from people laughing at you and not with you? What if most of your followers enjoy hating you and carry on following so they can find reasons to hate you more? We are wising up to the dangers of overconfidence in quantitative data: that numbers aren't necessarily neutral; that calculations can be loaded in favour of the mindset and motivation of the people who came up with the formulae.

I am not a numbers person. I am not an economist, an actuary or a statistician. There's barely any maths in this book. Think of this as a non-numbers person's guide to the prices. My job is to talk to people and hear their stories. And while I can't be dispassionate about my encounters with them, I have started to realize that to understand human beings today, and the injustices we face, we need to explore how the prices of our lives are determined. I am going to take you into different worlds where the basis of those figures is revealed.

My adventure with these numbers began just before the pandemic, in November 2019, when I was inspired to fly across the Atlantic to investigate the price of saving a life, as recognized by the wealthiest philanthropists on the planet. Back then – to me – any approach that sought to calculate it seemed like an incredibly hard-hearted way of doing good. But, within a few months, thanks to Covid-19, every nation on the planet would be undertaking cost–benefit analyses about the price of life, and every citizen would be asking the same uncomfortable questions. How much should the economy suffer to save lives? Is it right for some to make huge sacrifices so that others don't die? Are some lives worth more than others? Determined to try to answer these questions, I embarked on a journey that took me into dark yet illuminating territory, to places that were often preposterous, and sometimes surprisingly funny.

This book tells the story of twelve prices put on a life, but it's really a book about people: encounters with characters, not numbers. I will look at the person or people who came up with these prices, how they did it and why, and also what it's like to be the individual at the other end of their calculations. I'll use each price tag as an entry point into different ethical dilemmas. Talking about money can be a grubby business, particularly if you've grown up with British sensibilities. Americans are much better at it, which is why I make several trips to the US to uncover the figures.

These twelve numbers vary enormously. Sometimes your age,

nationality, race, sex, gender or sexual orientation will make a huge difference to the price put on your life; sometimes the price will be painfully equal for everyone. Who pays these prices? Taxpayers, businesses, the charitable foundations of the super-rich or insurance companies? The depth of the pockets being delved into matters as much as the lives being saved, taken, created and sold.

We'll start off by looking at the cost of taking lives, and compensating for a life lost; this is where criminals, governments and the insurance industry come into play. This is followed by the creation of life: the cost of biological parenthood, wanted or unwanted. And then the cost of saving a life, which is the kind of territory where economists and moral philosophers are most comfortable. We'll investigate the cost of a human being – where a price is explicitly put on a specific person's life – because, no matter what we like to tell ourselves, human beings can be bought, after all. We'll finish, appropriately, with the price of a life after death – the price of a human body.

My twelve prices are not the only values to be put on human lives; this is not a comprehensive list. I've chosen these specific figures because of the contrasts they reveal about how human life is evaluated in different circumstances. The numbers themselves are a snapshot of a particular time: most of the prices will go up and down, according to inflation and market forces. The point is not the numbers themselves, but what the differences between them can tell us about what matters, and who matters.

These numbers will reveal hidden and sometimes uncomfortable truths about who and what we really value. They will expose fault lines, prejudices, exploitation and unfairness. Some of the numbers will be cruelly unequal, others will be brutally standardized. They will demonstrate the limitations of our governments, our societies, our morals. And the pursuit of them will lead me to ask questions that make me squirm, and reveal injustices to people who have already suffered more than I could bear.

In a world obsessed with numbers, the quality of things can get lost. I'm determined to put human experience back into the equation. Are we letting ourselves down by expecting numbers to give us answers to the toughest moral questions? Or are numbers the quickest, fairest and most pragmatic way to make decisions in a world where global catastrophic risks of competing magnitudes loom larger than ever before?

What can these prices tell us about human values, rather than monetary ones? What do we gain and what do we lose of our humanity when we put a price on life itself?

PART ONE

TAKING A LIFE

CHAPTER ONE
£15,180

The average hitman

In 2005, Bob Innes was in his early thirties and bursting with enterprising tech ideas. He owned a portfolio of thirty or so domain names that he'd buy and sell in the hope that one day he'd 'flip' one for serious money. He was taking courses at a business trade school in Santa Rosa, northern California, learning how to test networks for vulnerabilities. After graduation, he and three friends planned to start an IT security consulting business.

During a paintball game one afternoon, Bob and his buddies started to bounce domain names off each other for the smart new business they were going to run together. Inspiration struck Bob like a paintball pellet on his back. What about RentAHitman? *Rent,* as in *hire us. Hit,* as in *traffic, analytics, network vulnerabilities.* He even came up with a tag line: *Rent-a-Hitman – your point and click solution.* As luck would have it, the domain was available. So he snapped up rentahitman.com.

But that's as far as the idea went. When two of his team of friends landed jobs in Texas after their graduation, the business never got off the ground. The rentahitman.com domain became just another in Bob's portfolio that he put up for auction, and he was willing to part with it for as little as $50. He made a basic homepage, bearing the image of a cartoon figure holding up a sign saying *This domain is for sale – contact@rentahitman.*com. And then he forgot about it.

By the time he remembered to check the inbox he'd created, two or three years had passed. And there, waiting for a reply, were around 300 emails from all over the world, many asking the same, urgent kinds of questions. *Do you operate in my country? Do you perform asset extraction? Are you hiring?*

Bob had no idea what to do with these messages. He didn't reply to any of them, but was intrigued by them, astonished that so many people were prepared to go to the trouble of taking down the address from the cartoon and composing an email in search of murder for hire. He began to keep a regular eye on the inbox.

Then, in 2010, a message arrived from a British woman called Helen. She said she was stranded in Canada, irate at three family members who had 'screwed her out of her inheritance', and she was very persistent: her first email came at 9 a.m., and her second, at 4 p.m., had the subject line 'URGENT', and detailed the names and addresses of the people she wanted taken out.

Bob felt he had to engage with this woman. This time he had to respond. He wrote back with two simple questions: 'Do you still require our services?' he typed, followed by 'Would you like me to place you in contact with a field operative?' If the email bounced, or Helen didn't reply, then he would leave it there.

But Helen did reply. Yes, she said, she did still require RentAHitman's services. She gave her full name, her mobile number and the address of the Canadian hostel where she was staying, plus details of funds held in a safe deposit box. Bob spent the night checking Google Earth, MapQuest, online electoral registers, anything he could find to corroborate her story, and it all checked out: the targets were three real people living at the addresses she'd given in the Cotswolds. He printed out his research and took it to a police sergeant friend the next morning, who alerted the Canadian police so they could perform a welfare check on Helen.

'She's right where she says she's going to be. She's using her real name. The Canadian authorities are running her for warrants and they determine that she was wanted out of the UK on extraditable charges. She spent 126 days in a Canadian jail before being shipped back to the UK,' Bob tells me, shaking his head, still in disbelief. 'That's when I realized: this simple $9.20 website has just prevented the murders of three people.'

Bob's life also changed that day: he became Guido Fanelli, the catfish hitman whose flashy website has led to around a hundred police investigations and more than fifty arrests. It's a role he relishes: when we were emailing to set up this interview, he unfailingly replied as Guido, even though my emails were always addressed to Bob.

We're talking over FaceTime; he's in Vacaville, California, parked up during his lunch break. 'My real gig is in pest control. I guess you could say I'm licensed to kill,' he says, with a grin.

Rentahitman.com now has everything a very naive person in search of contract killing would want, and plenty more besides: there's a detailed service request form, customer testimonials, group and senior discount offers, and even a merchandise page where you can buy a $20 souvenir T-shirt. 'GOT A PROBLEM THAT NEEDS RESOLVING?' screams the homepage. 'THE DARK WEB IS NOT SAFE, BUT WE ARE!'

The site is obviously bullshit, but Bob tells me in the twelve years since he developed it fully he's had close to a thousand genuine inquiries. 'I got one that came in this morning that I'm going to look at when I get home. I spend fifteen to twenty hours a week on this.'

Submissions come from all over the world, from men and women of all ages. Many want their spouses or business associates taken out. Some are kids asking him to murder a school bully or a teacher. He's currently working on a case where a father 'is not happy with his son's new-found gayness and wants him dead'. He's already passed that on to the Feds.

Bob is wary of talking money with the people who contact him. 'When people have brought up how much it will cost, I always say it's between you and the field operative to discuss. I would much rather be state's best witness than a co-conspirator,' he declares solemnly. 'In the past couple of cases, the solicitor has actually struck a deal with the undercover agent for the cost, and $5,000 has been the typical figure, with a down payment of $500. Which seems *really* cheap,' he says, shaking his head again.

Every time there's an arrest linked to Bob's website, there are headlines. It doesn't take much online sleuthing to find out that Guido is Bob. If you even squint at rentahitman.com, it's clear that it's fake.

'Do you ever worry that you're just trapping the dumbest potential clients?' I ask him.

'The website does go after the low-hanging fruit,' Bob concedes. 'But if these people are seeking out the website, and taking the time to accept cookies and fill out the webform, and they *still* want to have a field operative contact them, I will help them *to the end*. If I don't get that solicitation and handle it, somebody else will.'

I can see his point. While Bob doesn't get involved in the price of taking a life, his experience shows there are a surprising number of people willing to pay it – and he only sees the most gullible ones. I think of all the people who must be considering commissioning a murder for hire right now, as we speak, their faces aglow behind their laptops.

Ever since he started monitoring that inbox, Bob tells me, he's looked at people differently. 'I was really troubled by it. How could somebody want to do this to somebody? It's scary because they walk among us. Right now, I have a case out of the very city in which I live. In fact, I've driven past that address a couple of times in the last week.' His eyes are wide. 'I started to go to church four or five years ago, just to add a little balance to my life, because I read these solicitations and they're so negative.' But amid such darkness, Bob has found his calling. 'Everybody's got a purpose in life. I guess my purpose is to continue to advocate for these people who may never even know they need it.'

If you want to find a hitman, don't google. Don't go on the dark web, either: the contract killers advertising services there are pretty much always scammers or FBI agents looking to entrap you. Real hitmen operate through criminal networks and personal connections; if you want to get in touch with one, you need to know the right people.

In my quest to discover the price of taking a life, I've spoken to ex-police officers, crime reporters and former prison governors, all of whom claim to have had the right connections at some point or other. I've sent far too many emails to the National Offender Management Service, asking for the prisoner numbers of some of Britain's most notorious murderers so I can write them letters asking about their pricing structure. They either couldn't help, or they didn't reply to me. But one night my phone rings at 10.22 p.m. It's John Alite, calling from New York.

John spent thirty years as a hitman for the Gambino dynasty – one of the notorious 'Five Families' of the Mafia that controlled organized crime in New York City – at the time when the clan was under the reign of John Gotti senior and his son. John Alite's Albanian heritage meant he could only ever be an associate of the Mafia: only Italians can become 'made' men. John worked for the mob from when he was a teenager until 2003, when he got word that the FBI was closing in on him and decided to go on the run. Interpol tracked him down to Copacabana and arrested him on murder, kidnap and racketeering charges. He spent two years in a wretched Brazilian jail before being flown back in chains to the US in 2006. Hearing that Gotti Jr and many of his old associates had been informing against him, John made a deal with the prosecutors: he'd plead guilty and testify against members of the mob in exchange for leniency. He got a ten-year sentence.

Now fifty-nine, John has put his criminal life behind him. He's a motivational speaker, an author and a youth advocate. He's also the host of several podcasts (*Mafia Truths, The Alite Show*, and *The Mob, The Mafia and The Man*) and that's why he's happy to talk to me: he knows I've been a guest on Joe Rogan's podcast, and wants to know if I'll introduce them. It turns out I do know the right people, after all.

A few weeks later, I arrive at the Club A Steakhouse in Manhattan, on the border of the Upper East Side and Midtown East. I'm early, but John is already there, waiting upstairs in a pale designer suit, with a striped black and cream silk handkerchief folded in his breast pocket. His black shirt is unbuttoned enough to reveal a hint of faded neck tattoo and a glint of gold medallion. There are flecks of white in his hair, but he looks

At dinner with John Alite.

young for nearly sixty, with the broad shoulders of someone who still spends a lot of time working out. He flashes a dazzling smile of expensive teeth, and motions for me to take a seat next to him on the red devoré banquette. I am determined not to glamorize John, or glorify the world that he represents, but he's asked me to meet him in a haunt that looks like something out of *Goodfellas*, and he's come dressed like a character straight out of central casting.

John orders us both steaks (he likes a filet mignon, medium) and martinis (dirty). Bruno, who owns this place, is also Albanian, and treats John like a king. John tells me he used to do business from here sometimes, and Bruno would bring up a corded telephone for him to use at his table.

'I started working with violence since about, I guess, 1978,' he begins, as if he were an artist describing how he found his medium. A sports betting operation was being run out of a deli in Queens where he worked as a teenager, and John was recruited to fetch takings for the mob there. 'While I was still a good kid, I was collecting for Lucchese, a gangster. He asked me to collect with a little bit of violence, so it started then.' John was a talented baseball player at school, and won a baseball scholarship to the University of Tampa, but his dreams of going pro were thwarted by injury. His skills with a bat made him particularly attractive in his fallback career as a mob enforcer.

'In the mob world, everything you're doing revolves around money. It's not about personality – who you like, dislike – it's always around finances. So, when you're hurting somebody, it has something to do with either someone not paying loan shark money, union money dues, or shakedown money from an operation they're running,' he explains, as sizzling porterhouse steaks are delivered to the tables around us. 'Whoever my boss may be at the time, if they're asking me to go and collect money from somebody, you're not asking questions, you just go and do what your superiors tell you to do.'

John says he killed people over debts that could be as small as $1,000. It was never about the sums owed, he tells me; it was about enforcing the mob's authority. 'If you read *The Art of War* and Machiavelli, these books all explain that, to rule, you have to rule with fear. What people fear is *violence*. And if I'm the guy doing the violence, I'm the one that's in control.' It's an image he clearly still cultivates, along with the cream suit and silk handkerchief. 'There's two things they respect in the street: the ability of making money and the ability of taking someone's life. And if you're good at those two things, you're going to be the guy calling the shots.'

The thick steaks arrive: charred on the outside, yielding and bloody within. John has creamed spinach instead of fries and doesn't touch the breadbasket: he's watching his waistline.

'How many people have you killed?' I ask, the words surreal and absurd as soon as they leave my mouth. The first glow of dirty martini is in my veins, and I can't quite believe I'm here, having a steak dinner with a killer.

'My answer in court was, I'm not a computer, I didn't know I had to keep count,' John replies, with a wave of his hand. He pleaded guilty to charges that included two murders, four murder conspiracies and eight shootings. He probably shot forty men, he tells me now, but didn't keep track of how many of them subsequently died. Then there were the ones he killed by other means. 'I batted the first guy I killed with a baseball bat. He was a vegetable, they had him on life support, and I'm not sure why they didn't charge me with that murder – they were aware of it.' In total, he thinks he was responsible for taking well over a dozen lives with guns and baseball bats.

John was never expected to provide his bosses with evidence that the jobs had been done. Gotti Jr sometimes liked to come out and take a look at the scene of the crime, John says, but it was more out of morbid curiosity than anything else. 'They were almost impressed – mesmerized by what you do that they *can't* do. I think they wanted to feel like they're part of it, for some reason.'

And then John starts talking about Gotti Jr, and it's impossible to stop him. There is no love lost between them. When Junior was prosecuted for racketeering, drug trafficking and conspiracy to murder, John testified against him, but a jury failed to reach a verdict four times in five years, and the judge declared a mistrial in 2009. Whenever he is asked about John, Gotti Jr describes a rat and a fabulist who is cashing in on exaggerated tales of his gangsterism; John points out that 'the timeline is undeniable': Junior ratted on him by speaking to the Feds when John was still in prison in Brazil, remaining silent and loyal. He explains all this assuming that I'm familiar with all the big names in the Mafia canon. He is used to being surrounded by people either steeped in that world or utterly fascinated by it. I try to take it all in and nod in the right places.

John earned himself the street nickname 'The Calculator'. 'I was good with numbers,' he explains. He passed the Series 7 stockbroker's test, but the burgeoning criminal record he'd been cultivating since his teens meant he couldn't get very far on Wall Street. His business acumen made him a particularly effective hitman. 'Any dummy can hurt somebody – you've got to have the attributes of being intelligent. In the street you don't find a lot of smart guys.'

He orders another dirty martini for himself, and I ask him about prices. 'There isn't a fee for your services, but there's *opportunity* because of your services,' he explains. 'So, if a nightclub is going to open up and there's guys looking to get involved with that nightclub, you'll be the first guy involved. The opportunities are different for you when you're successful at what you do.'

There were 'union no-show' jobs – where he would get paid a salary and benefits for doing nothing at all. He had nightclubs in three states, and parking lots and valet businesses in six states. There were catering halls, candy stores, glass companies, all sorts of real estate investments. 'By me doing what I did, there would be phone calls made to people that owned the establishments to tell them that John's coming by, give him your contracts for the lease on your lots, or make a deal with him to purchase your property so he can use it.'

Determined to get the numbers, I ask how much money those opportunities earned him in total.

He leans back. 'Well, put it this way, my parking company was sold at 17.6 million. I had four nightclubs – the last one I lost was making about three to four million a year. I owned an estate on Route 73 and Vorhees' – in New Jersey – 'that's worth about ten million now. I lost that. I had houses in Manhattan that were worth a couple of million. I had properties in Princeton in New Jersey. I lost everything, or I sold it real fast for a penny on the dollar before the government took it. I made millions, I spent a couple of million on lawyers, I sent a million to a guy in Brazil when I was trying to hide money and he took it and cooperated and helped Gotti put me in prison. So I never got that money back. But I made, I don't know, one hundred million?'

If John's telling the truth, that would mean each hit was implicitly worth millions of dollars to him. But John never put price tags on the lives of the individuals he killed. He didn't think about their lives at all.

'Since I was three years old, I was groomed as a fighter by my father, to be successful and not to be bullied. My father comes from Albania – it was a rough, third-world, kind of communist country. He wanted to make me tough. At a very early age, I learned a detachment from violence and blood because I grew up in it. I was never haunted by what I saw, what I did. There was no feeling about it. It was just another day at the office for me, unfortunately.' He sinks a gulp of martini and lowers his voice. 'The problem is, after you're not doing that anymore, there's a haunting. There's a consequence for everything you do in life. Just like anything else, there's a bill at the end. Eventually you're going to have to pay. The bill is for me now.'

'What price are you paying?' I ask.

'You don't sleep well. You have thoughts of some of the

family members. You may come off like you're fine but you have some psychological issues. I have PTSD. I think that anybody that's seen the amount of action and blood that I've seen . . . it's not a normal human thing that you're dealing with.' He has reached out to the families of some of the people he's killed, met up with their children, cried with them, he tells me. 'I'm still the same person – don't get me wrong, I have the capability of killing at any moment if I wanted to. I don't want to.'

John now makes his living recounting stories about his criminal past. Much of what he's telling me over dinner is a cascade of mobster names, places and numbers that I know are supposed to impress me, but I'm no Mafia obsessive, and most of it goes over my head. And some of his numbers don't stack up. He says he's spent eighteen years in prison in total, and served eight and a half of his ten-year sentence, but this doesn't tally with being extradited in 2006 and released, as he was, in 2013. It would be naive to take this former gangster at his word. But there's a thoughtfulness to John, a warmth and an openness that makes him seem sincere, even gentle. At this moment, over our shared dinner, it feels impossible to me that the man sitting next to me on the banquette could have killed anyone at all. He's clearly either a reformed man or a talented operator. He's probably both.

Despite what John might be telling me about the psychological burden of the crimes he committed, it wasn't guilt that made John face up to what he'd done: it was betrayal. He had been determined to give up everything to keep the promises he made to the Gambino family, such was his loyalty. He had abandoned his wife and children to be a fugitive. Languishing in a Brazilian jail and facing the death penalty on extradition, he had been prepared to die for the mob, he says.

'One after another, every made guy in the Gambino family was talking against me. I'm sitting in the penitentiary in a third-world country, getting tortured while these guys are all making deals with the FBI. I said, "OK. The loyalty I give, by leaving my children and my family, I'm not receiving." I'm an Albanian that's actually doing the violence that these guys aren't capable of doing, yet when there's a problem they point the finger at me. My life was a lie in that world. I believed in rules that didn't exist.'

Prison changed him, he says. He was baptized while he was in jail. He decided he wanted to be present for his three sons and his daughter. And when he was on parole he started giving talks to inner-city kids alongside former FBI officers and chiefs of police, warning them of the dangers of making the wrong choices in life. He discovered he had a talent for this kind of motivational speaking, and found it rewarding. 'I've been doing it for a decade now. I'm dedicated to saving each kid.' He tells them they need to find a healthy way of getting an adrenaline rush. 'Whether that is going ice skating or going out with a group of guys and playing ball, boxing in the ring. Find a new hobby. If you want a rush, jump out of an airplane. (Not for me – I'm scared of heights.)'

He smiles at me.

John's a grandfather now. His eldest son is thirty-two, and in prison, John says, after he was found asleep in his car with a gun he uses for protection in case any of his dad's old enemies should turn up.

'Are you scared of repercussions for speaking so openly?' I ask.

He flashes another dazzling grin.

'Not at *all*. You know why? First off – we all die sometime. And second, the guys in the mob world – most of them are frauds. They're nepotism kids, it's like a father and son union almost now. I was a killer. If anyone gets in the ring with me, I'm still that same guy. I don't fear anybody at all.'

We don't order dessert, but Bruno brings it anyway: a trio of profiteroles, chocolate cake and tiramisu for us to share, on the house. John forgets about his diet. Bruno takes a photo of us sitting together, prints it out, mounts it on card and gives it to me as a souvenir. It's as if I've just taken a ride in a theme park.

'John,' I ask, 'do you think we romanticize gangsters?'

'A hundred per cent. I lived in the real world out on the street where it's dangerous. I've seen blood and I've seen tears. The reason why people fantasize about this stuff is that they really don't grasp the reality of it. They don't see the actual bodies. They're not actually seeing the person's last breath. They don't see that on TV. If I brought some of these people with me when I was actually killing somebody with baseball bats across the head, the screams, the blood, and you've got blood all over yourself, then they wouldn't be so keen on romanticizing that life.'

'You sell signed baseball bats on your website, don't you?' I say. 'Do you make a good income out of that?'

'Yeah, I make good,' he says, with another wave of his hand. 'Listen, I've been a businessman my whole life. They called me *The Calculator*. I understand how to market myself. Some people buy the bats because I was a great ball player, other people buy them because I battered people. Whatever their reason for buying the bat, that's their thinking process – I can't change that – but I'm a businessman and I believe in capitalism, I want to make money legitimately. I'm not committing crime anymore and it's just the way I make money.'

I had planned to pay for dinner but John won't let me, which makes me uncomfortable, but he is really insistent, and it's clearly not up for discussion. He worries about me taking the subway back to my hotel and tells me I have to take a cab. He waits outside the steakhouse until my Uber arrives, and then leans in through the driver's window to tell him to take care of me. We say goodbye and shake hands. He has remarkably soft palms.

John may not have had a price list, but some Mafia hitmen do. When Italian nightclub bouncer and hitman Giancarlo Orsini informed on his Mafia bosses in exchange for leniency, he told prosecutors in Rome he'd been paid €3,500 (around £3,000) to kneecap sixty-one-year-old beautician Cinzia Pugliese outside her tanning salon in July 2013, plus €17,000 (£14,500) to kill cocaine dealer Federico Di Meo in September of the same year, and €25,000 (£21,000), shared between him and an accomplice, to kill loan shark Sesto Corvini in his van that October. Orsini would travel to his target on a scooter, wearing a helmet and sunglasses, before shooting precisely five times. It was his trademark. 'There were always two parts to me, there was the one who could watch from a distance and the one who wanted to remain human,' Orsini said at the time.

I know about Orsini and his prices because his story was published in the Italian press. No country releases official data on contract killings, who commits them and what they get paid. Criminologists seeking to understand the economics of murder for hire have to rely on the details revealed in court documents and news reports when hitmen are brought to justice. Just as Bob's website catches the low-hanging fruit among those who want to commission murder, our public understanding of hitmen is based on the ones who don't get away with it.

'My research acknowledges that, in a sense, I'm looking at failures,' Professor David Wilson tells me. 'I'm probably looking at hitmen who aren't very successful, aren't very skilled, and therefore what they might charge is as a consequence quite low. The most successful hitmen – obviously I could never meet them, because they didn't get arrested, they didn't get stopped.'

David is emeritus professor of criminology and the founding director of the Centre for Applied Criminology at Birmingham City University. He's also a bit of a murder celebrity, and his jowly, sombre face will be familiar to any British true crime aficionado. He's written at least ten books on murder, including *My Life With Murderers,* his memoir of how he moved from prison governor to top criminologist; he presents his own TV show, *David Wilson's Crime Files,* on BBC Scotland; and he's ringing me up early in the morning because he's on location in Dundee, shooting another series of *In the Footsteps of Killers,* the Channel 4 true crime series he presents alongside *Silent Witness* actress Emilia Fox.

He has written several academic papers on hitmen, but the one we're talking about today, *The British Hitman 1974–2013*, specifically examines the going rate for murder for hire. It is one of the few pieces of research into the price of taking a life in a contract killing.

David's team trawled through thirty-nine years of newspaper archives and compiled a list of twenty-seven hits in England, Scotland and Wales, committed by a total of thirty-five people (there were more hitmen than murders because some worked in teams). They consulted court transcripts and conducted off-the-record briefings with offenders, ex-offenders and current and former employees of the criminal justice system to find out as much as they could about each specific hit. They found that the average British hitman was male and thirty-eight years old, that his victim had an average age of thirty-six, and that the average price of a hit was £15,180. 'That's what it would cost you to buy a small second-hand family car,' David points out dryly.

Some context, before we go any further: their sample size is small, the hits occurred over several decades yet the data isn't adjusted for inflation and the sums they found ranged from £200 to £100,000 a hit. 'The figures that we came up with had a wide disparity, but it masked a cost that was frankly within everybody's reach. If you wanted to commission a hit, you could commission a hit.' And people were commissioning hits for what David calls 'the most banal of reasons': business disputes, marriage breakdowns, custody battles. 'It was really rather sadly familiar and ordinary.'

The only other in-depth academic investigation into murder for hire – an analysis of 163 contract killings in Australia between 1989 and 2002, published by the Australian Institute of Criminology in 2003 – found the average price per hit to be AU$16,500, which is around £9,700. The authors found that 2 per cent of all murders in Australia had been committed for money, and that 20 per cent of hits involved disputes between former romantic partners – confirming that murder for hire is much closer to home than we might imagine. This is a crime conducted for mundane reasons, by unremarkable people, for relatively little money. 'It's within the pockets of ordinary people. That's the frightening thing,' says David.

Santre Sanchez Gayle was both the cheapest and the youngest hitman in David's sample. He was fifteen, and ultimately paid only £200 to kill twenty-six-year-old Gulistan Subasi in Clapton, east London, in March 2010, although police believe he had been promised £2,000. Gulistan had flown to the UK from Turkey and was staying with relatives while she sought to regain custody of her nine-year-old son; Gayle was commissioned to kill her before she could take the boy home with her. He was so meticulous in his methods that the police were sure they were dealing with a seasoned killer; he was only caught because he bragged to a friend afterwards. In security camera footage of the murder, Gayle rings the doorbell and waits calmly for Gulistan to open the door before shooting her at point-blank range with a sawn-off shotgun. 'When we saw the CCTV we all thought it was a professional hitman,' the senior investigating officer said at the time. 'There was no hesitation and he shows no nerves. It did not look like a fifteen-year-old boy.' Gayle was sentenced to a minimum of twenty years in 2011.

'Gayle bought a fake Gucci hat with the £200,' David tells me. 'It wasn't really about the money at all; he saw accepting the commission to do the hit as a way of establishing his reputation within a street gang – the Kensal Green Boys.' It wasn't about the price of taking a life – it was about Gayle proving he could take one, proving his *own* worth. But Gayle was an outlier in many ways, David says: hits are almost always about money.

David and his colleagues devised a typology of four different kinds of hitmen. *Novices*, like Gayle, can be very professional, but their lack of experience makes them cheap. *Dilettantes* have no specific skills and are driven to murder by desperation over gambling debts or other money problems. 'They would literally go down the pub and say, "I'd do anything to get five grand", and somebody in the pub would say, "Well, I know somebody who's looking for x, y and z,"' David explains. *Journeymen* are also cheap: they are criminals who establish a reputation for easy violence in prison. 'If you are prepared to stab somebody in the showers in exchange for phonecards or half an ounce of tobacco, then when you've been released you're used in exactly the same way.'

The *master* hitmen are the ones who are expensive, successful, and therefore still a bit of a mystery to criminologists. They are well established within national or international criminal networks; they arrive at the scene of the hit from out of nowhere, and disappear as soon as the job is done. All this travelling and expertise adds to the substantial cost of their services. But their prices fluctuate according to supply and demand. 'When the peace process happened in Northern Ireland there were a lot of men who had access to firearms and had used them regularly. They saturated the market, and therefore the price came down,' David says matter-of-factly. 'They were trading on their fearsome reputation as IRA men. Now that reputation has gone to the Russians, or to the Albanians.' Just like Hollywood movies, you can date a master hit by who the biggest baddies are at a given time.

It's the master hitmen who are glorified in films, TV box sets, novels and true crime podcasts. Both Bob Innes and John Alite trade off the place these kinds of hitmen hold in our collective imaginations – and David does too, to some extent. But the vast majority of murders for hire are conducted by the other types of killers – the cheap ones. 'They are much more common,' David says. 'You've got to be in quite a sophisticated criminal network to even identify master hitmen who could successfully undertake the hit. That limits the amount of people who'd know who to go to.'

The price of taking a life tells us nothing about the value of the person being killed, but it lays bare the circumstances of the person doing the murder: their desperation for money or desire for opportunity, their ease with violence and ability to detach themselves from death. And it reveals something about the person who has commissioned it too: the extent to which they really want someone dead, and their eagerness to be removed from the act of killing.

Before David hangs up to go and film his TV show, he tells me to call Dr Mohammed Rahman, senior lecturer in criminology at Birmingham City University, who worked alongside him in his research on hitmen, to see if there's been any further work on the price of taking a life in the years since the 2014 paper was published. Mo seems to be much more immersed in that world at the moment, which makes me excited to talk to him. It might also be the reason why he's so hard to get hold of: I try him for several weeks before he picks up the phone.

'Ultimately the role of the hitman is to shoot to kill, not to maim, harm or injure. You're paying someone to do it because you're confident that they can do the job. It's a fusion of distance and having a reliable pair of hands,' Mo tells me when I finally manage to reach him.

Mo specializes in serious and organized crime, gangs and violence, but when I listen to him describe the hitmen he studies, I realize that he's using the same sort of language that anyone else would use if they were describing soldiers. For as long as there have been armies, there have been professional killers. The difference between being a soldier and being a hitman is simply whether the state sanctions the kind of killing you do for money. 'Contract killing is the extreme end of criminal enforcement,' Mo explains. 'The enforcers are essentially an alternative form of justice.'

I immediately think of John, the former Mafia enforcer, trained by his father to be clinical in his violence, suffering PTSD after his years of service. Like all hitmen, John was effectively a private soldier, a paramilitary, sent out to enforce the rules in the alternative system of justice imposed by the Gottis and the rest of the Gambino clan. 'My life was a lie in that world,' he had told me. 'I believed in rules that didn't exist.' Once John realized how contingent and arbitrary those rules were, he saw how foolish it would be to continue to keep to them.

Mo tells me the main thing that has changed since the 2014 paper is not the price of taking a life but how it's paid, in a world fast becoming cashless. The days of being handed large sums of banknotes stacked in holdalls or suitcases are numbered, because cash is becoming ever more conspicuous, harder to spend, far less useful. The kinds of business opportunities John was prepared to kill for are also more difficult to conceal, now that almost every transaction leaves a trace; Mo says those who commission hits are wary of leaving any kind of digital footprint at all.

As the allure of cash payments diminishes, maybe the price of life will too: instead of being commissioned for money, hitmen may kill in exchange for debts being written off or slates being wiped clean. The people who murder for hire may increasingly be just the desperate and the beholden. If so, the price of taking a life may become cheaper than ever, because these hitmen will be prepared to kill in exchange for nothing more than their own freedom.

CHAPTER TWO

$100m, or $150m – or $400bn

The world's most expensive weapons system

I am standing on a metal platform several metres above a factory that is 1.6 kilometres long. Below me are orange robot arms, yellow ladders, blue metal workbenches, trolleys and scaffolds and gangways, all clustered around hulking fuselages the colour of oxidized copper. The hundreds of glaring halogen strip lights suspended far above me, the loud colours, the sheer vastness of this space leave me dizzy. It's like peering down into sixty Olympic swimming pools filled with half-completed sets of Lego.

'Smile!' shouts the Lockheed Martin photographer who's been assigned to take a shot of me at the one position in the entire factory where pictures are allowed.

But I don't feel like smiling. This place is so unfathomably huge, so complex and bustling, that I'm completely overwhelmed. Plus, it would be kind of perverse to smile here. Lockheed Martin is the world's largest defence contractor. The machines being assembled on this production line are for killing people.

The F-35 Lightning II is more than just a jet; it is a weapons

Courtesy of Lockheed Martin

On the Lockheed Martin F-35 factory floor (courtesy of Lockheed Martin).

system, 'the most lethal, survivable and connected fighter aircraft in the world,' according to Lockheed Martin's marketing department. But it's also the most expensive ever built. Today, there are over $3 billion-worth of F-35s being built in front of me in this assembly plant.

'Smile!' he says again. So I smile: a too-large, bewildered, goofy grin.

'I just can't get over the size of this place,' I say.

'Well,' he says, checking his shot, 'this *is* Texas.'

Size is definitely a thing around here. The Lockheed Martin Aeronautics facility in Fort Worth, aka Air Force Plant Number Four, spans 679 acres in total, a complex of enormous hangars and seemingly infinite corridors. My tour of the F-35 production line is taking place in a golf buggy. Perhaps this is because there is so much ground to cover; perhaps it's to stop me getting too close to the world's most expensive killing machines, or wandering around the assembly plant and overhearing some trade or military secrets.

My driver and tour guide is Kevin McCormick, who handles 'customer engagement' for the F-35. He's in a navy suit, a gold tie, signet rings, a neat side parting and a flesh-toned headset microphone that makes me think of Britney Spears. Kevin loves his job and knows his stuff. He wields a laser pointer like a lightsabre, and is a blizzard of acronyms and jargon.

Here's a typical exchange between us:

ME: Why are those guys over there wearing white suits?

KEVIN: If they're avionics technicians they will wear the white smocks to minimize electrostatic discharge while they're populating circuit cards and performing systems check-out.

While much of what he says is a foreign language that I only just understand, it is peppered with extraordinary numbers that I pick up immediately: 33,000 parts made by 1,900 suppliers worldwide. A production line that runs seven days a week. Thirty-six months between the signature on the contract and the keys being delivered. But in the two hours I've been here, one figure is conspicuously absent: the price tag. I've flown over to Texas to find the price of life taken by the most expensive weapons system ever made, yet whenever I ask about current prices, price changes over time, or price variations between models, I'm told those numbers will be given to me – in due course.

But some prices – those paid by the US military – are already out there for anyone to find, and they are notorious. US Department of Defense documents show that each F-35 cost an average of $110 million in the 2021 tax year. In 2021, the US Government Accountability Office found that it will cost the US government $400 billion to buy the 2,500 F-35s it plans to acquire by 2036, putting an average price per aircraft at $150 million. And that's just the purchase price: operating and sustaining those planes will cost another $1.25 trillion. The biggest item to come out of this factory is the bill.

The only thing here that doesn't appear supersized and dazzling to me is the F-35 itself. It has to be small, because it's a fighter jet: it must be subtle enough to pass by undetected, nippy enough to win dogfights – close combat with other military aircraft. But to my very unsophisticated eye it is – dare I say it – underwhelming. For $150 million apiece I'd expected these machines to look like a work of art, or a vision from the future, the kind of sci-fi prototype Tom Cruise flies at the beginning of the second *Top Gun* film. But the F-35s on the production line just look like fighter jets. Sleek fighter jets, good bits of kit, not much more.

But there is a lot more to the F-35 Lightning II than meets the eye. In fact, its USP is what you *can't* see. Its stealth, supersonic speed and surveillance capabilities allow it to be omniscient yet invisible, so Lockheed Martin says. 'The bad guys are dead before they even know you're there,' as Kevin puts it. And the F-35 can do it all: it can drop nuclear bombs, shoot missiles, dogfight and conduct reconnaissance missions. It's been dubbed 'the Flying Swiss Army Knife' – the only fighter you'll ever need.

There are three models of the F-35, depending on which branch of the military is using it. The F-35A is made for the Air Force and designed to land on runways. The F-35B – the

Marines' variant – is the big showstopper: it flies like a jet but can perform short take-off and vertical landing like a helicopter, it can fly backwards, and it can dead-stop, hovering eerily over the ground like a flying saucer. The F-35C is the Navy variant, made to land on an aircraft carrier; its wingtips fold up so it can be stowed away at sea. All three can carry machine guns, advanced medium-range air-to-air missiles, a heat-seeking missile and laser-guided bombs for air-to-ground attacks.

I am not going to be seeing any F-35s shooting rounds, dropping bombs, folding wings, dead-stopping or performing vertical taking off and landing today. I am not even going to get close enough to see inside a cockpit, stuck as I am in a golf buggy, trundling down the central aisle of the factory with Kevin. But I remind myself that I am lucky to get a glimpse of anything at Lockheed Martin Aeronautics. I had to be cleared by the US Department of Defense before they allowed me anywhere near the compound. They didn't have to let me in here at all.

Each jet on the production line has its own monitor displaying which variant it is, its serial number, the number of hours spent working on it, how close it is to completion, the base the aircraft will be delivered to, the service that will be flying it, and the flag of the nation that ordered it. 'Here's one of yours,' Kevin says, parking up so we can take in BK-31, #977, an F-35B, 79.4% finished, Union Jack flag.

I get the sense that Kevin expects me to feel patriotic in front of this fuselage, or some kind of kinship with or ownership of the machine, but I don't really feel anything. Perhaps I should: I've paid for it. British taxpayers are spending £2.2 billion on a fleet of F-35Bs; forty-eight have already been bought, and there are a further twenty-six in the pipeline. Kevin flashes his laser pointer beam at the system that allows the B to perform its vertical take-off and landing party trick. It's behind the cockpit, so it gives the B a chunkier profile than the A or the C, as if it has muscular shoulders. 'Like a linebacker's neck,' he nods appreciatively.

Lockheed Martin's website promises that the F-35 'strengthens national security, enhances global partnerships and powers economic growth,' and Australia, Belgium, Denmark, Italy, the Netherlands, Switzerland, Poland, Norway, South Korea and Israel are among the sixteen countries that have so far agreed that the path to security, growth and global partnerships depends on spending billions on these lethal machines. First proposed in the 1990s and formally approved in October 2001, the F-35 programme's big selling point was that using the same airframe for Army, Navy and Air Force variants would mean the jet was affordable. The US Department of Defense originally planned to buy 2,852 F-35s in a contract worth an estimated $233 billion, putting the average cost per plane at just over $80 million apiece. They were supposed to be ready for combat by 2010.

But delays and costs quickly spiralled out of control. There were problems with the high-tech bespoke helmet, a kind of virtual reality headset made from a 3D scan of each pilot's head, with the plane's ejector seat, and with cybersecurity (at one point the 'stealth' jet couldn't transmit data without revealing its location to the enemy). With every setback came reams of increasingly negative headlines across the globe. By the time the F-35 was ready to fly off the production line and into combat it was 2018, and the enemy was now most likely to be a terrorist militia that was inconceivable back in the nineties when the jet was dreamed up. The trade-offs necessary to put so many functions into a one-size-fits-all machine made it look like a jack of all trades and master of none. That's the thing about a Swiss

Army knife: it may be able to open tin cans, but given a choice, most of us would rather use a simple can opener.

Eight international programme partners (the USA, UK, Italy, the Netherlands, Australia, Norway, Denmark and Canada) had already paid billions upfront so they could be involved in the development and manufacturing process; the UK alone put up £2.5 billion. With so much already sunk into the programme, the partners stuck with it. Now that the F-35 has finally been used in combat, in Afghanistan, Iraq and other parts of the Middle East, Lockheed Martin wants to put its long and drawn-out labour pains behind it. There have been few grumbles since it was first deployed in 2018, and the more units are sold, the cheaper each one will be, so the marketing department says. Those international sales matter more than ever. And, as we linger next to BK-33, I realize that's why they've allowed me in here: because I am British. They need us to fall in love with this much maligned plane, so that we keep on ordering.

The golf buggy trundles out of the main hall and into another colossal space, full of dazzling artificial light, like an operating theatre. Final finishes are applied here: the light green base coat is sanded, the F-35 is covered with primer, and then robots spray on what Kevin is calling 'low observable coatings', as if it was an invisibility cloak. Key to the F-35's stealth is how its surfaces are designed with hardly anything for radar to bounce off: no antennas or sensors, internal weaponry, sawtooth edges instead of straight lines where panels meet. In its final topcoat, the F-35 is gunmetal grey and looks as if it's been moulded in one single piece.

Kevin pauses the buggy in front of an F-35A with a kangaroo on it. 'As you can see, there's a roo painted on this Australian F-35A aircraft. Still part of your Commonwealth, isn't it?' he asks earnestly, as if we're standing in front of my cousin's new car.

A minibus is waiting to take us to the flight line, the final destination on the production line. We drive along an almost endless taxiway, past hangar after hangar, each containing a single jet. Under normal circumstances, each F-35 spends forty-five days here undergoing final tests before Lockheed Martin pilots take them to the skies for a minimum of two flights. Then the US government flies them away, either for the military to use, or to distribute to other countries.

But these are not normal circumstances. Every hangar is full today because of a hiccup involving a magnet made with a banned Chinese alloy recently discovered to be present in every F-35 ever made. The Pentagon has suspended deliveries until Lockheed Martin sorts its supply chain out and removes this Chinese interloper from their flagship fighter jet. Kevin shrugs it off as if it's no biggie, but the flight line is clearly running out of storage space. There are thirty F-35s sitting here – $4.5 billion-worth of military muscle – just waiting.

'Let's do a slow drive by to look at one of the UK B models out here,' Kevin tells the minibus driver. And there's the final highlight of my tour: the UK's thirtieth F35-B, BK-30, with its gunmetal super-stealth coating and chunky linebacker's neck, the most lethal fighter aircraft in the world, ready to perform aeronautical wizardry but unable to fly away.

'I will tell you straight up, as a veteran of twenty-one years in the United States Air Force, the things we do here are about saving lives. It's about deterrence. That's what we're in the business for: to deter the use of *any* type of military force,' Joe LaMarca, Lockheed Martin Aeronautics' Vice President of Communications, declares in his rich Texan drawl. 'But if you do have to use it, you want to have the very best, and this is the very best.'

We're sitting at one end of an enormous boardroom table, next to a huge whiteboard and opposite a screen that takes up most of the back wall, along with Tara Lause, Director, Global Pursuits, Northern Europe. I've just asked Joe why the F-35 is so expensive, and it's opened some kind of floodgate.

'This is a very complex programme, nothing like this has ever been undertaken before. We've learned a lot of lessons in how we do maintenance on this airplane. That is the big cost in *any* weapons system. And you're talking about an airplane that has a forty-year lifespan, maybe more, depending on how much it's flown.'

'You're expecting each plane to last forty years?' I ask.

'I mean, it can go longer,' Joe replies.

'I think it's easier to measure in hours . . .' Tara interjects.

'Yes,' nods Joe, 'because it all depends on how many hours you fly. But we've tested the airplane up to three lifetimes.'

'How long is a lifetime?' I ask.

'We'll get you the exact numbers,' Joe assures me. 'We take it into a test cell and we measure it. We stress the airplane – more stress than you'll ever put on it in a real-world environment, and we test everything, and we've measured it out to *three lifetimes*. That's *a lot*.'

I don't know how I'm supposed to be impressed if I don't know what a lifetime actually is. The communications team have so many figures to give me – more than 840 F-35s delivered to sixteen countries so far, more than 3,000 on order, as many as 153 jets due to be delivered this year, a factory that could deliver 175 annually. But when it comes to basic specifics – the cost of a plane, how long each jet will last, how much fuel it uses and how much it will cost to maintain over a lifetime – they just don't have the numbers to hand.

'That's what you're getting when you buy an airplane like an

F-35,' Joe continues. 'You're getting three lifetimes' worth of airplanes, and the ability to upgrade it.' The F-35 is only going to get cheaper, because of 'economy of scale', he adds. And the more countries buy, the better off everyone will be. 'As we're selling the airplane around the world, we ask – how do we create jobs? In this factory alone we have 16,000 people. Where do you think they live? Where do you think they go to the store? Where do they buy their cars? Where do they buy their food? You think of the local economic impact.' Some of the 1,900 suppliers who manufacture the 300,000 parts employ thousands of people, Joe tells me, equipped once again with the necessary numbers. 'Look at Pratt & Whitney, who built the engine.'

'Rolls Royce,' Tara interjects.

'Rolls Royce.' Joe nods approvingly. 'BAE Systems.'

I get it. British companies depend on this, as do all their thousands of employees, their families, communities, local businesses. Brits like me need this to work as much as Lockheed Martin does.

'I guess that's my answer when people say, "Wow, it's really expensive",' Joe continues, sipping his coffee. 'People say, "It costs this much, so Lockheed Martin is making all this money . . ."' He chuckles and shakes his head ruefully. 'It doesn't work that way. We're certainly making a profit on the airplane because we're a business, but we take that profit and we turn it back into the business.'

'We invest,' Tara adds.

'We invest in R&D. It's not like we're throwing big parties every week.'

Perhaps I shouldn't be surprised that a weapons manufacturer can be so defensive. But everyone I've met so far at Lockheed Martin seems genuinely proud of the work they do. It must have been painful for them to see all the bad press the F-35 has had.

'The criticism was one of the reasons why I was hired thirteen years ago,' Joe says, when I ask him about the coverage. 'There have been some challenges along the way, things we didn't anticipate: it could be a part issue, it could be a manufacturing issue, it could be the supply chain. It's a steep learning curve but now we're at the peak – we've learned a lot and we're really starting to settle into our groove. We're humming on all cylinders.'

For a moment I am lost in the peaks, grooves and cylinders of his metaphors. But then Joe – who's been so relaxed and welcoming and warm and friendly this far – changes gear.

'For some, their whole job in life is to criticize government, or big business, or the industrial complex. Whether you're a critic or not I don't know, but my challenge to you would be – *learn the facts* and then write your story.' There's a quiet menace in his voice as he says this. 'I went to a journalism school, and I was taught that journalism is about fair and balanced reporting, have more than one source, two or three are best, and then validate those sources, OK? If you're a true journalist and you do that, I'm confident, I'm *confident*, that you will come away with a story that says, *Yeah, these airplanes cost a lot of money but there's a good reason why they cost what they cost.*'

The gauntlet thrown down, Joe leaves the rest of the briefing to Tara. 'I've said way too much,' he says, handing me his business card with a broad smile. 'We're happy to answer any question that's not classified. Anything that we can tell you, we will.'

Everything except the price, it seems.

Tara seems to exhale a bit with Joe out of the room. She has a serious demeanour, befitting someone who began her twenty-year career here writing the code for the F-35's safety system, but a soft voice that clearly can't compete with Joe's.

She talks me through Lockheed Martin's different business areas, and her eyes light up when she tells me about the Skunk Works, the enigmatic California-based 'factory of the future' where cutting-edge technology is dreamed up.

'We're testing out new and intriguing capability,' she enthuses. 'Here's a factoid: the F-35 is going to be in service until 2070. The pilots who are going to fly it are not alive today, and, in a lot of cases, neither are their *parents*. We need to be constantly anticipating where technology is going to go in the next fifty years. That's what our Skunk suite is about.'

'Isn't that really hard?' I ask. 'We're talking about planes that were designed twenty years ago. How confident can you be that the F-35 will be useful in 2070?'

Tara blinks. 'You do as much advance appreciation of technology as you can. If you go past ten years or so into the future it's really hard to anticipate, it's kind of anybody's game. That ten-year window is what we tend to focus on.'

So how can they promise that the F-35 is an investment that will still be paying dividends in fifty years' time – how can they possibly know? It may still be able to fly, but it's very likely to be obsolete given advances in artificial intelligence, automation, and an ever-changing definition of the enemy. Who has any idea who or what we'll be keeping safe from in 2070?

'You can't know for sure?' I say, somewhere between a statement and a question.

She briefly closes her eyes and nods. 'We don't know what that battle space is going to look like, but I do feel pretty confident that there is a need that the aircraft itself will fill through that time. You need a lot of different tools in your toolkit. But you're still always going to need a screwdriver, for the foreseeable future.'

So much for the Swiss Army knife. But at least Tara is going beyond the PR patter and giving me a nuanced answer to a direct question. The F-35 may well be the ultimate piloted fighter jet – literally; it may be the last. What will supersede it, and how soon? This is all beginning to sound like a massive gamble: that the F-35 won't become obsolete before 2070; that enough people will buy it to keep costs down.

Then Tara tells me about the high-tech helmet that receives data from sensors all over the aircraft and displays them in front of the pilot's eyes in a virtual reality display. 'They can just turn their head and see what's happening, with all the threats mapped,' she continues. 'F-35s are able to share images *between them*. If I'm an F-35 flying several hundred miles away, I can pass back information about what I'm seeing in real time for the pilot to react to or use.'

I don't like the sound of this at all. I've presented live radio programmes where producers are talking in my ear at the wrong time, and it can be massively distracting; that would be nothing compared to flying a plane and being shot at while someone hundreds of miles away pushes things into my field of vision. But I guess pilots are made of sterner stuff than me.

I've read that the helmets cost half a million dollars apiece, but Tara can't confirm it, or tell me whether it's included in the cost of the plane.

'I know that your focus is on costs,' she says. 'I wondered if you had heard about the Mitchell Institute Study on costs per effect? It's all about how we measure cost on aircraft systems. Historically there have been measures like cost per flight hour . . .'

'Yes. And I want you to give me all of that.'

'Yes,' Tara laughs, without giving it to me. 'We need to think holistically about how we measure cost. The Mitchell Institute is arguing, if the effect that's desired is to go strike an enemy base out in a country, you should measure everything it takes along a value chain to do that. That's the real cost comparison that you want to draw.'

Unsurprisingly, the Mitchell Institute report finds that the F-35s represent good value when measured according to this metric. But we can all think of ways that we'd like to be measured, the ones that are most likely to show us at our best. The metric I am after is the price of life, and for that I need to work out the money spent per life taken, or saved. They can't, or won't, give me any costs at all. On this vast compound, it feels as though they're hoping that if they obfuscate long enough while bamboozling me with an array of other astounding figures, I'll give up and just focus on how big and important the F-35 is. But there's no chance of that.

Still, Tara is determined to continue with other numbers. This time, it's employment figures: hundreds of British companies involved in producing the aircraft; at least 20,000 jobs created in the UK because of the F-35; more than 298,000 direct and indirect jobs in the US. The F-35 programme generates over $65 billion annually, she says. 'The continued success of the programme is beneficial to everyone who is part of it, because the more orders there are, the better position that industry is in.'

One in twenty jobs in the city of Fort Worth depends on Lockheed Martin's F-35.* It's been Tara's life's work, and she has spent over two decades determined to make it a success. So I choose my next words carefully.

'There's no doubt this is a very important business – you've

* Lockheed Martin says it has created 56,000 indirect jobs in the city. The population of Fort Worth is around 950,000.

made a really good case for that,' I say. 'So many countries have spent so much money on it. Is the programme now too big to fail?'

Tara smiles. 'We won't *let* it fail. I wouldn't say it's too big to fail; everyone is so personally invested in making this successful that there is no other option. And it has demonstrated that it has not failed.'

Failure may be in the eye of the beholder; there are some big numbers out there that certainly suggest the F-35 programme is not a success. In 2021, the Pentagon's testing and evaluation office registered 871 software and hardware problems that could undermine the F-35's readiness for battle. In 2019, *Defense News* reported thirteen issues that posed a risk to pilot safety, including cockpit pressure spikes that leave pilots with 'excruciating' ear and sinus pain, and stealth coating that blisters when the F-35 flies at supersonic speed.

But Tara is right in one respect: the F-35 has been used in combat since 2018 (eight times, according to Lockheed Martin) and continues to be bought, which is evidence that it has not failed – or rather, that it's not a white elephant. Whatever those hundreds of problems may be, they've not stopped the F-35 going into battle.

To find out the price of a life taken by the most expensive weapons system in the world, I need to know how many people were killed on those missions. What threat did those people pose? How much safer is the world without them? But finding out where, how and what happened is even more difficult than getting a price list from Lockheed Martin. The military doesn't tend to make the number of lives it has taken public, if it bothers to measure them at all.

Here's what I've been able to find out: Israel's air force was the first to use the F-35 in combat, in May 2018, against unspecified targets in the Middle East. This is public knowledge because Israeli Major General Amikam Norkin boasted about it. 'We are flying the F-35 all over the Middle East and have already attacked twice on two different fronts,' he said at a meeting of heads of twenty foreign air forces in Israel. 'You know that we just won the Eurovision with the song "Toy"? Well, the F-35 is not a toy.'

Next, a Pentagon press release announced that the US Marine Corp deployed F-35Bs in Afghanistan in September 2018, 'in support of ground clearance operations'. The F-35A got its first outing in April 2019, in a strike against a network of ISIS tunnels in Iraq. The Royal Air Force's 617 Squadron, the Dambusters, first flew the British F-35Bs in May 2019, for a three-week period, as part of operations in Iraq and Syria against ISIS. The RAF used them again in 2021, in the same region. Then, in March 2021, the Israeli air force shot down two Iranian drones approaching Israeli airspace. There was no mention of casualties in any of these six operations – but that doesn't mean no one was killed.

The most high-profile use of F-35s in combat came in September 2019, when the US-led Operation Inherent Resolve (OIR) coalition against ISIS dropped 36 tonnes of bombs on a suspected ISIS stronghold on Qanus Island in Iraq. OIR released an aerial video of the F-35 attack that is both horrific and mesmerizing: explosions bloom across the entire length of the island like amber cherry blossom. The Iraqi counter-terrorism service told reporters a few weeks later that around twenty-five ISIS fighters had lost their lives. I emailed the OIR press office three years after the attack to ask if they could confirm this, but no one replied, and the OIR press release on the operation mysteriously disappeared from the internet within days of my inquiry.

The only death I can definitively link to an F-35 is that of forty-one-year-old Major Akinori Hosomi, a Japanese pilot who was killed during a training exercise when his F-35A crashed into the Pacific Ocean at 690 miles per hour.

All of which is to say: it's pretty much impossible to give even a ballpark figure of the price of a life taken by the world's most expensive weapons system. There is no way of finding out the price of the system accurately, or the number of lives it has taken. Given the cost of the F-35 programme so far, it is likely to be in the billions. These are the most expensive lives ever taken.

'It's like if you get into a new car – that new car smell. The buttons are really crisp. There's no dirt, no bug splats. It is *beautiful*.'

The last item on my itinerary at Lockheed Martin is a meal in the boardroom with Monessa Bahlzhiser, aka Siren. For twelve years, Siren flew with the US Air Force, in combat against ISIS over Iraq and Syria, before becoming one of Lockheed Martin's fifteen in-house pilots. It's her job to fly F-35s off the production line and airborne for the very first time, taking them supersonic, maximizing the angle of attack, bringing them up to a G force of nine, a gravitational pull nine times stronger than she'd experience on the ground, testing them to the edge of their capabilities. 'One of the best jobs in the world,' she tells me.

I can't imagine anything I'd want to do less; I'd be terrified even to be a passenger in a jet that's never been flown before. But Siren has a cool ease about her that suggests she's not easily fazed. She's forty but looks younger, tall and striking in her

With Siren, the pilot, aka Monessa Bahlzhiser (courtesy of Lockheed Martin).

khaki jumpsuit, her hair pulled back in a tight bun, with a broad smile that softens her face. She has aviator Ray-Bans – of course she does – which she lays down next to her plate as we tuck into grilled chicken and rice together.

Siren earned her call sign after repeatedly setting off fire alarms making popcorn when she was a young officer. 'It has nothing to do with Greek mythology,' she smiles. 'I love it. Generally you get to keep your call sign if you've employed weapons in combat.'

The subtext is clear: Siren is fun enough to make the popcorn, but she is also prepared to kill you if she has to.

'I have about eighty hours in the F-35 now, and I'm just getting my feet under what this jet is capable of,' she says. Key to it all is the ingenious tech, beginning with the magic that takes place within the helmet. 'It provides us with a tremendous amount of situational awareness that I never had before.' It doesn't distract her, she says; the jet is made easy to fly, so the pilot can devote his or her attention to the sensors. 'You can let go of the controls and manipulate the buttons, and the jet will stay where it's at.'

Then she tells me about the auto ground-collision system Lockheed Martin pioneered with the F-16 jet, and which is now in every F-35. If a pilot passes out, from the effects of G-force or anything else, and the jet determines that it's within three seconds of crashing into the ground, it will automatically recover. She swoops her palm up from the table. 'In the F-16, it has already saved twelve pilots' lives. I had a friend personally saved by it.'

They can't have it both ways. They can't be arguing that greater automation saves lives, but then promising this jet – this manned jet – will be operational until 2070. If the F-35 is clever enough that the pilot can let go of the flight controls to manipulate buttons that lead to bombs being dropped or rounds being fired, won't it just be a question of time before jets are clever enough to do the bombing and firing too? Siren could be talking herself out of a job here: if the objective of this plane is taking enemy lives and saving pilots, then the safest plane has no pilot at all. The safest plane is a drone.

'What's the future of pilots like you?' I ask. 'Do you not think we're close to a time when we'll expect a machine to do it all?'

Siren smiles. 'I'm biased, but I don't think you can ever replace how a pilot thinks inside a cockpit. You can model it, but there's always going to be those few situations where you need a pilot, whether they are experienced or not, to react in a certain way. Let's just say you're getting targeted, and you have to figure out who's targeting you. How does a robot know that at that very moment there's a civilian right there? I've had situations in combat where I've had to make the tough decision to drop a bomb knowing that somebody could get hurt, but either they get hurt from my bomb or they get hurt by getting shot by terrorists.'

But humans don't always get it right. The US Air Force has targeted Afghan wedding parties at least three times (once in 2002, and twice in 2008), leading to the deaths of over a hundred innocent people. That's just weddings: tens of thousands of civilians were killed and ultimately classified under the Orwellian phrase 'collateral damage' during the war in Afghanistan alone. And even if human judgement were infallible, then it could still be used to operate drones remotely. In an era of unmanned aircraft, when no one has to be in the cockpit at all, how will governments ever be able to justify the deaths of pilots?

'How does it feel to make decisions like that?' I ask.

'You really have to trust your training, trust yourself,' Siren says, nodding to herself. 'That's why fighter pilots are the way we are. We're a little gruff. A little weird.'

On my way out of Air Force Plant Number Four, the communications team promises to send me the F-35 price list in writing, over email. Nothing has arrived by the time I fly back to the UK. I send six messages chasing the numbers up, and each time I'm assured the figures will be coming my way. Two months after my visit to Fort Worth, I'm still waiting.

It turns out the answers I'm searching for are much closer to home. In fact, I get them at home, sitting behind my laptop in London, on a Microsoft Teams meeting with another British person.

Air Commodore Ian 'Cab' Townsend is the Assistant Chief of Staff, Air Capability Delivery Combat Air, and Senior Responsible Owner for F-35. 'What a mouthful – let me put that into lay terms,' he says with a warm smile. 'I effectively own the chequebook. I own the money. I pay for F-35.' Cab is in charge of management and leadership of the F-35 programme in the UK. If anyone in the country knows the going rate, it's him. After weeks of badgering the UK's Ministry of Defence, I'm finally granted an audience with him.

'Each F-35B at the moment costs about $100 million,' Cab tells me – just like that, a straight answer. 'The original air vehicles would cost something like $150 million, and we are on this progressive decrease of cost. Aircraft always cost more to begin with. That's the trajectory we expected.'

The numbers keep coming. Cost per flying hour? $33,000. Maintenance costs? About $10,000 per flying hour. I'm beginning to feel a little silly for travelling all the way to Texas to ask these questions.

I tell Cab about my trip to Fort Worth, about the tour of the factory, about how Joe and Tara told me the F-35 would be in use for the next forty or fifty years. 'I absolutely buy that,' he says with supreme confidence. The great fighter jets of the past – the Harrier, the Tornado, the F-16 and the B-52 – have all been in service for many decades, he explains. 'Are you familiar with a programme called *Only Fools and Horses*?' he asks.

'I am aware of it, yes,' I say, trying to imagine how a sitcom about Peckham wheeler-dealers will inform my understanding of the F-35.

'Are you familiar with Trigger's broom? There's a scene where Trigger's really proud that he'd had his sweeping brush for twenty-five years. He said in that time he'd replaced the handle five times and the head ten times. So it wasn't the same broom.'

I get it – the world's most expensive weapons system is Trigger's broom, and the Ship of Theseus.

The jet gets a significant upgrade every four or five years, Cab says, keeping it at the cutting edge of capability. 'I *absolutely* believe that the F-35 will be in service up until our published out-of-service date of 2069. As a nation, we have *absolutely* committed to this air system as a fifty-year project.'

Cab is a former fighter pilot. Like Siren, he can't envisage a time when fighter jets aren't flown by human beings. (I find it hard to imagine a future when robots will go on reporting missions and write non-fiction books, despite mounting evidence that AI might very soon do this as well as I can.) For him, the great power of the machine lies in its potential to prevent dogfights altogether. 'You've got such a capable air system. It informs the enemy of the risk calculus they have to go through if they wish to joust with NATO and a collaboration of F-35 operators; it really does increase the risks on their part.' And then there's the importance of the F-35 to the British economy: the UK gets back 15 per cent of the value of every F-35 built and sold, he says.

Pilots have to be confident, decisive, assertive. But Cab seems to have no doubt at all that the F-35 is worth it. 'Over the course of fifty years, for the return that you get on your investment – militarily, through the supply chain in the UK, and through our influence with countries like the United States – I think there's an awful lot that comes out of the F-35 programme that's incredibly positive.'

*

Joe had been convinced I'd fly away from Texas agreeing that, while the F-35 costs a lot – whatever it may cost – there are good reasons why it's so expensive. And he's right: I do. But I'm equally convinced that it's a waste of money. Even if the F-35 really is versatile enough to replace the need for any other jet, even if it can still be relevant and useful in 2070, even if there's still a demand for piloted aircraft during that time, this jet is built in wilful ignorance of the biggest enemy humanity will face over the next fifty years.

The F-35 runs off JP-5 and JP-8 military jet fuel, two of the most carbon-intensive on the planet. In five minutes, the F-35 will produce as much CO_2 as an average UK petrol car driven for an entire year. Annual jet-fuel use by the US military alone generates emissions equivalent to six million US passenger cars. In a world on the brink of climate disaster, the F-35 itself may well be the enemy.

Many countries with F-35s on order have promised to cut their greenhouse gases to as close to net zero as possible by 2050. Some are aware of the dissonance in making these two commitments: Britain's Ministry of Defence announced in 2020 that it's looking into sustainable fuels that might one day be used to power the jets. Cab says they are aiming for 70 per cent of all training to be conducted in simulators rather than burning fuel in the air. Even if F-35s are one day run on solar power or cooking oil, the F-35 cannot keep rising sea levels at bay, rescue people from wildfires or transport personnel to help with hurricane relief. The money spent on these machines could have gone on flood defences, renewable energy, planting trees, carbon capture – anything to counteract the biggest existential threat humanity has ever faced. But perhaps that wouldn't create as much global employment.

And maybe that's what this is all really about: a jobs

programme. A form of welfare devised in a country that doesn't really do welfare very well. Military spending is a way to put public money back into the economy while cultivating a fearsome image of technological might that may give enemies pause. And deterrence and job creation do both save lives. But if this is the point of the F-35, it feels like an uncosted solution, a way of throwing money at a problem without considering whether more lives could be saved were it to be spent another way.

The enormous numbers Joe and Tara gave me in Forth Worth leave me convinced that the F-35 programme is a mistake that became too big to correct. Lockheed Martin's biggest innovation was to make so many nations complicit in it, and unable to back out.

CHAPTER THREE
£3,217,740

An average murder

Every week, the routine was the same. On Thursdays, Jessica Plummer would soak the white shirts, and on Fridays she would wash, dry and iron them, so her children's uniforms were pristine and ready for school on Monday morning.

On the evening of Friday, 30 January 2015, Jessica was in her nightshirt in the kitchen of her home in Finsbury Park, north London, finishing the ironing and chatting to a friend on the phone, when there was a knock on the door. It was not a normal knock. It was forceful: very loud, very persistent. She thought it must be Shaquan, her seventeen-year-old middle child. She shouted out that he should be using his key to let himself in. But the knocking didn't stop, and whoever was behind the door was using the letterbox flap as well as the knocker and the doorbell.

Jessica told her friend she'd call back. She went into the living room, which overlooks the street, and pulled back the net curtain. She saw the flash of a blue light.

Two police officers were on her doorstep. They showed her their IDs.

'Are you the mother of Shaquan Sammy-Plummer?' the male officer asked.

Jessica said yes.

'We need you to get your bag and your coat,' said the female officer. 'You need to come to the hospital with us.'

'Is my son OK?' Jessica asked.

'We don't know,' came the reply.

Jessica's legs crumpled underneath her. The female officer helped her up, and followed as she somehow climbed the two flights of stairs to her bedroom. As she tried to get dressed, she wet herself. The female officer helped her again. She asked Jessica if anyone else was at home with her. Jessica called out to her youngest, fifteen-year-old Andre. He perched on the stairs as the officers explained they were taking his mother to the hospital to see his brother. 'I don't do hospitals,' Andre said. Jessica asked him to call his father, Jerome, and tell him to meet her there.

As they sped off into the night with blue lights flashing, Jessica crossed her fingers tightly and prayed. '*Please*, Lord God, *make* him be OK, Lord.' When the police officers asked if she was all right, Jessica couldn't break her prayer to answer. Her fingers were so tightly entwined in crosses that she couldn't pick up her phone. The fifteen-minute journey was an agonizing eternity. 'Lord God, make me reach there,' Jessica pleaded.

When they finally arrived at the Royal London Hospital in Whitechapel, Jessica saw throngs of police behind the double doors of A&E. She clutched at her clothes. The female officer took her to a room where Jessica paced up and down, beseeching, imploring. When Jerome arrived, he asked what had happened, but the officer said she couldn't tell them anything. Left alone with the father of her children and no answers, Jessica felt like this little room was a bubble, and they were floating inside it, suspended above the real world and its horrible possibilities.

Then a tall man in a bright orange jumpsuit came into the room. He asked Jessica to sit down. He knelt in front of her.

'I'm sorry, but I have awful news,' he said. 'Your son is dead. He was stabbed in the chest and died.'

'You are lying,' Jessica said. 'It's not true.'

'Yes, it's true,' he said. 'Would you like to come and see him?'

'And I said *no*, because I was *scared*,' Jessica tells me, her eyes in the middle distance, deep in the memory of the night everything fell apart. 'I really and truly regret that, because I never got to see my son. And I will never see him again.'

Shaquan was killed after he refused to hand over a plastic bag containing a couple of cans of soft drink and a packet of sweets. In that moment, he became one of 570 homicide victims in England and Wales and one of fifteen teenage boys to be stabbed to death on London's streets that year. He also became part of a data set used by economists working with the Home Office to calculate the price of a murder. They totted up the economic burden that each crime put on the public purse in 2015/2016, and concluded that the average homicide cost £3,217,740.

We will get to what exactly happened to Shaquan, and how meaningful that figure of £3,217,740 is. But first, we need to get into who put that price on his murder, how they came up with it, and why.

Every few years – and quietly – civil servants working for the UK Home Office calculate the cost of a long list of crimes. They have been doing this for over two decades, without much notice or fuss: the reports are published online and get little press attention. But the enormous job of costing all the different crimes against individuals and businesses – from murder to arson to cybercrime to theft from a commercial vehicle and beyond – is considered worthwhile enough to set a team of economists onto the task whenever the figures need updating.

In July 2018, the Home Office published *Research Report 99*, 'The Economic and Social Costs of Crime,' by Matthew Heeks, Sasha Reed, Mariam Tafsiri and Stuart Prince. It was the fourth time these costs had been calculated since 2000, and it used 2015/2016 crime figures and prices from England and Wales. Civil servants aren't supposed to talk to journalists. I tried to contact all four authors, and Matt Heeks sent me a very polite reply saying he couldn't really say anything beyond what was in the paper. And indeed the paper speaks for itself. 'The unit costs of crime estimates are designed to help policymakers and practitioners weigh up the crime reduction benefits of policies and help assess the cost-effectiveness of particular interventions,' it reads, in the dry, technocratic language of cost–benefit analysis. 'They demonstrate the relative magnitudes of the economic and social costs of different crimes.' The costs are supposed to be treated as tokens to be compared with each other, rather than accurate, itemized costings. But *Research Report 99* uses very precise numbers from official sources, and it would be difficult to read it without absorbing the idea that there are specific costs to the public purse every time someone commits a crime.

The approach is strikingly simple. The authors add up the costs 'in anticipation'* of a given crime (like buying insurance, or installing CCTV and burglar alarms), the costs 'as a consequence' of crime (property stolen or damaged, physical and emotional harm to the victim, lost productivity from time off work, health services and victim services), and the costs 'in response' to crime (the police investigation and costs of the trial, prison and probation). They take the total, divide it by the number of incidences of that crime committed in a year, and come up with the cost per crime. Basic maths.

Murder is the most expensive. Rape comes in second, at

£39,360 per offence. Violence with injury costs a total of £15.5 billion a year, but given that there were over 1.1 million incidences in 2015/2016, the cost of each was put at £14,050. 'Violent crimes make up the largest proportion of the total costs of individual crime – almost three quarters – but only one third of the number of crimes,' the paper reads. 'This is mainly due to the higher physical and emotional costs to the victims of violent offences. These costs are particularly high for crimes that are more likely to result in emotional injuries, such as rape and violence with injury.' In other words, hurt people cost society more than damaged things.

As they seek to tot up all the costs incurred when a crime is committed, the authors of *Research Report 99* go into almost ridiculous detail. A chipped tooth is said to last 0.0192 years and costs the victim £20 in harm; a dislocated joint lasts 0.154 years and costs £650. It took a bit of head scratching for me to work out how they could give death a duration of 39.8 years, but the figure refers to premature death, calculated by subtracting the average age of a murder victim from typical life expectancy. Physical harm to a murder victim is put at £2,082,430, based on the number of quality-adjusted life years, or QALYs, lost when the average-aged victim is killed. Lost output is £254,710, calculated using an average number of 13,902 working hours that will not be worked, paid at the average rate.

Reading these figures makes me queasy. It feels inhuman to see this degree of abject pain and misery – the worst of human suffering – reduced to digits. The authors of *Research Report 99* don't try to justify putting a price on murder and other violent crimes. Instead, they direct readers to the first paper ever to calculate the cost of crimes in England and Wales – the granddaddy of this approach – which made a big argument for it in 2000.

'Crime imposes a huge cost on society . . . The potential savings to individuals and households, businesses and the public sector from effective crime reduction measures are therefore extremely large,' write civil servants Sam Brand and Richard Price in 2000's *Home Office Research Study 217.* Estimates of the social and economic costs of crime are intended to focus minds on the most cost-effective solutions, it continues. They can 'increase the awareness of both policymakers and the public in general of the full impact of crime on society and the potential gains that could result from reductions in crime'.

This 2000 report is very much in the spirit of the times. In the middle of the first term of a New Labour government, cost–benefit analysis in the most sensitive areas of public spending was no longer taboo – it was part of responsible decision-making. Brand and Price say it provides 'a good basis for answering many key questions about crime and crime prevention, such as: how can we use our existing resources in the most effective way? How can we reduce the total cost of crime to society? What is the correct level of resourcing for crime reduction activity? Should we concentrate only on preventing crime or should we do more to mitigate its consequences?' These seem like reasonable questions.

This approach has continued under successive governments of every political stripe. And while the UK has been a bit of a pioneer at this, it's certainly not a British thing: around the world, public servants, charities and campaigners all do it as a way of getting the right people to pay attention to a given cause. Estimates of the cost of pretty much any violent crime, anywhere in the world, can be found with only a few mouse clicks. In an effort to encourage investment in policing, the RAND Corporation has calculated that the average murder costs America $8,649,216. The European Institute for Gender Equality concluded that gender-based violence cost EU member states €366 billion a year in 2019. The Institute for Economics and Peace concluded that, in 2021, homicide cost the Mexican public purse US$105.5 billion, with violent crime in general costing US$243 billion, equivalent to 20.8 percent of Mexico's GDP.

It's a strong way of making a point. But what does it say about how political decisions are made today? Is the only way to focus powerful minds to present them with a bill? What do we lose when we flatten the worst of human experience and turn it into an average price? Can there ever be such a thing as an average murder?

I live less than ten minutes' drive from Jessica's house. She told me I'd know which one it was because of the picture of Shaquan in the window that her neighbours won't let her take down. But it's actually impossible to miss. It looks like a shrine.

There's a memorial bench in the front garden, with a weather-beaten teddy bear and an almost entirely faded photo in a frame on the seat. Much of the front window is taken up by a picture of Shaquan. He looks dashing in his work uniform (striped shirt, green satin tie, dark fleece jacket with the Waitrose logo embroidered on one side and his name tag pinned to the other), his carefully shaved eyebrow slits, immaculate hair and sparkling ear studs suggesting he probably knew how good-looking he was. His face smiles out from three mugs placed on the inside windowsill, interspersed with open-palmed ceramic Jesuses, and poems taped to the glass. It's September, but there's an unlit neon sign hung beneath the first-floor window saying *Merry Christmas*.

Jessica answers the door in nightshirt and dressing gown, and leads me up to the living room. Seven years after his death,

Jessica's front window.

Shaquan is everywhere, in that same pose in his Waitrose uniform: on the face of a clock, gazing out from an enormous frame on the wall, in smaller frames in a glass cabinet in the corner. The floor is covered with toys: teddies, dolls, a ride-on plastic car, a huge easel with an abacus. There are two stars in this house: Shaquan, and Jessica's two-year-old granddaughter, Shamiyah.

'The kids wanted us to move, but I didn't want to,' she says, pausing the TV and motioning for me to sit on her cream leather sofa. 'I felt like I'd be leaving Shaquan behind.' Jessica's twenty-seven-year-old daughter, Shantel, lives here along with Shamiyah, who's at nursery down the road. Andre, now twenty-three, stays over every so often. Jessica came to the UK from St Lucia in 1989. She moved to this house with her three children in 2001, when she was thirty-one, and earning a living scrubbing floors at McDonald's.

When I ask what Shaquan was like, a smile blooms across Jessica's face. 'He was like the dad to the house. His name is on everything. If you go into this television – the passwords are all his. My phone, my iPad – Shaquan's name is there, his recordings are there, I'm only discovering some of them now.' Shaquan loved tinkering with computers and gadgets, trying to fix things. And he loved girls. 'He was *so vain*! He would stand in this mirror' – she points to one on the wall – 'and he would say to me, "Mummy, Mummy! Look at your *peng* son, Mummy." If we were going out he used to say to me, "Mummy, when you're going out you need to have a bit of *swag*." Those were his two words – *peng* and *swag*.'

'You say he was vain . . .'

'*Very* vain!'

'. . . but I would say, looking at his photograph, that he was very handsome.'

'I know.' Her eyes sparkle. 'That's what everyone says. He had girls like it was wildfire. This boy! He was a *darling*.'

Shaquan also loved to eat, and Jessica loved to feed him. She'd cook him a full English every Sunday, and he'd eat it here in the living room, in front of the rugby or the football, while she began preparing his dinner. Sometimes he would dart into the kitchen and steal a piece of chicken. 'He would run up the stairs and say, "You cannot catch me, Mummy!"' She gazes across the corridor into the kitchen, and her face falls. 'After Shaquan died, I found it hard to cook.'

Jessica has debilitating arthritis, as well as a condition called intracranial hypertension which leaves her with vision problems and agonizing headaches. From an early age, her children became her carers, helping her around the house, scrubbing her back in the shower. They did it gladly, Jessica says.

'Shaquan used to say to me, "Mummy, listen. I want to get a job, I want to make you rich",' she tells me. He did a paper round in secondary school, getting up at 5 a.m. to make his deliveries in Archway before coming home to get ready to go to school in Enfield. Aged seventeen, he was doing his A-levels in Camden, and had offers from five universities to study human resources, Jessica says. He was also doing two jobs: serving food at Tottenham Hotspur football ground on Saturdays, and stacking shelves and working the tills Wednesday to Friday at Waitrose. 'The day when he put on the uniform, I took pictures of him, just to show off. I felt so good: my son was working.'

They were close, the two of them. 'If something happened outside, if his friends were doing things that were wrong, he'd find a way to tell me. I used to say, "You cannot follow them, you can't do what they are doing." And he'd say, "Mummy, I'm not stupid. I know what I'm doing."'

The last time Jessica saw Shaquan was at 3 p.m. on 30 January 2015, when he left home to go to work. Jessica didn't know it then, but he planned on going to two house parties that evening. The first was in Winchmore Hill, Enfield, with two old friends he hadn't seen in a while: Christopher Nzeh, known as CK, and another boy whose name I've never been told, for reasons you'll soon understand.

CK was going out with a girl called Amber, and there was a party at the home she shared with her mother and older brother on Berkeley Gardens. The three boys ate dinner at McDonald's, and CK called Amber to check it was OK for him to bring two friends along. Amber said she'd have to ask her nineteen-year-old brother, Jemal. Half an hour later, she hadn't rung back, so they called her again. She told them to make their way over: Jemal would talk to them there. They stopped off at Costcutter, and Shaquan bought some sweets and soft drinks. There's CCTV of the three of them, laughing and play fighting, as they make their way to Berkeley Gardens.

When they arrived, Jemal came downstairs to inspect the seventeen-year-olds on his doorstep. His eyes were red; he looked wasted. He was irritated that CK had brought along boys he didn't know. There were already too many people at the party, he said.

'What are you bringing next people to my house?' Jemal asked CK. (This comes from a report of what was said in court; *next people* means *strangers*.) He sneered at Shaquan. 'You've got five seconds to get away from my door.'

'What's this guy's problem?' Shaquan said.

They argued outside the house for a few minutes, before Shaquan told his friends to forget about the party. He turned to walk away, and Jemal demanded to know what was in his carrier bag. Shaquan said it was none of Jemal's business. He carried on walking down Berkeley Gardens.

Jemal ran upstairs, picked up a knife, ran out into the street after Shaquan, and stabbed him. Then he jumped the fence at the bottom of his back garden and disappeared.

*

Shaquan's life was taken by a single stab wound. The cost of trying to save it was likely far greater than the £1,110 estimate for health service costs after a homicide given in *Research Report 99*.

At 9.33 p.m., someone on Berkeley Gardens rang 999 to say that a young man had been stabbed outside his home, and he was trying to give him CPR. When paramedics from the London Ambulance Service arrived, they called for help from the London Air Ambulance service, and headed to the Royal London Hospital's specialist trauma unit.

The Air Ambulance fast-response car joined them on the way, with a team made up of Tom Konig, a surgeon, and two specialist paramedics, all dressed in stab vests and orange jumpsuits. Konig is an army major: he worked at a British military field hospital in Afghanistan before becoming one of five duty surgeons on the Royal London's trauma team. Stab wounds make up 30 per cent of his workload.

'What we found was the all too familiar scenario of a young boy with a single stab wound to the chest, who was in cardiac arrest,' Konig wrote the day after the murder, in a piece for London's *Evening Standard* newspaper. The team immediately cut through Shaquan's ribs to open up his chest so they could simultaneously diagnose and treat his injuries. 'The heart struggled to beat again and as it did it bled from its wounds and a significant wound from the aorta, the main artery that leaves it to take blood to the rest of the body,' Konig continued. 'The wounds were sutured, warmed blood was transfused directly into the heart and adrenaline infused to stimulate it to beat again. We held the heart of a young boy in our hands and willed it to beat and to survive.'

Their will was not enough. Shaquan was pronounced dead at the hospital at 10.56 p.m. It was Konig, in his orange Air Ambulance uniform, who knelt before Jessica to deliver the news.

'I feel like people are judging me all the time,' Jessica says, her voice breaking. 'My son wasn't involved in gangs!'

'I know,' I say. It was the first thing she told me on the phone when I first contacted her.

'It's the first thing people think. The liaison, even the barrister, they all said to me, "If you're going to do anything public, *always* use that picture to show the world that your son was a good boy."'

'Which picture?'

'The picture of him in the Waitrose uniform,' Jessica says, gesturing towards the enormous frame on the wall. 'That's what's on Shaquan's grave.'

Of all the devastating details that Jessica has told me today, this is the one that floors me. As if losing Shaquan were not enough, Jessica must bear the judgement of others, the loss of her family's reputation, because of the assumptions people make of how he must have been taken from her. It is a double tragedy.

I think of the grid of faces I've seen in newspaper coverage of the fifteen boys stabbed to death in London in 2015. Only two of them were white.

'When people assume that Shaquan was in a gang, do you think it's because of racism?' I ask.

'No,' Jessica replies immediately, 'it's just because he was stabbed. People think everyone that gets stabbed is in a gang. But the person who stabbed Shaquan *was* in a gang.'

*

'It was relatively clear from an early point that Shaquan was not involved in anything, as far as criminality was concerned,' Jamie Piscopo tells me. 'It was wrong place, wrong time.'

Piscopo is speaking to me over the phone from Northampton, where he's now a detective superintendent. He used to be a detective chief inspector at the Metropolitan Police, and was the on-call Senior Investigating Officer when Shaquan was killed. He tells me they knew who'd done it from day one. But when they finally found Jemal, after a nine-day manhunt, the CPS solicitor said they had insufficient evidence to charge him. Piscopo remembers being 'incredibly annoyed and frustrated'.

Even though Shaquan was killed in front of his two friends, even though Jemal ran down the stairs with the knife he used to kill him in the middle of a packed house party, no one at the scene said they saw anything at all. Shaquan's friends were so uncooperative that the police considered them suspects and arrested them. Jemal's sister, and his mother, who had been home at the time, were also arrested.

The police knew Shaquan had been killed by someone at the party: a blood dog followed a trail from where he collapsed to Jemal's house. They knew Jemal had been previously arrested for knife crime and had connections to a local gang. They knew he had fled. But there was no forensic evidence at the crime scene, they couldn't find the murder weapon, and house to house inquiries didn't reveal any witnesses. There was no CCTV footage of the stabbing. When Jemal was eventually arrested, his phone was clean, and he answered *no comment* to every police interview question.

'In hindsight, it was absolutely the right decision at the time not to charge,' Piscopo says. 'You've got to make sure that there is sufficient evidence to get it to trial and get it *through* the trial. The last thing you want is for the judge to turn around at the first hearing and go, "Why is this even in front of me?"'

Everyone was released on bail. Piscopo knew that the key to the investigation was breaking through what he calls the 'wall of silence' and getting one of Shaquan's friends to talk. CK had a criminal history and had been particularly hostile to the police.

(He's currently serving twenty-one years in prison for murder: less than six months after Shaquan was killed in front of him, he stabbed a man with a hunting knife during a robbery.) But the other friend was a different prospect: he had no criminal convictions, and had kept in touch with Jessica since the night of the murder. And he'd made a comment to the officer who'd released him from custody that suggested he knew more than he was prepared to say. They had to win the boy's trust, and make it easy for him to come forward and make a statement. Old-fashioned policing, or, as Piscopo calls it, 'good coppering'.

Jessica tells me that the reason Shaquan's friends wouldn't talk to the police was because they wanted to get their own kind of justice. 'They had their plans. But I had to call them and say to them, "No, don't." I didn't want that.'

With Jessica's encouragement, the friend who'd seen it all began to speak to the police. He said the main obstacle to giving evidence was fear for his family's safety. He was about to move house, but was still waiting for everything to be finalized. Piscopo's team wrote to the council, saying they hoped the process could be concluded quickly. As soon as his family moved, he made his statement. In October 2015 – more than eight months after Shaquan was stabbed – Jemal was rearrested and charged with murder.

Research Report 99 puts the cost to police of dealing with and investigating a homicide at £11,960, which it rather opaquely explains is 'the opportunity cost of police time and resources taken up by investigating a certain crime rather than engaging in other activities, such as responding to non-crime activities'. The figure includes call handling, investigation, crime scene management, custody duties and family liaison, but not police overheads.

Piscopo says twenty detectives would have been working on

the case at first, including an exhibits officer, scene of crime officers collecting forensic evidence, and specialist search officers looking for the murder weapon. Then things begin to taper off. 'By the end of the first month there were probably two detectives working on it. When it goes to court, you've got half a dozen who are working to support it. It's fits and starts.'

While there were some challenges, this was an average investigation for the police. 'It was typical. To be honest, it was a relatively straightforward job,' Piscopo tells me. Homicides are categorized, he explains. Category C murders are open and shut cases, where the suspect is found with the weapon in their hand and all the police need to do is put the evidence together and get it to court: 'Your domestic homicides and suchlike.' Category B murders are more challenging. 'You kind of know what's gone on, you've probably got a suspect, but you've got to work on it, and a bit of resources have got to be thrown into it.' A Category A murder is 'a whodunnit-type job. You haven't got a clue what's happened, you don't know who's done it. There's media scrutiny, you're in it for the long haul. Lots of resources, lots of complexities.' Shaquan's murder was a Category B: middling, average. 'Unfortunately, it's one of many, many, many cases that you see, especially in London,' Piscopo says.

Jemal Williams' trial at the Old Bailey began on 18 April 2018 and lasted a week. Shaquan's friend – the lone prosecution witness – gave evidence from behind a screen. In his defence, Jemal claimed Shaquan had pulled the knife on him, and was stabbed with his own weapon while Jemal tried to defend himself. Under cross-examination, he admitted it was normal for him to carry knives. 'Everyone does,' Jemal said.

The trial, too, was pretty typical. *Research Report 99* estimates the total costs incurred by the average murder to the criminal justice system to be £800,980, including the costs of the crown court, the CPS, jury service, defence, and the cost of prison and probation. The trial was relatively short, with a regular sized legal team (and with Jemal's defence covered by legal aid).

Sentencing Jemal Williams to life imprisonment with a minimum tariff of twenty-four years – a fairly average sentence for murder – Judge Richard Hone said, 'This is yet another profoundly sad case of the needless loss of a young life through knife crime on the streets of London.'

Yet another; one among too many.

But, seven years later, this average, typical case still sticks in Piscopo's mind. 'Two points in this case were genuinely two of my best moments while serving on the homicide command. The first was when I was able to go and see Jessica in person and tell her that we'd charged him. That was a good day. The second was when we got that guilty verdict in court. Not only did we get justice for Shaquan and Jessica and the rest of the family, it also was an illustration of my team's good work. There were a few drinks after that.'

I've been straight with everyone I've spoken to about Shaquan; they knew before they agreed to talk to me that I'm looking into the price of life, and trying to work out how the price civil servants put on a homicide relates to the real cost of murder. Still, when it comes to actually discussing it, I really don't want to. It feels callous, inhuman, abhorrent. But if anyone might see the benefit of this kind of analysis, it's a detective. It could mean more resources being directed to their team. It could mean they're better able to do their job. It could mean more justice for families like Shaquan's.

'How useful is it that the Home Office estimates the economic and social costs of homicide?' I manage to ask.

'Hmmm.' There's a long pause. 'That's the last thing on my mind. I've got no interest in that kind of stuff.' Piscopo then says, 'I have the resources that I've got; if I need extra, I'll ask for them. Hopefully, I'll get them. If I don't, I'll just manage with what I've got. You're there to solve murders.'

Research Report 99 values the loss of Shaquan himself at £2,337,140: £254,710 in lost output from average unearned wages, plus £2,082,430 from an average number of quality-adjusted life years lost. But, at seventeen, Shaquan was younger than average; he had more years taken away from him. He was also his mother's carer, and the loss of that care isn't accounted for. The price of £2,337,140 is too low for him.

But what about the cost to Jessica?

'I found Shaquan's loss very, very difficult to cope with,' she tells me quietly. 'I felt like everything of mine had gone, like he was the only child I had.' Andre used to complain that she only thought about Shaquan, but Jessica couldn't stop him monopolizing her thoughts. 'All I wanted was to just end my life.'

Today, it's as raw as ever. 'Every day it's like you're carrying this burden. You're carrying this *pain*. And the pain is *not going*. When Shamiyah is around, it kind of occupies your mind, but it's still there.' She points to her hairline. 'My hair is falling out.' Her fingers move down to her jawline, which is pocked with dark scars. 'I pick my chin – can you see? I have to stop.' She sighs. 'I just want to be normal like everybody. I cannot be like you because I've got this thing inside of me that's *not going*.'

Someone came over to see her from victim support (valued at £5,480 per homicide in *Research Report 99*), but Jessica says he wasn't much use. 'He was just telling me things that he googled.' She had to wait three years for the little counselling she's had. Andre had some counselling too, but he didn't like it. 'Andre cannot cope with . . . He hasn't accepted Shaquan's death. He doesn't really do much talking about Shaquan.'

While we've been talking, Shantel has been sorting out the washing in the kitchen. Jessica calls her into the living room, and she greets me with a huge smile, her delicate face an echo of her handsome brother in the frames. Shantel never had any counselling. 'I just keep it inside and leave it there,' she tells me. 'For me, the biggest thing is Shamiyah doesn't have her uncle. She's basically lost two uncles: Andre is so isolated within himself. He was always quiet, but not *this* quiet. Andre's very angry at the world, he's very irritable, every little thing annoys him, he runs away from *everything,* he doesn't speak to *anyone.* He just likes to be by himself. Shaquan was the life of the house. A middle child. And then he wasn't here, and everything disintegrated.'

After Shantel goes back into the kitchen, I feel I have to do it now. Could there ever be anything more grotesque than showing a mother the bill for her son's murder? But Jessica knows that's why I'm here.

'You remember I told you about the study some Home Office economists did?' I begin. 'They calculated each murder costs society about £3,217,000.'

Her eyes widen. 'I think that's a lot. Of course it is. Wow.' Jessica takes it in for a few moments. Then she shakes her head. 'I don't see the point of that,' she says.

'These economists are trying to show politicians which crimes they need to focus on, by looking at what's costing the most.' It's strange to hear myself rationalizing it, just like Brand and Price did in the first paper.

Jessica frowns. 'Of course they need to invest more into knife crime. We need to take a different approach to it. When the Queen died, there were so many killings, and it was put to one side because the news was focusing on *her* death . . .'

The capricious news cycle isn't a good way of focusing the minds of politicians on things that matter. There has to be a better way. But is putting a price on life the answer?

'To be quite honest, I don't know what to say,' Jessica continues. 'The government just worries about the money and nothing else. If you are rich and your child is killed, they will be with you. If you are a privileged person, it will be on the news 24/7 for a while. But if you are poor – no. And if it's a Black kid killing another Black kid . . .' She shakes her head.

'People focus on the white victims?'

'*Of course* they do.'

When I looked in more depth at the fifteen teenagers lost to knife crime in London in 2015, I could see the two white boys had had reams of coverage. Fifteen-year-old Alan Cartwright, stabbed by a Black boy, less than a month after Shaquan, five minutes from where we are sitting now, had his story told in long form magazine features. Alfie Stone, eighteen, stabbed by a woman in Ickenham in a row over stolen food, made national television news bulletins. The other victims, the Black boys, got a story or two in their local paper, but rarely anything more.

No matter how much the economists crunching the data for the Home Office may seek to use numbers to take the idiosyncrasies out of human experience, some people's murders are clearly worth more to society. A Black boy stabbed is often worth less. Calculating averages does nothing to reflect that inequality, or address it.

Like many parents who have lost their children to knife crime, Jessica has set up a foundation in her son's memory. She gives talks to schools to warn children about the dangers of carrying knives; she raises funds for the London Air Ambulance. It gives some meaning to the senseless thing that happened to Shaquan.

'I'm so sorry to make you tell this story again,' I say.

'But I have to,' she replies. 'It's a way of making me better.'

She leads me to her front door, and stands in her nightshirt with bare feet on the cold stone doorstep. 'My neighbours saved up for that bench, you know,' she says. 'The sun has bleached that photo. I'll have to put a new one in.' She smiles. 'Never mind. God is good.'

On 5 July 2003, my friend was murdered. Richard Wild was the first journalist to be killed after British and American forces supposedly won the war in Iraq. He'd been reporting outside the Museum of Iraq in Baghdad, when someone came up behind him and shot him in the back of his head at point-blank range.

Rich and I had been students together. He was twenty-four when he was killed; so young and gorgeous, so popular, talented at so many things, so smart. Twenty years on, I've accepted that my friend was murdered, but the void he left remains. As I have got older, had kids and the experiences of adult life Rich will never see, I get a sense of the contribution he didn't get to make to the world. His death feels like a robbery, as well as a murder.

I know there must be hundreds of people who have been robbed by the taking of Shaquan's life. The ripples caused by his murder go further than any economist could accurately measure.

'It's seven years now and I don't think there's a day that's gone by where I haven't thought of his name at least once,' Perciss Frimpong tells me over the phone. He's twenty-six and went to secondary school with Shaquan. They were at different sixth form colleges in 2015, but they hung out all the time, playing football ('although he was absolutely terrible at that, man'), jumping on the Xbox, going to house parties together – 'typical stuff'. They were supposed to go to the second party together on the Friday night Shaquan was killed.

Perciss heard the news on the Saturday morning. He didn't eat or sleep over the weekend. He thought he could go to school the following Monday, but it was too much for him. Across London, in all the schools that Shaquan had attended throughout primary, secondary and sixth form, hundreds of young people were struggling. 'He was so popular. So many were touched by it. So many people couldn't go into school.'

Perciss's college organized grief counselling. 'They were really supportive in trying to help me process things. I was with the school counsellor quite a bit until I finished up my A-levels.' This kind of help would never be accounted for in *Research Report 99*, but kids in several schools would have needed it; students at Shaquan's sixth form college would have been at school with him only hours before he died.

The cost of victim support in *Research Report 99* doesn't include the community support that does so much to help people bereaved by murder. Shaquan's friends were the ones to receive it, at first. Now they provide it to Jessica.

'Things can be difficult for Auntie Jess. Any support that she needs, we're there for her. If one man can't do it, there's another man that's ready to go there.' Every year, they play a football tournament in Shaquan's name, raising money for the foundation and giving Jessica an excuse to cook for them all. 'There's a *lot* of us, close to twenty-five of us. If we all put down £20 each, if my maths is correct, that can turn into £500 towards helping her to do whatever she needs, or helping put the tournament together.'

And in providing that unofficial, unconditional safety net for Jessica, these young men have made something precious for themselves. 'It's mad because as the years have gone on, we're all still together. I think that's the main plus that we gained from Shaquan's passing – the strengthening of the brotherhood.

It's a double-edged sword. We're all so much closer together now. The way things are is just so good.'

Another life was taken away because of that single stab wound in Berkeley Gardens on 30 January 2015. Sentenced to life in prison for twenty-four years without parole, the earliest Jemal Williams can be eligible for release is 20 April 2040, when he will be forty-five. Allowing for changes in accounting and inflation, the most recent set of figures from the Ministry of Justice say it costs £49,888 a year to keep each inmate in a public sector jail. The price of Jemal's life in prison is £1,197,312.

PART TWO

A LIFE LOST

CHAPTER FOUR
£200,000
Life insurance

By the time the call came in to the police, on 1 October 2011, the body was already decomposing. An adult male, apparently dead, had been reported at the roadside on the outskirts of the Moldovan village of Cojușna, forty minutes north of the capital city. The officer dispatched to the scene found no visible signs of injury on the body, and the man was well dressed, with his passport, hotel key card and a list of contact numbers in his pockets. At the state morgue, the Moldovan medical examiner gave the cause of death as a heart attack. The body was identified as Igor Vorotinov, a recently divorced forty-seven-year-old Moldovan national and Minnesota resident, who'd been in the country dealing second-hand cars.

The news was broken to Irina Vorotinov over the phone a few hours later, five thousand miles away at her home in Maple Grove, a suburb of Minneapolis. She was distraught, barely able to function. The elder of her two sons, twenty-one-year-old Alkon, wanted to accompany her on the journey to Moldova to formally identify his father, but Irina insisted on travelling alone. She arrived at the small morgue accompanied by Igor's cousin and a representative from the US Embassy, and confirmed their worst fears: it was her ex-husband. She organized a cremation in Odessa, Ukraine, on 20 October, and flew the ashes home to the USA a few days later. At Igor's funeral on 4 November, the urn was placed in a niche at the mausoleum of Minneapolis's Lakewood Cemetery. Throngs of mourners from the local Russian-speaking community came to pay their respects.

It was a lot for Alkon to take in. He was bewildered by the sudden news, dazed by shock and grief, and overwhelmed with the responsibility of taking care of his family, who were now saddled with Igor's debts. And there was more bad news to come: days after the funeral, Irina learned that the breast cancer she thought she'd beaten had returned. She'd need chemotherapy, and a double mastectomy.

But there was a bright, shining silver lining that Irina now shared with Alkon: his father had left them a generous gift from the grave. Eighteen months before his death, Igor had taken out life insurance, and Irina was listed on the policy as the primary beneficiary in the event of his untimely death. She had submitted a claim to Igor's insurer, Mutual of Omaha, three days after the funeral, and in April 2012 a cheque for $2,048,414.09 made out in her name landed in their Maple Grove mailbox.

Alkon did what he could to look after the family while his mother underwent cancer treatment. At her request, he opened a trust account and began wiring money all over the world, to Moldova, Hungary, Switzerland and beyond. He sent $1.5 million to an account in Zurich for investment purposes.

While he waited for the dividends to come in, he paid a visit to Moldova in June 2012, to reconnect with Moldovan friends and family for the first time since he'd lost his father. At a dinner party hosted by a friend's mother, after the guests had already sat down to eat, there was a knock on the door. In walked Igor. The father he had spent eight months mourning was very much alive.

'I was very happy to see him but it was weird,' Alkon wrote in an affidavit to the US Federal Court in September 2016. (As you will soon discover, Alkon is a master of understatement. Laconic doesn't even begin to cover it.) 'I started to ask him some stuff but my dad said, "The less you know, the better you sleep at night."' They exchanged hugs, but Alkon never got a chance to speak properly with Igor that evening. He waited until his return to the US before breaking the news to his mother – and then he realized it wasn't actually news to her. 'When I told her she didn't seem surprised,' his statement continued. 'My relationship from this point forward with her has been strained.'

Alkon continued to make trips to Moldova to see his father, and brought his younger brother along to meet their dead dad at least once. On one of the trips, Alkon embarked on a whirlwind romance with a Moldovan woman called Olga: they were engaged within two months of meeting. He brought her to the US for the first time on 27 November 2013, but they were stopped at the airport in Detroit, and customs officials seized their computers, phones and cameras. Alkon thought they were just overzealous border officials doing due diligence on the Moldovan fiancée he was bringing into the country; it was only when he was finally arrested, in February 2015, that the penny dropped. Someone in Moldova had tipped the Feds off that Igor was out there, living it large. And there Igor was, in time-stamped digital photographs on Alkon's and Olga's phones and hard drives: posing with their baby daughter in a park in April 2013, splashing about in a pool in May 2013, bursting with life.

The FBI argued that this was a major conspiracy that went further than the Vorotinov family: there were no photographs of the corpse by the side of the road, or at the morgue, because both the Moldovan police and morgue staff claimed not to have any means of taking pictures the day the body was discovered. When the FBI removed the urn from Lakewood Cemetery and analysed its contents, the ashes were found to be human remains, but the true identity of the corpse found in Cojușna dressed in Igor's clothes and festooned with his ID documents remains a mystery.

Almost five years after Igor's 'death', Alkon pleaded guilty to the charge of misprision of felony, which means having knowledge of a federal crime and failing to report it. Prosecutors never doubted that he'd believed that his father had died; the issue was what happened once he'd learned he was still alive. After initially seeking a three-year jail sentence, they struck a deal with Alkon: in return for cooperating with the court and giving evidence against his own mother, he got three years of probation plus 300 hours of community service. A few months later, Irina pleaded guilty to fraud and was sentenced to just over three years in prison. Igor managed to avoid extradition until November 2018; he was sentenced to forty-one months in jail in July 2019. But the outstanding balance – the $2 million due to Mutual of Omaha – still needed to be paid back. The court decided the restitution money was Alkon's responsibility.

But why should it fall to Alkon to repay the money his father had stolen? How could the insurers justify valuing Igor's life at $2 million in the first place? And can any sum of money be worth pretending to be dead for the rest of your life?

The Vorotinovs have never given interviews before, but I try my luck. I manage to work out what Igor's email address must be and drop him a line, around the time I figure he must have served his sentence. And, to my delight, he replies the very same day to say yes, he'll talk to me.

'Hello dear Jenny, I will let you interview me,' he writes, 'after my probation is over.'

Joy turns to despair when I realize that's another year and a half away.

'Do you think Alkon might be happy to speak to me in the meantime? Or perhaps Irina?' I reply.

'Sorry but all 3 of us can't be able to talk to you until the end of probation,' he fires back.

So close, and yet so far. I rue my misfortune for a day or so, and then I remember that Igor is a convicted fraudster, and perhaps I shouldn't take him at his word. So I contact Alkon, and discover there are no restrictions on him giving interviews at all, other than logistical ones: he's working all the hours he can to pay the insurance company back, and to pay child support to his now ex-wife, Olga, so finding the time to talk will be tricky. But he'll talk. While we play phone tennis trying to work out a time to speak, I have a Zoom call with his attorney.

'I feel that Alkon really got screwed here – not by the Feds, but by his own parents,' Matthew Mankey tells me from his office in Minneapolis, in front of a mantelpiece adorned with certificates. Matthew has a neat beard and kind eyes. He tells me the Vorotinovs' story with the air of someone who knows it's true but still can't believe it himself. 'His mother literally had a memorial service for the guy, and let her two children anguish. What kind of people put their kids through this?' He shakes his head. 'This kid had the Hobson's choice of supporting his mom and dad or narking them out. And he was twenty-one years old. He didn't know what misprision of felony was – frankly, his lawyer didn't even either. But there's still $2 million of restitution owed, right? He's on the hook for two mil. Because who else are they going to hook?'

I still don't really get why this is Alkon's problem alone. What about his younger brother, who's never named in court documents but knew Igor was alive just as much as Alkon did? And what about Igor and Irina? Why didn't they cash in all those investments in Zurich and beyond to repay the insurance company?

'I guess karma is a bitch, because they lost everything,' Matthew tells me. 'They got taken advantage of by people in various countries.' Irina is still very sick, Igor was in Moldova and then in jail, and Alkon's brother has serious mental health issues that leave him unable to work, Matthew explains, adding that Alkon lost his job after his brother turned up at the car lot where he was working and damaged a number of vehicles. Alkon had to foot the bill for that too. The price he's paying for his parents' criminality goes way beyond the restitution money, Matthew says. He has been ostracized by the Russian-speaking community. He was evicted from his apartment after receiving a handwritten note which read, 'We know what you did. Go to hell.'

'Are you familiar with Winnie the Pooh?' Matthew asks me. 'You know Eeyore? Dealing with Alkon, it was constant hopelessness. He owes $2 million, he's a felon now, he can't get a frigging job, his ex-wife was horrible to him, meanwhile he's taking care of his brother and trying to parent his two children.' He sighs. 'At one point, Alkon was so distraught that he drove his car at 140mph into a bridge abutment trying to kill himself. He walked away unscathed, and then said to me, "I can't even do that right." I think he's got a really good heart. It's just a cascade of crappy things that happened to this kid.'

But Alkon wasn't quite a kid back then. He was mature

enough to be able to wire dodgy money around the world and instruct investors in Zurich; he was twenty-one, soon to become a husband and a father. Matthew is Alkon's attorney, paid to paint him in the most sympathetic light possible. Could anyone be as unlucky, and as gullible and guileless, as the man Matthew is describing?

'He really didn't benefit financially at all from this?' I ask.

'Not a goddamn bit. He doesn't have the sophistication to concoct a scheme like this, even though it was stupid. He doesn't have it in him,' he replies. 'One of the big problems when the US attorneys were prepping him for testimony was that they just got really frustrated with him. I don't know whether he's monumentally shy or what, but they hated the thought of having to use him as a witness.'

I understand what Matthew means when Alkon finally has time to talk to me. Alkon speaks in painfully short, almost comically understated sentences, with a strong Minnesota accent. I start off by asking him how he felt at the dinner party when his dead father walked into the room, and he pauses, before replying, 'Surprised. Shocked. Like – what the hell.'

'You must have had mixed feelings,' I say, determined to get a proper answer out of him.

'Exactly,' comes his reply.

If he is a scheming mastermind, he hides it very well.

The first opportunity he has to call me is on Boxing Day. And no, he didn't have a good Christmas: both his kids had vomiting bugs.

'I'm working my ass off, like I got to,' he says. 'I have to make money. It's been tough getting jobs.' At the moment he's the manager of a car-buying centre, sourcing second-hand cars at auction for dealerships, but he has to pay the insurance company $500 a month, as well as child support to his ex-wife. 'On top of taxes,' he adds. At his current rate, it would take him well over three centuries to repay Mutual of Omaha.

Alkon is desperate to put all this behind him, but nobody will let him. 'Pretty much everywhere you go, people have heard about it. They're quick to judge. I've definitely lost a lot of friends and family along the way. People have turned against me, but my brother, who obviously didn't know either, they've kind of left him alone.'

After a tough few years, his brother is finally doing better now, Alkon says.

'There's people that are able to get pardoned and forgiven for much worse than whatever I've done. It sometimes feels like I've been paying a heavier price.'

Yes, Alkon tells me, he does have his own life insurance policy. 'It's through work and stuff,' he says. 'I mean, it *is* a good idea to have. You never know what could happen.'

After being made to grieve at his dad's phoney funeral, after testifying against his mother, after losing friends and jobs and his home, and now staring into a future where he'll have to pay back the money his parents embezzled for the rest of his life, Alkon says he still talks to them. 'Things are better. But it's still tough. We were definitely a lot closer when I was growing up.'

'It's amazing that you have a relationship at all,' I say.

'Well. We don't get to choose our family. Right?'

If you think the Vorotinovs' story is extraordinary, think again. For John Saunders it's mundane; his bread and butter, his daily in-tray. John has spent many of his seventy-four years being sent around the world to investigate scams just like Igor's. Fraudulent life insurance claims are made *all the time*; what makes Igor's slightly unusual is that it was successful, at first:

the insurance company paid out. John reckons his work has led to at least £300 million of claims being refuted, and thirty or forty people being convicted of fraud. You could write a book about the hundreds of scammers he's unearthed. And he has: a self-published memoir entitled *Go Away, I'm Dead*.

Written during the enforced break from visiting morgues caused by the Covid lockdown, the book is a travelogue of his experiences on dirt roads and in dodgy hotels across Africa, Asia, Latin America and Europe, investigating the putatively deceased. I was looking forward to a detailed examination of his caseload, an insight into the mindset of insurance scammers from someone who knows them better than anyone, but it's not that kind of book; there are surprisingly few details on the cases he's debunked. Hundreds of anecdotes, but very few names or dates. Pages of photos of John standing alongside officially dead people who are very much alive, but their heads are entirely obscured with large black squares. John writes it's to 'protect the guilty', but if they're guilty, I can't see why he thinks they deserve his protection. Perhaps he's worried about getting sued.

When we finally talk, in the dining room of his home in Windsor, it's clear that it's times, places and sums of money that matter to John, not characters and personalities. He has a neatly trimmed moustache, bristly white hair and the air of someone who has no time for nonsense – perhaps no time for verbs and definite articles. He's just returned from a recent work trip (he doesn't want me to reveal where), and when I ask him how it went, he says, 'Good. Hard work. Long hours. Huge fraud. Three million.'

In pretty much any given country in the developing world, John can tell you which morgues are dodgy, which registrars are prepared to issue a death certificate without a body, which doctors and police officers are the most bent, and how to spot a fresh grave that's been dug just for his benefit. But John investigates claims in the UK too – when people have supposedly died at sea, or are claiming critical illness cover for a condition they were aware of and didn't declare when they took out insurance. He has a highly developed nose for fraud, he tells me. 'With 90 per cent of the claims, I can tell within seconds if the claim is genuine. It's a battle of wits.'

John has always got a buzz from unmasking liars. He's semi-retired now, but companies still send a steady stream of claims to him for his perusal. He tells me about a critical illness claim he recently investigated in the UK. 'Two million. I found that it was nonsense. Immigrant on the dole, benefits – why are you insured for so much? Another guy, very educated, two million for motor neuron or something like that. It's sad, he has it, but I proved he *knew* he had it when he took the policy out. It was *obvious* he knew. So I quite enjoy the work, really.'

I can't get a word in even if I wanted to, but I don't really want to. What can you say when someone tells you how much they enjoy denying the claim of a man with a terminal wasting disease? I guess John isn't thinking about how all this sounds. In his world, fraud is fraud, and any tragic circumstances of the person committing it are irrelevant.

Sometimes people try and pass off suicides as accidental deaths to make a claim. Sometimes people are even murdered for their life insurance: it's one of the many reasons people hire hitmen. But the most common kind of life insurance fraud is faking your own death overseas, John says. Road traffic accidents are the most popular method. 'Trouble is, they forget they need a police report,' he tells me. 'It's easy to get the death certificate, but they don't know how to get the rest of the stuff.' Paperwork can be faked or stolen. John has his own death certificate – a blank one he picked up on his travels and filled in with his own name, just for fun.

So what kind of person is prepared to fake their own death? John says it's generally men, first-generation migrants to the UK who've worked and saved some money, maybe bought a house and got a pension, and then realize they could disappear and 'live like a king' in their country of birth on the insurance payout. 'A new start. Start a new business. Import cars – that always used to be the thing.' And I think of Igor, dealing cars in Moldova, one of the poorest countries in Europe. I'm beginning to see just how humdrum his scheme was. 'They think they're clever,' John says, licking his lips. 'They think they've come up with a new idea; they don't realize it's been done before.'

The children and grandchildren of migrants are less keen.

'I often talk to second- or third-generation Indians, Pakistanis, Nigerians, Ghanaians. They say, "I couldn't fake *my* death. I couldn't go and live in India. I've been with my parents a few times, but I couldn't live there."'

As John has got older, he's noticed a different kind of fraudster emerging: younger, more desperate, more naive. 'Immigrants who've not been here long. The Indian one I did recently, one and a half million. Unemployed, debt, struggling,' he says. 'Most of the people who fake their deaths have got loans, massive credit card debts. You think, how on earth did they get the loan in the first place? In fact, how does an insurance company give a twenty-one-year-old immigrant £2 million in insurance? They do a health check, blood test, does he smoke – did they do a financial check? No. Unbelievable.'

This is the first time John has been anything close to critical of insurance companies, and it chimes with my big question. How do they value a life? Why don't they investigate whether people are worth the sums they're insuring their lives for? How could Mutual of Omaha take one look at Igor the debt-ridden second-hand car dealer and see $2 million?

'So it's partially the fault of companies for insuring people who really shouldn't have that level of cover?' I ask.

John pauses and takes a deep breath. 'Well, if they checked everything out when the policy was taken out it would delay it, it would make the policy more expensive, people wouldn't take out life insurance. For every 10,000 policies, there's probably one where there is a problem. When that problem arises, deal with it. It's much cheaper to do it that way around.' You can't blame John for not wanting to bite the hand that feeds him. 'I've got to be very diplomatic here,' he adds, a little sheepishly.

A normal level of cover is probably £200,000 now, John says. 'The fraud cases tend to be more towards the £500,000 plus.'

While John won't reveal most of the names and faces of people he's investigated, he's happy to give me details when the fraudsters have previously been exposed in the press. There's Thulile Bhebhe, the nurse who claimed her husband, Bekezela, had died on holiday in Zimbabwe; John found that Bekezela – also a nurse – was on duty at London's Charing Cross Hospital on the day of his 'death.' There's Ecuadorian Alfredo Sanchez, who was unmasked by John when his fingerprints were discovered on his own death certificate. There are plenty of British fraudsters too: Paul Early, who was supposed to have died at sea but who John found hiding under a bed in Bournemouth; Anthony McErlean, who was supposed to have been killed by a cabbage truck in Honduras but was spotted shopping in Sainsbury's in Kent.

And of course there's John Darwin, aka Canoe Man, the most famous of them all, the debt-ridden prison officer who was supposedly lost in the North Sea during a kayak trip near Hartlepool (it was actually a kayak) in 2002, before his wife, Anne, claimed on his £250,000 life insurance policy. He lived in a bedsit next door to Anne for a while before secretly moving back in with her; then they moved to Panama. When John was closing in on him in 2007, Canoe Man turned up at a London police station pretending to have lost his memory. The truth was revealed when pictures of the Darwins, taken in 2006, were spotted on the property website movetopanama.com. For five years, they had allowed their two sons to believe their father was dead.

The story has prompted countless podcasts, at least five books (including one by Canoe Man himself and another by his now ex-wife), a BBC Four dramatization in 2010, and a four-part prime-time ITV miniseries in 2022. But John practically yawns when I mention it. 'It's probably one of the most boring ones,' he sniffs.

'Do you think people would be surprised if they knew how un-unique John Darwin is?' I ask. 'Why don't people know about how widespread this kind of fraud is?'

'There aren't that many convictions. There have also been several convictions that have not been in the newspaper.'

My mind boggles at the scale of it all. 'Would you say that for every one of these cases of fraud that you've uncovered, there must be more that go undetected?'

'Do some get through? Possibly, but not if they come to me,' he says, with such supreme confidence that I think he must be joking, so I laugh.

'No, I mean that,' he adds, unsmiling, and perhaps annoyed that his self-belief should surprise anyone.

John has a very definite sense of what's true and untrue; of right and wrong. And he has no truck for those who might think defrauding an insurance company is a victimless crime, a bit Robin Hood, a bit less wrong than other forms of theft.

'If the insurance company pay, *we're* paying, aren't we? We all pay for it,' he says sombrely. And he's right, of course: we're subsidizing all this criminal activity with our premiums. A recent study by Coalition Against Insurance Fraud found it costs $308.6 billion a year in the USA. The Association of British Insurers (ABI) estimates that fraud adds around £50 a year to the insurance bill of every policy holder.

I think about how Bob had to start going to church after so many years of looking at the rentahitman.com inbox. 'Having spent so many decades investigating fraud, do you still have faith in people?' I ask.

'I do,' he replies immediately. 'But I do think . . . how can I put this? I know people who'll exaggerate an insurance claim for a burglary or a car or something. There's a general sense of opinion among what I would regard as *honest* people that getting a bit extra from an insurance company is fair game.' He looks straight at me. 'It does surprise me. But it is, unfortunately, common.'

In the UK alone, the ABI detected £1.2 billion of fraudulent claims in 2019. Most of us are somewhere in the middle of a continuum that begins with John and ends with Igor. By exaggerating any insurance claim, even by a tiny amount, or by massaging a detail to ensure the claim goes through successfully, we are all prepared to enter the same waters as Canoe Man.

In January 2022, the German supermodel Heidi Klum appeared on one of the final episodes of Ellen Degeneres's talk show and discussed why her legs are officially worth $2 million. She was dressed in a low-cut shocking-pink latex minidress, but it was her legs that stole the show, tanned and endless and tightly crossed as she perched on Ellen's white armchair.

'I didn't insure them, by the way – it was a client that insured them,' Heidi explained. 'And one was actually more expensive than the other, because when I was young, I fell into [some] glass and I have, like, a big scar. Obviously I put so much spray tan on you can't see it right now. But yeah. One was more expensive than the other one.'

Rumours abound of celebrities that have bits of them insured for ridiculous sums: J-Lo's bum ($17m), Gene Simmons from Kiss's tongue ($500,000), Julia Roberts' smile ($200m). It's not just for the rich and famous either. Companies sometimes insure the prized body parts of significant employees. In what may be a clever marketing exercise as much as prudent risk management, Cadbury owner Mondelez announced in 2016 that it had insured chief chocolate taster Hayleigh Curtis's tastebuds for £1 million with Lloyds of London. That makes them only 10 per cent as valuable as those of Costa Coffee's chief taster, Gennaro Pelliccia, whose tongue was insured for £10 million seven years earlier. These limbs, bottoms and mouths are insured as part of a personal accident policy; they're not part of any life insurance. And, believe it or not, there's some logic to it all.

I ring up Charlie Boyd, an underwriter at Lloyds of London, who has made a career out of insuring the body parts of male strippers and female 'models of various sorts,' as he puts it. 'It's insuring yourself against being disabled and not being able to do your job – it just happens that your job relies on one or several body parts,' Charlie tells me. 'We will look at the income they generate through the profession they rely on their body part for, and then we will typically give a maximum of ten times that income.'

But when it comes to how insurers value a human life, income doesn't seem to come into it. Getting good figures on the average value of an insured life is tricky. The ABI has data on the average claim paid in the UK (it was £80,485 in 2021), but when it comes to group assurance – life insurance paid by companies on behalf of their employees – that figure is £116,414. Both these numbers relate to amounts paid out, rather than the amount covered; they can't be seen as estimates of the value of human life insured. Levels of cover vary enormously according to time, place and person. Research published by the insurer Royal London in 2021 showed how much gender is a factor: while the average sum assured on a life insurance policy in Ireland was €177,409 for women, it was €291,162 for men.

With such huge figures at stake, there must be some logic to all of this. Where do these numbers come from? How can the average man be worth 64 per cent more than the average woman? How can a supposedly sensible sector like the insurance industry put up with such variations in value?

I find some much-needed sanity in the form of Dr Simone Krummaker, an insurance underwriter-turned-academic who's now a senior lecturer in insurance at Bayes Business School, City University. Simone has a sweep of long blonde hair and a soft German accent. She has a fake backdrop of the exterior of her campus behind her on our Zoom call, a modernist grey building, reassuringly sober.

When it comes to how a human life is valued in insurance, Simone tells me, there are two separate perspectives at play. 'If you're the one taking out the life insurance policy, you're thinking about what you need to cover. It's about balancing what you can afford and where you want to end up, for most people,' she explains. This is about what the rest of the family needs to survive without a massive loss of lifestyle if one of the breadwinners gets seriously ill or dies. It's the sort of thing you'd chat through with a broker when you decide what level of cover you need and can afford; it might explain the discrepancy between the average levels of coverage between men and women: men value themselves more highly than women do.

There is some logic to this: the gender pay gap means that women are paid 14.9 per cent less than men on average, and are more likely to take time away from paid work after they have their first child. But it's strange to think that becoming a mother might diminish the value of a woman's life when viewed in terms of insurance coverage.

The other perspective, Simone says, is that of the insurer, who is interested in how likely it is that they are going to have to pay up – or rather, how likely it is that you're going to die before the end of the policy. 'That is more of an actuarial and statistical exercise. There are mortality tables, life expectancy tables. This is also why we have to fill in long questionnaires about risk factors, lifestyles, health, behaviour, all that kind of stuff,' she continues breezily. 'They can cite with pretty good accuracy what your average rest of life expectancy is for your given age and condition.'

I decided to get life insurance after I had my kids. I think about the endless forms I filled in, assuming they needed all that information so they could check I was healthy. I didn't realize I was giving them data so they could calculate when I was going to die.

'Does that mean my insurer has a pretty good idea of how long I'm going to live?' I ask.

Simone nods. 'Yes. If you have insurance, they have your risk factor, your number, your likelihood of an early death.'

Insurers care about whether you're likely to die before the end of the term covered by the policy, not how much they will have to pay if you do. That's why they don't do financial checks: the level of cover doesn't matter. You could take out a massive policy – like Igor's $2 million with Mutual of Omaha – even if it's far more than your family would ever require to maintain their lifestyle without you, and no one would ever stop you, so long as you can pay the monthly premium. Your premium would be adjusted accordingly, Simone explains. 'The risk element in that – that you die – doesn't change independently of how much money is being covered, but of course, the premium element that goes towards the payout increases in line with how much you want to take out.'

In the twenty-first century, your risk of death is being calculated in increasingly sophisticated ways. 'Insurers are looking into artificial intelligence and credit scores to predict behaviour, and from there predict risk factors,' Simone says. The underwriter is looking for reasons to reject you: anything that indicates you're a non-standard risk, increasing the likelihood that they'd have to pay out before the policy ends. 'This is where big data comes into play.' It can work in the customer's favour, she says: an eighty-nine-year-old woman would normally never qualify for traditional life insurance, but if bank data shows she's making withdrawals at the cashpoint on the high street every other day, then she's probably fit and mobile enough to be offered a certain policy. If someone has already been diagnosed with diabetes – the kind of pre-existing condition that would normally preclude you from cover – but regularly posts gym photos and fitness tracker data on social media, it could be taken as evidence their condition is well managed, and they might be in with a chance of being offered a regular policy.

I shudder a little at the thought of the exponentially more intelligent algorithms churning through the vast and swelling reservoir of data I leave in my wake, to build up an ever more accurate picture of when I'm expected to die.

Simone seems unfazed. 'The more data an insurer can get hold of, the more accurately they can figure out what the potential future losses for them are going to be. Because that is always the long-term worry – more payouts than expected.'

If they really wanted to go there, the industry could use genome sequencing and genetic testing, but so far they've chosen not to. 'The fear always is that you will find a marker for breast cancer or something else, even though it might not manifest. Again, it's just probabilities. There are ethical and moral questions with that.'

You can say that again. It turns out that there's a voluntary moratorium on genetic testing in insurance, reviewed every year when the ABI writes a report for the UK government on the state of the insurance market and development of genomic technologies. But in an era when genetic testing and personalized medicine are becoming routine, it's easy to imagine this being dropped one day, and a strand of hair, a drop of saliva or a vial of blood being as necessary for insurance as those long, dull questionnaires.

I thought getting to grips with the theory part of this would be like brown rice: necessary, good for me to know, but difficult to get excited about; certainly after speaking to someone whose father faked his own death and a man who hunts down the undead. But it turns out that insurance – even the non-fraudulent, straight-down-the-line kind – is fascinating when Simone is explaining it.

And there's more: life insurance is unique precisely *because* of the price of life, and how it's calculated. You can take out as many life insurance policies as you like as long as you can afford them, Simone says, but you can only insure your possessions once. 'The key idea with insurance is that it should put you back into the position you would have been in if a loss never happened. It shouldn't make you better off, because then you would have *gained* from having a loss. That's why I only insure my bike once; my house once. In life insurance, though, the situation *can't* be restored as if the loss hadn't happened.'

While you can put an accurate price on property, a price on life is much more subjective in insurance, so it's up to you to decide how much you want to invest in covering it. It falls to you to put the price tag on your life, because a life can't be replaced, and your insurance company has no way of assessing the true value of your life to the people left behind when you die.

Simone has convinced me that insurance does depend on clever logic, even if it's only on the side of calculating the likelihood that a person will die, rather than valuing their life. But this all still relies on risk factors and odds. How is any of this different from gambling?

'There's a difference – that's what I teach my students in their first lecture,' she replies, clearly delighted to be asked this question. 'You should not be able to *win* from insurance. It only covers you if the bad stuff happens, and then it will restore you to your initial wealth.' When you go into a casino, you know you'll either come out richer or poorer, but when you sign up to an insurance policy, you know you will stay where you are, minus the premium.

'Although you can have multiple life insurance policies,' I say. 'You can maximize your chances of getting a lot of money if something bad happens.'

'Yes. But life insurance – *you* cannot win, it's your beneficiaries that can win.'

'Unless you fake your own death.'

Simone smiles. 'If you fake your own death, and you get away with it, lucky you. If they find you out, you'll end up in prison, and the money will be gone as well. Now, *that's* a gamble.'

CHAPTER FIVE

£11,000 – if you're British

Criminal injury compensation

Sara Zelenak was brutally unlucky.

Her parents can reel off all the different reasons why she shouldn't have been walking down the pavement at the junction of London Bridge and Borough High Street nineteen seconds after 10.07 p.m. on 3 June 2017.

'She was never going to be in London,' Mark says, wide-eyed. 'She was going to be an au pair in Milan.' Ten days before she was supposed to leave Brisbane, with her flights already booked, the job got cancelled. 'She wanted to have that whole European experience – not so much English speaking – but in those ten days she was able to pick up something in London, so that's where she went.'

Sara loved London: the fashion, the nightlife, even the cold. She was twenty-one and the world was her oyster. 'She came completely out of her shell,' Julie tells me. 'You know how people get worldly from travel? You could just see her change in the space of three months. She blossomed.'

On Saturday, 3 June 2017, Sara was meant to be staying at home in Victoria with the kids she au paired. 'She was supposed to be working,' Mark says. 'But the grandma said, "I'm going to have the two children tonight, so you can have the night off."'

First, Sara planned to go to a rooftop bar in Soho with Priscila Goncalves, a friend from her WhatsApp au pair group, but they couldn't find it. Instead, they headed to London Grind, a buzzing place close to Borough Market, right on London Bridge. Sara had made plans to go on a first date with a guy who was watching the Champions League Final nearby; he said he'd call her once the match was over.

'Her phone rang. He said, "It's finished, come and meet me,"' Julie tells me. 'It always plays on my mind: if he had rung one minute later, she would have been one minute behind. She walked out into a terrorist attack.'

'There were so many sliding doors,' says Mark.

'Every door slid to make her there,' says Julie.

Sara stepped out of the bar moments after a white Renault Master van containing Khuram Butt, Rachid Redouane and Youssef Zaghba made a U-turn at the northern end of London Bridge and sped back towards Borough High Street. Less than ten minutes later, eleven people were dead and forty-eight had been seriously injured. Three terrorists had been shot and killed by armed police, at the end of a rampage where eight people were murdered. Sara was their youngest victim.

But there was one final piece of bad luck that only emerged after Sara's death. Because of the way criminal injury compensation is calculated, some of the eight lives taken by the terrorists were worth far more than others. The price of Sara's life turns out to be a small fraction of others killed in the same atrocity, by the same people, only seconds before they killed her.

*

At pretty much any time of the day, there are throngs of pedestrians on the broad pavements of London Bridge. Looking across it, the glory of London ancient and modern is set out before you. It's the oldest river crossing in the capital, overlooked by the jagged glint of The Shard, with Tower Bridge resplendent and draped in lights just along the river to the east. Tourists pose for photos, oblivious to the atrocities that have happened here. (There have been two in recent memory: the attack that took Sara's life is now known as the 2017 London Bridge attack because there was another here in 2019, which began at Fishmongers' Hall on the north-west side of the bridge and ended with the terrorist being shot in the middle of it.) But there's something about this landmark that makes you look beyond immediate history. I travelled along London Bridge on my way to work three times a week for two years, and it never occurred to me to think about the

Looking south down London Bridge.

lives lost here so recently. Their only memorial here is the temporary barriers installed after 2017 to prevent vehicles from swerving onto the pavement and mowing down pedestrians.

The evening of Saturday, 3 June 2017 was warm, and London Bridge was full of tourists. The white van, hired by Butt for £70 a few hours earlier, was weighed down with bags of gravel, with thirteen wine-bottle Molotov cocktails and blowtorches also in the back. Zaghba was behind the wheel as it hurtled along the bridge and mounted the pavement three times in fifteen seconds. Holly Jones, a BBC journalist, had been crossing from south to north and could see his face as he ploughed into people. 'It was very intentional what he was doing. He was angry, demented,' she told the inquest into the attacks. (A pre-inquest hearing found that all three terrorists had taken large quantities of steroids before their rampage.)

The first time the van mounted the pavement, it struck and injured three people. The second time, it hit Xavier Thomas, forty-five, and Christine Delcros, forty-three, a French couple who'd arrived in London on the Eurostar that day, and were taking a romantic walk before cocktails at The Shard. Christine was seriously injured but survived; her fiancé, Xavier, was knocked over the bridge's granite balustrade, and his body was recovered from the Thames two miles downstream three days later. Ten seconds after hitting Xavier and Christine, the van careened onto the pavement a third time, striking Chrissy Archibald, a thirty-year-old Canadian who was walking with her fiancé, Tyler Ferguson. Chrissy became trapped under the van's chassis as it travelled over the bridge's central reservation. When she came free, Zaghba ran her over. She died shortly afterwards, in Tyler's arms.

The van then crashed against wrought-iron railings at the top of Borough High Street, next to the Barrowboy and Banker pub, a few paces from London Grind. It was seconds after Sara and Priscila had left the bar. Priscila later told the inquest that they became separated in the chaos as people ran away from the crash site. The three terrorists emerged from the wreckage dressed in what turned out to be fake suicide vests, with twelve-inch pink ceramic knives they'd bought from Lidl for £4.62 strapped to their wrists. They set upon Sara, stabbing her in the neck several times, from behind. She died on the pebble-dashed concrete at the top of the steps down to Green Dragon Court, her phone buzzing in her hand as Priscila tried to find her.

At the top of the steps to Green Dragon Court and Southwark Cathedral, where Sara Zelenak was attacked.

James McMullan, thirty-two, who had stepped out of the Barrowboy and Banker for a cigarette, was the only British person killed by the terrorists. He was stabbed in the back; a witness told the inquest he may have been trying to help Sara after she slipped and fell in her towering heels. Alexandre Pigeard was a twenty-six-year-old French waiter at the Boro Bistro in Green Dragon Court, below street level. A shower of rubble had fallen down into the courtyard following the crash, and Alexandre headed towards the stone stairs to see if he could help anyone, only to be stabbed in the neck at the base of the steps. Tracing a wall with his fingertips, he managed to make it back to Boro Bistro, but was pursued by the terrorists and stabbed again. Sébastian Bélanger, a thirty-six-year-old French chef who'd been watching the football with friends in Borough Market, was killed in the dark archway close to Boro Bistro, and Kirsty Boden, a twenty-eight-year-old Australian nurse who was out with friends at the Bistro, was circled by the attackers and stabbed to death as she tried in vain to save Alexandre's life.

The attackers then ran back up the steps and onto Borough High Street. Ignacio Echeverría, a thirty-nine-year-old banker originally from Spain, had spent the evening skateboarding with friends. They were cycling towards the river when he saw the terrorists attacking a police officer and a woman under the railway bridge. He threw down his bike and swung his skateboard at Redouane. Redouane stabbed him, and when Ignacio fell to the ground, Zaghba joined in the assault. His was the last life taken by the terrorists.

The best and worst of humanity was on display during those frenzied ten minutes. Ignacio and Kirsty gave their lives trying to save others. British Transport Police officer Wayne Marques confronted the attackers armed only with his baton, and was stabbed in the eye, leg and hand. Off-duty Met PC Charlie

Guenigault ran to help PC Marques, and was also seriously injured. When the terrorists moved on into Borough Market, Romanian baker Florin Morariu threw crates at them and then gave shelter to twenty people in his bakery. And when they began stabbing diners at the Black and Blue Steakhouse, forty-seven-year-old Roy Larner attacked them with his bare fists, shouting, 'Fuck you, I'm Millwall.' He was stabbed in the neck, back and chest, but survived.

Armed officers from the City of London and Metropolitan police forces fired a total of forty-six rounds at Butt, Zaghba and Redouane on Stoney Street. They were shot dead eight minutes after the first emergency call was made.

Perhaps mercifully, there is no CCTV of the attack on Sara.

'They assume Sara slipped in her high heels,' Julie frowns. 'Sara could do a *backflip* on a *tightrope* in high heels.'

'Sara's high heels were *serious*,' Mark says, extending his arms to the top and bottom of the frame of our video call. 'What she was wearing on the night were like running shoes, really.'

'It made her out to be a blonde bimbo, and that's really annoyed me. People have no idea what my daughter was like.'

Julie and Mark are speaking to me from Fraser Island, off the east coast of Australia, where they moved from Brisbane a few months ago to look after three holiday homes as caretakers-in-residence. Curled up on their sofa together, they've clearly settled into beach life: Julie has sun-kissed curly hair, and Mark is in shorts, with a bushy beard.

'She was very streetwise. She was always looking after everyone else,' Julie tells me. Sara was athletic and adventurous: she loved basketball, she'd done avalanche survival training in Canada. She left school at eighteen and worked alongside Mark for a while as a crane operator, wearing fake nails along with her hardhat and high-vis jacket. Mark was Sara's stepfather, but he calls her his daughter: he brought her up from the age of eighteen months. He worked in the drilling industry and Julie was a personal trainer; they were both self-employed and worked odd hours, and Sara would look after her older and younger brothers when their parents weren't around.

'She was a mini me,' Julie continues. 'But she was better than me – nicer, and kinder, and younger – and beautiful. She had the most beautiful pale blue eyes, and when she laughed, her eyes would laugh as well. But she was very humble and shy, and she didn't see her beauty. It was a shame she didn't see it.'

Sara was on Westminster Bridge the day before 22 March 2017, when a terrorist drove a hired SUV into pedestrians, killing four people, before stabbing an unarmed policeman to death outside parliament. She had tickets to go and see Ariana Grande at the Manchester Arena on 22 May 2017, when a terrorist detonated a suicide bomb in the foyer, killing twenty-two people and injuring over a thousand, but she wasn't able to get the night off work, so she didn't go.

'It was two in a row that she'd just missed,' Julie says. 'I said to her, "Sara, be careful with all the killing going on in London." And she goes, "Mum, I'm *fine*."'

The news of what had happened trickled through to Julie and Mark agonizingly slowly. The blonde woman lying in St Thomas' morgue looked nothing like the photos on Sara's passport and driving licence, when she had dyed brown hair and a seventeen-year-old baby face, so the authorities at first refused to classify Sara as anything other than a missing person.

'You know when you lose your toddler in the supermarket and you can't find them for three seconds? It felt like that for three days,' Julie says. The Australian Federal Police (AFP) eventually contacted them to say there was a body, and suggested they fly to London. As they landed on their stopover in Abu Dhabi, they got a WhatsApp message from Sara's older brother saying it had been confirmed: Sara had been identified using DNA from hair left on her comb.

Then things happened fast. The Met Police, the AFP and DFAT – the Australian Department of Foreign Affairs – all worked together to guide them through every part of the process in baby steps. Before they went to view her body, they were told exactly what each room would look like, who would be there, what they would see and what would happen. They were briefed about every detail of the inquest in advance: where the judge would sit, when they would be called to give evidence, what the CCTV would show. 'All those things were very meticulously planned,' Mark says. 'There was a lot of care to step us through everything.'

But when it came to claiming the compensation they were entitled to as parents of someone killed in a terrorist attack, Julie and Mark were left on their own.

'You would expect that that would be the next conversation, a couple of months after burying Sara. Not even so much a conversation, more a "Let's step you through this process, because you're well qualified, and let's do it for you,"' Mark says.

'No one told us about it,' Julie says, with a shake of her head. 'We never had any help or support.'

A friend of Julie's happened to read something online, did some googling on their behalf, worked out that they qualified and sent the application form over to them. 'But it was something that she found by chance,' Mark says. If she hadn't seen it then, Julie and Mark may not have got any compensation at all. 'Under their guidelines, it's *you* that has to apply. And it has an expiry date on it: two years. You're in grief and you're just trying to find your feet. I think five years down the track there's still shit that we've missed.'

Compensation can't bring the dead back, but many governments acknowledge that a person shouldn't be left out of pocket if they lose a relative because of terrorism. There will be earnings lost due to bereavement; expenses to pay, dealing with the administration of death. Plus, it's arguable that victims of terror belong in a special category: they have been targeted as symbols of a state, nationality or government. They represent a particular way of life that's being attacked. Who they actually are as individuals doesn't matter to the terrorists: they are killed because they could be you or me.

The eight victims of the London Bridge attack are all citizens of countries that have compensation schemes for the families of those killed in terrorist attacks. After a bit of digging, I found out that the sums involved vary enormously from country to country, and according to how the compensation is calculated.

In the UK, any victim of a violent crime can claim compensation from the British government for physical or mental injury, and if they are killed their families can claim for the loss of their life. The Criminal Injury Compensation Authority (CICA) decides who is eligible and how much they should get. 'The Scheme is intended to be one of last resort,' say the CICA guidelines. 'Where the opportunity exists for you to pursue compensation from another source you should do so.' The guidelines are over a decade old as I write this, and the tariffs haven't been updated or adjusted for inflation since 2012.

I would have found the cold 'Tariff of Injuries' set out in Annex E of the *Criminal Injuries Compensation Scheme 2012* shocking, were I not already wearily familiar with the Home

Office's *Research Report 99* and the cost of a murder. The list goes on for twenty-eight pages and is strikingly detailed: £16,500 for a severe burn to the neck; £55,000 for loss of fertility; £33,000 for the loss of a leg below the knee; £44,000 for the loss of a leg above the knee. Mental injuries qualify for lower compensation tariffs than physical ones (£6,200 for disabling mental injury lasting two to five years – less than double the £3,500 you'd get for a permanently clicking jaw). The seriously injured are eligible for far greater compensation than the families of the dead. And perhaps that makes sense – they will have specific, life-changing and ongoing needs to manage – but it's jarring to see it written down in black and white.

A life lost is valued at only £11,000. (Interestingly, when forces of the British state are responsible for taking innocent lives, the price of life paid by the British government is much lower. The average compensation for an Afghan civilian killed between April 2006 and May 2014 was £2,380, according to analysis by Action on Armed Violence. But the sums vary widely. One family received £586.42 after British soldiers killed their ten-year-old son.)

The CICA payment makes no distinction between a death from terrorism, domestic violence or a random attack on the street. Shaquan Sammy-Plummer's mother, Jessica, would have been able to claim the same £11,000 as the parents of James McMullan, the only British victim of the 2017 London Bridge attack. (Jessica did claim it. 'By the time you take that money, pay back all the bills that are outstanding, the money you've borrowed, it's gone,' she told me. The Home Office's calculation of the cost of a murder includes only the administration costs of CICA, not the compensation payment itself.)

You're supposed to make a CICA claim as soon as possible after the incident – amid grief, or serious injury in the case of a personal injury claim – and you can be turned down for all manner of reasons. 'We will consider any evidence available about your character . . . which makes it inappropriate for us to make a full or reduced payment,' the guidelines read. 'This includes evidence of involvement or association in illegal drugs, crime, tax evasion and benefit fraud.' The mental and physical injuries sustained by Roy Larner – the *Fuck you, I'm Millwall* hero dubbed the 'Lion of London Bridge' after he fought the terrorists with his bare fists – should have made him eligible for tens of thousands in CICA compensation. But he had previous convictions for racially aggravated common assault, drug possession and breaching a restraining order granted to his eighty-year-old mother. He got nothing.

Unlike the UK, Spain, Canada, France and Australia all have specific provisions for the families of victims lost in terror attacks. Chrissy Archibald's family was entitled to CA$10,000 (£6,000). Ignacio Echeverría's family would have qualified for a quarter of a million euros (around £220,000) from the Spanish government. France has a special fund called FGTI (*Fonds de garantie des victimes des actes de terrorisme et d'autres infractions*) that calculates compensation in terms of the impact of losing a specific relation to terrorism. Family members of the three Frenchmen killed would be compensated accordingly: any spouses would get €35,000, children could get up to €25,000 depending on their age, parents get up to €35,000, grandparents up to €11,000, grandchildren €10,000 and siblings up to €15,000. The French system seems to be framed in terms of the price of bereavement, rather than the price of life.

Sara Zelenak's and Kirsty Boden's families were eligible for the Australian Victims of Terrorism Overseas (AVTO) payment, which is AU$75,000 – just over £40,000.

'That's nothing, for the rest of her life,' Julie says with disdain.

'Seventy-five grand? That would be one year's work. She was a healthy, vibrant person. She had her whole life ahead of her – no injuries, no illnesses. And they put $75,000 on that?'

Julie sees the price of Sara's life in terms of the cost of the years she didn't get to live. And I can see how, measured that way, the AVTO does seem pathetic. Insulting, even. It's hard to see what the figure represents. Something to help her kids, if she'd had any?

'If she did have dependents, seventy-five grand is going to get her kids – what?' Mark replies.

Still, it's several times as much as they would have got from the government had Sara been British or Canadian. But it's not citizenship that makes compensation for the 2017 London Bridge attack so incredibly unequal – it's the manner in which lives were taken. The families of Xavier Thomas and Chrissy Archibald – the two people killed by the van – were able to bring a significant compensation claim against Hertz, one of the largest vehicle rental companies in the world. The families of the six people who were stabbed to death had no one to sue.

'There is no simple compensation for being caught up in a terrorist attack, therefore people will reach around to discover what could be available as an alternative,' Robert Muir-Wood tells me over Zoom. 'The London Bridge attack is the most glaring example of why this is so strange and unfair.'

Robert is the chief research officer at a company called Risk Management Solutions. He analyses risk on behalf of the insurance industry. 'We develop risk models for catastrophic loss, both natural and man-made, and we license these models,' he tells me, clearly used to having to demystify his job title.

I chanced upon an article Robert wrote for the Insurance

Day website in 2019, entitled 'Crossing the Terrorism Casualty Protection Gap'. Midway through, he observes: 'Those stabbed and slashed by the London Bridge attackers can expect five or ten percent of the compensation awarded to those run over by the same terrorists driving the van.'

It made my jaw drop.

'The rental company has quite deep pockets and will themselves have significant insurance limits. So the compensation for those hit by the vehicle was, you might say, reasonable, or even generous,' he explains. But there were no pockets at all, deep or otherwise, for the stabbing victims to reach into. 'For those people, it falls back on other forms of compensation, or simply the willingness of the public to donate money in the aftermath of an attack of this kind.'

Robert wrote his article before the settlement with Hertz's insurer, Probus, was agreed in 2020. 'The amount has not been disclosed, but it's likely to be in the millions,' he tells me, pointing to the settlement paid by Zurich, the insurer of the Enterprise Rent-A-Car vehicle used to kill four people in the Westminster Bridge attack in March 2017: it's reported to have been in excess of £150 million.

France's compensation system is paid for through a levy on other insurance policies, Robert says. The families of the eighty-six people run over and killed in the 2016 Bastille Day attack in Nice might have been inclined to sue the rental company but the government prevented it. 'The government stepped in and chose to relocate the cost into the FGTI coverage, and €250 million was paid out to victims and their families. The French can point at a consistent process, whereas you absolutely can't do that in the UK, or the US.'

The inconsistency happens on a greater scale in the US. Robert's article was inspired by the enormous discrepancy in payouts after mass shootings according to their location. Gunmakers are legally protected from being sued in the USA if their guns are used in a mass shooting, but nightclub and hotel owners are not. When Stephen Paddock fired into a crowd on the Las Vegas strip in October 2017, killing fifty-eight people, he did it out of the window of the Mandalay Bay hotel, owned by MGM Resorts International. MGM has liability insurance across the whole chain, and compensation was set at the limit of the chain's insurance. Even after legal fees were deducted, Robert says that the settlement was worth $800 million.

'The guy researched a range of potential locations where he could have enacted this. He was exploring alternatives, including shooting people from a clifftop, or a rented apartment. There might have been absolutely no one to sue, or quite low limits. But he chose to do it from the window of a very large hotel, which was itself part of a very valuable hotel chain. He actually picked the location that had the highest compensation per death that he could.'

Compare that to the 2016 mass shooting at a gay club in Orlando, where fifty-six people lost their lives. The nightclub, Pulse, was independently owned; there was no one with deep pockets to sue.

'The Orlando nightclub shooting was $140,000 per death, based on charitable contributions,' Robert says matter-of-factly. 'It falls back onto passing the hat around. That's how things used to be in the seventeenth century. If you read Pepys, you'll find that when someone's house burned down, they would pass a hat around to contribute to the person who has suffered a misfortune. Pepys admits he's getting really tired of just how often he's being asked to put money into the hat. Insurance was invented in the late seventeenth century in order to compensate for this situation.'

It seems so arbitrary, so unfair, so totally unjust. 'Why isn't all of this more widely known, Robert?' I ask.

'I don't know. If all the victims in the London Bridge attack had been British, there might have been more awareness of this, as something needing redress.'

'If you've got no one to sue, it's not going to occur to you to think about how others might be able to,' I say.

Robert nods. 'And it's in no one's interest to actually tell you.'

I take a deep breath.

'You know, when I emailed you, it was about the different levels of compensation for the London Bridge families according to where the victims were from, and also the manner of their deaths,' I say. 'Were you aware of it before I told you?'

This is the first time since Julie, Mark and I started talking nearly ninety minutes ago that neither of them has anything to say.

'I didn't know,' Julie says eventually.

'We were not aware, and . . . we're not in a space where we're going, "What did we or didn't we get?"' Mark says. 'With everything in life, we pretty much take whatever comes.'

The Hertz payout had been reported at the time, albeit in the British press. I'd assumed they must have known about it. Now I want to back away. I don't want to be the person to bring this senseless fact to their attention.

'It's not that I would expect you to be comparing notes with other families,' I babble. 'I didn't think it would make you angry with other families. It's more that the system is so extraordinarily unfair.'

'The system fails,' Julie says, stony-faced.

There's another pause.

'Is the van considered a road accident?' Mark asks.

I'm not sure how to answer this. 'I think the families of the people killed by the van were able to get significant compensation from Hertz, whereas the families of the people who were stabbed would not have been entitled to that.'

They shake their heads.

'Yeah,' is the only thing Mark can say.

'See, I didn't know any of that,' says Julie. 'I don't know how that works. It's all the same attack.'

I don't know how it works either. 'It's manifestly wrong,' I say.

'Yeah,' Mark nods again.

Fieldfisher's ninth-floor meeting room is as generic and featureless as you'd expect for a city law firm, apart from its breathtaking view: the building is right on the Thames, practically on London Bridge itself. It's one of those cold, bright days in London where everything seems to sparkle. Jennifer Buchanan is explaining how different families can be eligible for different levels of compensation – Jenny is a partner in Fieldfisher's serious injury team, and represented Chrissy Archibald's family – but I'm finding the view distracting, because it overlooks the precise spot where Chrissy was so brutally murdered a matter of metres below us.

'It's genuinely unfair. It breaks my heart,' Jenny says, fixing me with her blue eyes. She tells me the firm acts regularly for victims of road traffic accidents or accidents at work who've been admitted to the Royal London Hospital. This is the specialist trauma centre where Shaquan was taken. But patients there who have been stabbed are only eligible for CICA payments – even if their injuries are more serious and life-changing than those of Jenny's clients who have been hit by a car.

In order to explain why Xavier's and Chrissy's families were able to win a settlement from Hertz's insurers, Jenny has printed out a flowchart to show me who is liable in any given motor accident scenario, which hurts my brain a little. In the end, the explanation is simple: Mark is right; those killed by the van were viewed in the civil courts as if they had been killed in a road accident. 'Chrissy was hit by a vehicle driven by a known driver and with an insurance policy in place, so we claimed against the insurers.'

The families of those killed with knives could never have made any claim against Hertz, even though the van delivered the terrorists to the scene. Only those injured by the vehicle itself would be eligible for compensation from the rental company.

There was no allegation that Hertz had been negligent in renting the car to Butt (who had tried to rent a 7.5-tonne lorry, and had only been denied because his method of payment failed.) 'There was a big call – Chrissy's family was leading it at one point – for lease hire companies to have stricter checks on who they lease vehicles to. Why is there such strict security going through an airport, but if you want to hire a van you just have to show a driving licence?' The 9/11 terrorists used planes as a weapon in the same way as Butt, Redouane and Zaghba used a vehicle, after all. 'Anyone it seems can go and hire any van, so whoever's insuring it has to be responsible for anything that happens, and the checks and balances in place.'

Jenny won't tell me how big the settlement was – 'It's never been in the public domain' – but does confirm Robert's hunch that it was comparable to the settlement for the Westminster Bridge attack. All solicitors go through the same criteria to make a claim, she says. 'The mantra for civil claims is using the "but for" principle: aiming to put everyone back in the pre-accident position as far as possible without betterment.'

Claims take the form of a dizzyingly specific and comprehensive itemized bill, some of which Jenny is prepared to share with me. Chrissy's parents were able to claim a bereavement award (nearly £13,000, Jenny says), secondary victim awards to cover any psychiatric help they might need, probate costs, an award for funeral expenses, and then the general damages award for every single injury Chrissy received. Jenny opens her laptop and brings up Chapter 1 of the Judicial College's *Guidelines For The Assessment Of General Damages In Personal Injury Cases*. 'You get different awards—' She interrupts herself and throws me a knowing look, as if to say, *you'll love this*. 'You get different awards depending on whether you're fully conscious at the time of death, or whether you survive for a short while and then die. If you're fully aware, the award is currently £12,000 to £23,000.'

Chrissy's family were able to claim aggravated damages because of the horror Chrissy suffered in her last moments. 'It was *so* horrific, so violent, and she could see it coming.' In addition to this, Chrissy's family were able to claim for 'the loss of love and affection for the sister and the parents. And we tried to recover some charitable expenses that were paid out to repatriate her back to Canada.' If Chrissy had had dependents (like Xavier Thomas, who had two children he was raising largely on his own), the award would have been much higher, Jenny says.

'Chrissy had the rest of her life ahead of her,' I say, with Julie's words in my mouth. 'Was that taken into account?'

'I think the courts really struggle with putting a price on a life, so they just make it a statutory amount that everyone gets: if you're a thirteen-year-old killed crossing the road or if you're in your eighties.'

On rare occasions, Fieldfisher will help clients who have no other recourse with CICA claims, but only for serious injury; the tariffs for fatal injuries are too low to make it worth anyone's while. But those claims take ages, Jenny says. 'Sometimes you have to go through appeals processes and tribunals. All the legal fees come out of that person's award, which is very unfair. We do end up doing a fair amount pro bono.' She tells me about an amputee client whose CICA claim has so far taken six years. 'He was self-employed and they wouldn't consider his loss of earnings position because he didn't have wage slips. We had to go to appeal.'

'If we had a system where the families of all of the eight people killed at London Bridge got the same amount, that would be morally the best outcome, maybe.' I'm thinking out loud. 'But even then, do you think people would still be looking at where else they could claim? A good lawyer will try and get whatever they can for their client.'

'Every person would have to be assessed on their injuries, their life at that time, and whether or not they had dependants. It wouldn't be fair to say you were all hit by a van on London Bridge so you all get a million pounds – that would overcompensate some people and undercompensate others,' she replies. 'What we offer is a very bespoke service. It takes a long time, but it's so important to get it right to ensure the process is fair and to enable people to continue living – as far as possible – their pre-existing lives and supporting their families.'

Fairness doesn't necessarily mean equality; in order for compensation to be fair, every life lost needs an itemized bill – but all prices need to be calculated in the same way. The injustice with London Bridge is not the different sums of compensation, but the fact they were arrived at by such different means.

'A bespoke scheme for CICA, mirroring something equivalent to a civil scheme, would be the only fair way,' Jenny continues.

'Going through a person's life in detail, looking at the losses, and replacing the losses.'

Perhaps it's easy for Jenny to sound reasonable when she talks about London Bridge compensation: she represented only Chrissy's family. Patrick Maguire had seven or eight clients following the attack; some were hit by the van and could sue Hertz, others were stabbed and had to make CICA claims. He represented Xavier Thomas's family, but none of the families bereaved by the knife attack, who had no need for a criminal injury lawyer.

It takes me three months to reach Patrick on the phone. He's now a partner at HCC solicitors, based in Manchester and London, and he specializes in the very worst of horrors, from the Westminster Bridge attack to the Salisbury novichok nerve agent poisoning. When we finally get to speak, he explains he's in the middle of the inquest into the 2021 Plymouth mass shooting, where a twenty-two-year-old man shot and killed five people and injured two others, before turning the gun on himself.

'What's it like having to explain to clients that they are entitled to compensation that's a tiny fraction of what other people killed in the same event might get?' I ask Patrick.

'That's a good question.' He pauses. 'If they've lost the breadwinner, that family will be in a very, very precarious financial position because of the death, on top of losing that person. There is no easy way of having these conversations; you've just got to tell them.'

Patrick doesn't mince his words about CICA compensation. 'The whole point of a civil claim is to, where possible, put the family or the injured person back in the position they were in but for the injury or death. The CICA doesn't go anywhere near reflecting that.'

'What's it for, then? A gesture of sympathy?'

'Yeah, basically. It's there to reflect that something's gone wrong when the offender doesn't have the means to pay a damages claim. It is just a small token. It's better than nothing.'

I wonder if that's actually true. Something can be worse than nothing if it means the government can say they've dealt with a problem, and it stops them from having to do better.

'If people disclosed the settlements they get, others would realize the incredible unfairness in all of this. Why don't they?' I ask.

'Well, I suppose it's like why people don't talk about their salaries,' Patrick replies, with a shrug in his voice. 'It's a matter of privacy for people. I don't think people would be going around saying what salary they're on, or what they've got in the bank.'

But if, as Patrick has argued, this isn't about financial betterment but rather putting bereaved families 'back in the position they were in but for the injury or death,' then this argument doesn't stack up. The families still have their own salaries and savings when they receive compensation; no one would be asking them to disclose their finances in full. If people were more open about how the price of their loved one was calculated, then there would be public awareness of the injustice, and public outrage, and perhaps change. But maybe it isn't in lawyers' interest for anything to change at all.

'Don't you think it would help, if this discrepancy were more widely known?' I ask.

'No,' Patrick says simply. 'I don't think so.' And it's clear he doesn't have any more to say about it.

The hat gets passed around whenever there's a mass tragedy, no matter what civil suit or government compensation might be available to victims' families. We give money to express solidarity and compassion, and maybe as an acknowledgement that it could have been any of us. More than words, money feels like the nearest thing available to us that can do any good. And it's charitable donations that often make the most difference to the lives of bereaved people. Where government compensation is palpably inadequate, public sympathy steps in.

Alex Klis took her little sister, Patrycia, to see Ariana Grande perform at the Manchester Arena in May 2017. Their parents, Marcin and Angelika, were waiting to pick them up in the foyer when Salman Abedi detonated his suicide bomb, killing them and twenty others, and leaving the sisters orphaned aged twenty and fourteen. The CICA payment would have entitled Alex and Patrycia to just £22,000 for the deaths of both their parents. Immediately after the news broke, crowdfunding fundraisers for them appeared online. I found five separate JustGiving pages that raised over £34,000 for Alex and Patrycia. The We Love Manchester fund raised enough in public donations to give £250,000 to the family of each person killed by Abedi, meaning that the sisters received an additional half a million pounds.

The UK Solidarity Fund established after the 2017 London Bridge attack gave £75,000 to the next of kin of every person killed, regardless of where they were from, or what weapon took their life. There were also individual grassroots campaigns on JustGiving and GoFundMe for the families of victims. When Sara was still a missing person, one of Mark and Julie's friends set up a GoFundMe that raised nearly AU$24,000 (£13,700) in a little over two weeks. Roy Larner, the Lion of London Bridge, may have got nothing from the CICA, but a single JustGiving page raised over £55,470 for him.

When we come to look at philanthropy, you'll see that many

of the world's richest donors look down on this kind of charitable giving; they see it as an inefficient way to make the world a better place. But there are other – and perhaps better – reasons to question whether charitable donations should be relied on to help victims' families.

Some tragedies (and victims) will get more coverage, public sympathy and donations than others. After the 2018 Pittsburgh synagogue shooting, $4.4 million in charitable donations was given to the families of the eleven people killed and the two seriously injured survivors – an equivalent amount per victim to donations received after the Manchester Arena bombing. But the families of the nine African Americans killed in the 2015 Charleston church shooting shared $1.5 million raised following the massacre. You do the maths.

But perhaps most urgently, charitable giving takes the pressure off governments to make things better for families when compensation schemes are inadequate or unfair. The compensation paid out by the CICA is still our money, just collected through taxes and distributed in a different way to a crowdfunding campaign. We shouldn't allow our donations to let the government off the hook. The UK's Ministry of Justice launched a review of criminal injury compensation in 2020, but as I write this, nothing has yet come of it.

The people who would benefit most from CICA reform are bereaved, traumatized and have no one else to claim from. They are among the most powerless in the country. Getting it right for them isn't a priority for the British government.

Julie and Mark spent the AU$75,000 compensation money setting up a charity in Sara's name. It provides emotional, spiritual and practical support to people living with traumatic loss, so that others won't have to scramble in the dark like they did after Sara's death.

Sarz Sanctuary was initially conceived as a live-in healing retreat, but morphed into a digital platform during the pandemic. 'We could help *more* people, and connect as many people as we want around the world,' Julie enthuses. 'Our digital platforms cost a few hundred thousand. We've spent everything. We've sold our house, our car, our boat, to fund it. Now we're caretakers here, just so we can reduce our costs and still do our digital work remotely.'

'It gives us purpose to get out of bed each day,' Mark says.

Julie nods. 'We have to normalize grief.'

Julie and Mark have become ambassadors for grief, speaking at UN events and the global Victims of Terror Congress, meeting Queen Elizabeth II at Buckingham Palace. They organize an annual London to Paris fundraising bike ride, and Christine Delcros, who was hit by the van on the bridge alongside Xavier Thomas, saw them off on their inaugural ride, from the bit of pavement where Sara was killed.

A piece of the pebble-dashed concrete from that spot sits in a vase in Mark and Julie's home. They wanted a way of taking Sara's spirit back with them from London. But Julie says ever since she visited Sara's body in the morgue, she's felt Sara beside her.

'She's guiding me with everything we do. I get a sign or a feeling that I should be doing something, and I do it,' she says, with sparkling eyes. 'We have the ability to make an impact and make that our purpose. I understand terrorism, and I understand the loss of a child. I speak from my heart. This is my lane. This is where I belong.'

The price of Sara's life is meaningless, arbitrary, unfair. But Julie and Mark are learning to live alongside the pain of their daughter's death, and they refuse to allow themselves to be victimized again by the injustice of the compensation they received for it. I've found our conversation so hard to bear, on the other side of the world, through a computer screen. Yet Mark and Julie won't be stifled by anger or bitterness. As long as it gives them purpose, Sara's death wasn't senseless.

'We're both of the opinion that we come on the earth with a contract that has a date when you're leaving – you don't know what it is, but you've agreed to it,' Mark says. 'She was leaving on that date, and that's why those sliding doors took her there.'

Julie nods. 'That's the only way, in my head – in both of our heads – that it can make any sense.'

PART THREE

A LIFE CREATED

CHAPTER SIX

£13,750 – or $200,000 if you're gay

Biological parenthood

It began with an Instagram ad, six months before the wedding. 'I got a targeted ad for an organization called Gay Parents To Be,' Nicholas tells me.

An 'informal resource and a starting point for LGBTQ parenting,' Gay Parents To Be is based in Connecticut, where gay New Yorkers have often flocked when they want to find a surrogate and begin a family. It was founded by a fertility doctor who also happens to be a gay dad. He was offering free consultations, 'to give you the rundown on the whole process,' Nicholas continues. 'We had the appointment and we were 100 per cent on the same page – let's move forward with this.'

Up until this point, the conveyor belt of life had always moved forward for Nicholas Maggipinto and Corey Briskin. They met in law school in 2011, were engaged by 2014, and had their 2016 wedding announced in the *New York Times*. They moved to a waterfront apartment block in Williamsburg, with a playroom on the ground floor full of toys and squishy shapes upholstered in primary-coloured vinyl for little ones to clamber over.

That bright, glass-panelled space is across the corridor from where we are sitting now, in their building's sombre communal meeting room. Corey is four years younger than his husband, and, with his striped blue and white shirt unbuttoned to the middle of his chest, he looks more relaxed. Nicholas is thirty-seven, with gelled hair and a furrowed brow. He sits forward in his chair, his shoulders stiff.

'We got married and then we wanted all the trappings: house, children, 401(k)* et cetera,' Nicholas says, tapping the boardroom table in sequence with the progression of each idea.

Corey grew up assuming he'd have children. Before he came out in college, he'd had relationships with women. 'Once I had come out to myself and others, I don't think my expectation of what my life would look like changed all that much,' he shrugs. With marriage equality won years ago, Corey and Nicholas expected to be able to have a conventional married life.

But at that free consultation with the fertility doctor, the conveyor belt ground to a halt.

'That's when we first learned about the timeline – eighteen to twenty-four months, minimum,' Corey says, with a sharp intake of breath. 'And also we learned about the cost.'

'How much does it cost?' I ask.

It takes them fifteen minutes to answer this question.

'Number one is egg donor compensation,' Nicholas begins. He tells me that the American Society of Reproductive Medicine's standard is that a donor's compensation should be no less than $8,000.

The most recent ASRM guidelines say they 'avoid putting a price' on human eggs, but previous guidance said: 'payments to donors in excess of $5,000 require justification and sums above $10,000 are not appropriate'. These words are nearly

* A 401(k) is a retirement saving plan in the US.

twenty years old, and they are just guidance – there's nothing enforceable about any of this. Fertility medicine is pretty much unregulated in the US, which is what makes it such a magnet for fertility tourists seeking procedures like gender selection or commercial surrogacy, which may be outlawed in their home country for ethical reasons.

'Then there is the fertility clinic fee, which encompasses all the services rendered by the clinic to intended parents, to the egg donor in getting the yield, and in impregnating the surrogate,' Nicholas continues, reeling off the list in a way that only someone who has fretted over every detail could. 'For the intended parents, that includes genetic testing and a panel of blood work and STD screening.'

I'm wondering why the intended parents need genetic testing. Straight couples aren't required to have their genes evaluated before they can become biological parents. But I guess I can see the point in doing something thoroughly if you're going to do it at all, and before I can ask, Nicholas is onto the next item.

'For the egg donor, that includes, again, FDA screening of blood and STDs, an evaluation of the donor's AMH – anti-Müllerian hormone – which is a measure of the potency of a woman's ovulation, the genetic panel to evaluate whether *this* particular donor with one of *these* two intending parents could produce a higher incidence of hereditary conditions. Then there's pharmaceuticals for the egg donor, which are used to stimulate fertility. Then there is the monitoring of the egg donor once she's been stimulated. Then there's the extraction of the eggs.'

'You didn't mention the costs associated with the psych evals,' Corey interjects.

Nicholas nods. 'There are psychiatric evaluations for us, and for the donor,' he says. 'Then there's the work the clinic does once they have the eggs: they evaluate them for abnormalities, the eggs are inseminated in a lab, and then they grow into what are called blastocysts over a period of five or six days that are evaluated for their health, and are graded. A blastocyst that has a chromosomal abnormality is immediately excluded, et cetera. The ones that survive are frozen. Those embryos are frozen until you find a surrogate. Who knows how long that will take.'

'And you have to pay for that too, by the way,' adds Corey, nodding in resignation.

'The freezing of the sperm also,' says Nicholas. 'Did I say that we gave sperm? That's part of the fertility cost on the men's side.'

'Also, they evaluated it,' Corey says.

'Oh yeah,' says Nicholas. 'Motility, morphology and count. Those were the three metrics.'

'If you're low in one area, you can take supplements to try to increase the likelihood of creating an embryo using that sperm,' Corey explains.

Nicholas and Corey have clearly pored over this shopping list of gametes, supplements, procedures and evaluations, and are presenting it to me as a necessary requirement for them to make a baby: an inventory of must-haves, a done deal. It doesn't sound like they've ever questioned whether the problem here might be the avaricious fertility industry as much as the inherent difficulties gay men face if they want to be genetically related to their children.

'So, those embryos are frozen,' Nicholas says again, keen to get back on track. 'The surrogate has to have a pysch evaluation and be cleared by your fertility clinic, and of course blood and STD screening. Then there's the implantation of the embryo in the gestational carrier.' (Surrogates are called 'gestational carriers' when they carry embryos created from another woman's eggs.) 'At that point, the fertility clinic's job is over.

Now the costs for that, excluding egg donor compensation, can run up to about $70,000.'

That's if it all goes well: if no embryos are created during a cycle, or if the embryos that are don't lead to a successful pregnancy, they would have to start again, from scratch. And that doesn't even include the most expensive – and controversial – part of the process: the surrogate.

Advances in reproductive technology mean that pretty much anyone can become a parent so long as they can get hold of the requisite gametes and access to fertility treatment, but someone always has to do the gestating. Surrogacy is always medically, legally and ethically complicated – a grey area where technology, reproduction, bodily autonomy and money collide. For now,* it's the only route to biological fatherhood for gay men, at a time when a growing number of gay couples want to create conventional families. (In England and Wales, where only altruistic – unpaid – surrogacy is legal, the number of parents using a surrogate quadrupled from 2011 to 2020, the decade when the Marriage (Same Sex Couples) Act was passed by parliament in 2013.)

Ukraine used to be the go-to destination for fertility tourists in search of commercial surrogacy. When Russia invaded in 2022, thousands of women pregnant with other people's children were left in turmoil, while the panicked intended parents tried to work out how to get them and their precious cargo out of the country. Now the US has been left as the prime location for commercial surrogacy, and there are far more people seeking

* I say 'for now', because artificial wombs are being developed that may mean it will one day be possible to gestate a baby without anyone being pregnant. I wrote about this, and took a deep dive into the ethics, politics and challenges of all forms of surrogacy, in my first book, *Sex Robots & Vegan Meat: Adventures at the Frontier of Birth, Food, Sex and Death.*

gestational carriers than there are willing surrogates. Surrogacy fees in America have soared since the pandemic.

Nicholas says they were told surrogates should be paid a minimum of $60,000. 'That doesn't include reimbursement for things like maternity clothing, lost wages if she misses work for doctor's appointments or is put on bed rest, transportation, childcare for her own children, lodging . . .'

Nicholas and Corey still haven't given me a final answer. 'This is all pretty eye-watering,' I say. 'Do you have a ballpark figure of what the entire process would set you back?'

'Just surrogacy?' Nicholas asks.

'Having a child as a gay couple.'

'Two hundred thousand dollars minimum,' Nicholas replies, drumming his index finger on the table with each word in disbelief.

Corey looks over to him. 'At the time we were quoted, I think $200,000 was probably at the high end . . .' he says gently.

'Oh no. $200,000 minimum,' Nicholas shoots back defiantly, 'because there are things we haven't mentioned. There's the surrogate agency fee for finding you the surrogate, which is $25,000, I believe.'

'And the egg donor agency fee,' Corey concedes.

'I forgot about that. I think it's between $8,000 and $10,000.'

They couldn't afford it. Nicholas is a corporate lawyer and earns a salary to match, but he has huge student debts, he says. Corey was working for the City of New York as an assistant district attorney at the time, earning around $75,000 a year. His employment benefits included generous health insurance, which, in theory, could have covered the costs of IVF at the fertility clinic, knocking $70,000 off their total bill. But when they read the policy, they discovered that they were the only class of people to be excluded from IVF coverage. Infertility was defined as an inability to have a child through heterosexual sex or intrauterine insemination. That meant straight people and lesbians working for the City of New York would have the costs of IVF covered, but gay male couples could never be eligible.

This is more than just an oversight, Corey says – it's outright discrimination. 'The policy is the product of a time when there was a misconception, a stereotype, a prejudice against couples that were made up of two men – that they were not capable of raising children because there was no female figure in that relationship.' He was working alongside colleagues who were happily availing themselves of the benefits he wasn't entitled to. One of his co-workers – an older, single woman – became a mother using donor sperm, IVF and surrogacy.

'It was hard,' he says. 'You want to be happy for people.'

'I was thirty when we got married,' Nicholas says. 'I was OK with not being a parent at thirty – I felt that was very normal for our generation and the current work-life balance ethos – but seven years later, I'm really not happy.' He twists his chunky wedding ring. 'There are younger LGBT people who work for forward-thinking companies that offer benefits. If you look at Instagram, #gayswithkids or #gaydads, you will see a remarkable number of people in their late twenties either planning their journeys or with really young children.' His eyes are filled with despair. 'I'm elated for them. But I'm sad for me.'

This is clearly more than Instagram-induced envy. Their frustration has turned to anguish in the real world. Nicholas describes having to 'enjoy other people's children vicariously'. His sister – more than six years younger than him – has just given birth to her second baby. 'We just took care of my nephew when my sister needed help. It's so awkward for me to wish my brother-in-law Happy Father's Day.'

'Did you always want a biological connection to your kids?' I ask.

I don't mean this question to be code for 'Why don't you just adopt?' But that's how Nicholas and Corey take it.

'I have never been opposed to adopting, and even to having a foster child to see where that leads,' Nicholas says, after a long pause. 'But as a couple we've come to a decision that having a child that's biologically connected to us is important.'

'I'm not wringing my hands here,' Corey says. 'I will take full ownership of the desire to be biologically related to my children. It is a decision that is entirely mine and ours to make.' He shakes his head. 'It really feels like such an affront to be asked this question. I find it deeply offensive. I help others in other ways – but that's just not how I'd choose to do it.'

I can understand why this bothers Corey so much. When I decided to try and start a family with my husband, no one suggested that we should consider adoption. I never had to justify why I wanted to see my own genes expressed and reflected back to me through my children; it was never implied that I was a narcissist for not finding other paths to parenthood. Straight couples going through IVF don't get routinely asked why they've chosen fertility treatment instead of adoption. It's assumed that if you have a chance at biological parenthood, you will take it, and no one will expect you to explain your reasons.

In April 2022, Corey and Nicholas filed a class action complaint with the US Equal Employment Opportunity Commission against the City of New York, suing Corey's former employers for unlawful workplace discrimination. Their struggle has become much bigger than one couple's drive to start a family: it's a landmark case with the potential to give gay men across the US the same access to fertility benefits as anyone else.

'I want to be really clear – if we could have afforded to have a child out of pocket, all of these costs, we would,' Corey says.

They've looked at what loans they could get, which subsidies they might qualify for; they've considered asking their families for money, or doing some kind of crowdfunding appeal. 'We're not willing to foreclose any of those options, because we are at a point of desperation,' Nicholas says ruefully. 'I almost feel embarrassed saying that. I think we are both accomplished people with great educations. We work very hard. And I don't think we should be in this position.'

'Not everybody wants to have children and I get that, it's not a necessary part of one's existence on this earth,' Corey says. 'But if you are among those who do have the desire to procreate, no one wants to be told there is no way to achieve that.'

'If you're determined to follow this route, are you vulnerable to exploitation?' I ask.

Nicholas replies by telling me about another advert, one he heard on the *Gays with Kids* podcast, for an at-home, DIY insemination kit. 'It's markedly less expensive. You're cutting out an enormous number of steps in the process. You're looking for a person, in a necessarily smaller pool, that's willing to have a child and give it to you,' he says. 'So yes, I think there's a lot of vulnerability that's introduced because people are looking to come up with ways to save money.'

My question had been about whether he and Corey would be vulnerable to financial exploitation because they wanted to have their own biological children so much. But he had understood it to mean that gay men would be vulnerable to legal and medical problems if they were tempted to save money by cutting out steps presented to them as necessary by their fertility clinic. The price of creating a life you are genetically related to, and doing it properly, as determined by the fertility industry, is taken for granted.

*

As their smiling doorman sees me out, I think about the look Corey shot Nicholas when he told me the bottom line was $200,000 minimum. Their legal battle gives them a vested interest in presenting the price of creating a life as beyond the reach of the average gay couple. Was Nicholas exaggerating for my benefit? Can it really be the case that every gay couple who's had kids through IVF and surrogacy had two hundred grand to spare?

The Gay Parents To Be website says it costs an average of $140,000 to have a child through IVF and surrogacy, but it varies depending on where you live in the US, from a minimum of $85,000 to a maximum of $207,500. The advice and advocacy group Men Having Babies publishes a budgeting guide that gives a minimum total as $113,050, but says the most common figure expected is around $194,100. Two hundred thousand dollars is probably on the money for a couple living in New York.

Today, biological fatherhood only exists for very rich gay couples – or very poor ones. Men Having Babies' Gay Parenting Assistance Program gives out over a million dollars a year in discounted and free medical services and cash grants to those in serious financial need. But Nicholas and Corey don't qualify. They are both too poor and too rich to have children that share their genes.

This problem goes beyond gay men in America. The price of creating a life is highest for men in same-sex relationships, but the enormous costs of assisted reproduction are taking an increasingly heavy toll on men and women, regardless of their sexuality – or whether they live in a country where fertility treatment is supposed to be free at the point of delivery.

One in six people worldwide are affected by infertility, according to the most recent WHO figures. For reasons not yet fully understood, sperm counts have declined by almost 60 per cent in less than forty years in Europe, North America and

Australia. Among women, fertility issues are strongly linked to age, and we are delaying motherhood more than ever before: women in the UK had their first child at an average age of thirty-one in 2020, compared with an average age of twenty-two in their mothers' generation. So the fertility industry is booming. The global market is expected to be worth $32 billion by 2029.

In the UK, most people undergoing fertility treatment are paying for it. In theory, women under forty should be offered three cycles of IVF on the NHS if they've been trying for a baby for two years without success, but the final decision about what treatment they actually receive is at the discretion of local integrated care boards (ICBs). The guidance refers only to women, which means that gay men aren't eligible to have any part of their fertility treatment covered by the NHS. And the boards often impose their own conditions: a woman generally must be under thirty-five, shouldn't smoke or be overweight, and shouldn't already have children (including stepchildren). It's common for ICBs to only offer one cycle of IVF instead of the recommended three. In a 2022 survey of 1,300 fertility patients, Fertility Network UK found that two thirds of people undergoing fertility treatment had paid for it privately, at an average cost of £13,750. Twelve per cent spent more than £30,000 on trying to have a baby, and a few (0.5 per cent of respondents) spent over £100,000.

'With five cycles, and all the travel, and £100 a month on supplements, we're over the £40,000 mark now,' Abbie tells me over the phone from Staffordshire. Her local NHS clinical commissioning group funded a single round of IVF, but when none of her eggs were fertilized, they told her they wouldn't be paying for more. 'If we'd lived twenty minutes up the road, we would have got an extra cycle on the NHS. If we had lived in another area, that first cycle would have been classed as a cancelled cycle, so we would have got another one. It was so unfair.'

Abbie's story, too, starts on Instagram – at least, that's where she became a spokesperson for the financial trauma of fertility treatment. She began posting about how she and her husband felt priced out of having a baby, and then realized that she was far from alone. But she doesn't want me to use her last name because, aged thirty-three and after four years of trying, she's finally fifteen weeks pregnant. Her baby was conceived in a Greek clinic using eggs from a Greek donor; she hasn't shared that part of her story yet.

'We basically went down to the breadline, to save every penny,' Abbie says. They sold her car to finance their fourth round of IVF; they had a loan on that car that they're still paying off. Their fifth round was at a clinic in London, because Abbie had heard 'so many miracle stories' about a particular consultant there. Her husband sold *his* car to pay for that round, and they took out yet another bank loan. 'We didn't go out. We cut out coffee, we cut out alcohol.' She missed friends' weddings and hen parties. 'My friendships took a nosedive.'

Even though Abbie has sacrificed so much to be pregnant, she tells me that one of the hardest parts of it all was realizing that she wasn't going to be biologically related to her baby. 'Accepting that the child was not going to share my genetics was very difficult,' she says quietly. 'I felt like I'm going to have a child with dark hair and features, and I wouldn't look like I was their mum.' The clinic is aware how much genes matter to people prepared to put themselves through fertility treatment. They offered Abbie two packages: either she shared the donor eggs with another couple, or she could spend an extra £3,000 and they would be hers exclusively. 'We'd just spent a hell of a lot of money. But then we started thinking about it: you're basically allowing for another child to share your child's genetics for the sake of £3,000. Then £3,000 does not seem like a lot of money.' So they paid the extra.

I guess when you've already spent so much, another £3,000 feels like a drop in the ocean. Abbie doesn't see it the same way, but it sounds to me like the donor eggs were being held to ransom.

'The difference between me having a child and not having a child was essentially how rich I am,' declares Nader AlSalim, father of one, and former executive director at Goldman Sachs. 'It's a very vulgar way to think about it, but it's the *only* way to think about it. The reality is you're *going* to get lucky if you have enough money.'

Nader has left the world of investment banking behind, but some of it lingers, despite the very deliberate decor in his west London office. There are water bowls for the office dogs, raffia rugs, trailing potted plants and a framed print bearing the words 'Brave Brave Brave' on his shelves. His thin bracelets and small, cryptic tattoos befit a startup CEO, but Nader's striped shirt, neat beard and recent haircut make him look every inch the finance guy. His company – Gaia – may be named after the ancestral mother of all life, but it's still an insurance company. Billed as 'the world's first IVF insurance,' it was founded six weeks after Nader's son was born following £50,000 of fertility treatment. Gaia insures its customers (or 'members,' as they're called here) against the risk of IVF failure.

Nader and his wife had five rounds of IVF. Three or four per cent of people in fertility treatment go to five rounds, he tells me. 'If you look at how many people have £50,000 in disposable savings, you'll find the same number – three or four per cent.

It's a process that mimics, essentially, how much money you have.' He shrugs. 'It's just unfair. How can you price someone out of a basic, fundamental right – the right to reproduce?'

But do we all have a basic, fundamental human right to reproduce, a right to become biological parents? Or is it a privilege, one that we should appreciate and cherish and feel grateful for? Do gay couples have the right to procreate, if that right demands a nine-month claim on a woman's body? Do single people have that right? There's certainly a drive to have children that we're biologically related to that many of us share. But whether that's a human right is still open to debate.

Nader presents it all so definitively, so I try and phrase my next question as diplomatically as possible. 'Some would say the right to reproduce is not a fundamental human right,' I say. 'Some would say, "If you want to become a parent, you can adopt."'

'I wish someone would explain to that person how hard the process of adopting is,' he replies, fixing me with plaintive eyes. When he and his wife explored it, they were struck by how understandably onerous it was. 'It's actually more exclusive than going through fertility treatment. I don't think it's an alternative, really. Everyone should have the right to a family. What *definitely* should not be the levelling field is your financial circumstances. Parenthood shouldn't be a luxury good.'

It's easy to agree with Nader. Being in his presence is a lot like attending a seminar given by a very charming and polished economics professor, who has logic and theory to back up his broad observations about humanity.

'The reason fertility treatments are expensive is because they're afforded a higher degree of price elasticity,' he continues. 'On the demand side, you have a wishful parent that is willing to pay money that they don't have, because no one can cap the price of hope.' A customer will continue to pay increasingly high prices for an ice cream up to a certain point where the pleasure of the ice cream is outweighed by the pain of paying for it, he says. 'In babies, that point is not clear.'

I'm just about keeping up. 'Because you can't put a value on a baby, you'll pay any price to have one?' I offer.

'Absolutely.' Nader smiles, like an encouraging teacher. 'You're pricing hope, and hope is infinite, subjective, circumstantial. In anything else in life, there is usually a very well-defined cap on how much you're going to pay for a service rendered that has a value. If the outcome of the service is a child, people can price whatever they want.'

The UK has a regulator, the HFEA – the Human Fertilisation and Embryology Authority – that has the power to shut down clinics found to be exploiting clients, but it does not oversee prices. In 2019, the HFEA chair admitted that some clinics were charging up to £20,000 for a cycle, four times more than it should cost, due to 'add-on treatments' of unproven benefit, like embryo glue and endometrial scratches. If hope is infinite, patients' willingness to maximize their chances probably is too, and they'll take all the add-ons they're offered.

This isn't just an issue for those who want to become parents, Nader says: it's an existential disaster for nations, an economic and political powder keg. 'Arithmetically, a lost life equals a life not being born,' he declares.

'How can that be true?'

'It's exactly the same,' Nader replies, delighted to be challenged. He picks up a black marker and writes '2.1' on the sketchpad in front of him. In order for a country to sustain itself – 'and assuming that immigrants like me do not exist' – households need to be producing 2.1 children, he says, but the average in England is currently 1.5. With low birth rates and a resistance to immigration, there's nothing to fill the deficit; there aren't enough taxpayers, which means we are sitting on a pension time bomb. The countries with the biggest pension holes are increasingly funding IVF at the national level. 'In Denmark, Israel, Japan, 10 per cent of all babies born are through IVF. In the rest of the civilized world, it's less than 2 per cent. It's a very clear message: if you make funding not the object, you will 5X the outcome,' he declares, articulating the formula with relish. In other words, when the state tries to tackle the pension problem by covering the cost of fertility treatment, five times as many babies are born through assisted reproduction.

Nader's innovation with Gaia is a clever algorithm that predicts the likelihood of IVF success over six rounds. 'You pay a personalized premium to reflect that likelihood, and you access the optimum number of rounds needed,' he explains. 'At the end of that journey, if you do not have a baby, you don't pay a penny. If you have a child, you pay back monthly.'

'Members' fill out a fertility profile so the algorithm can spit out a probability of pregnancy. 'It's not rocket science,' says Nader airily. The age of the woman is the major factor, but a whole host of others come into play: sperm count, BMI, levels of anti-Müllerian hormone, menstrual cycle, any history of endometriosis or polycystic ovary syndrome, previous pregnancies and miscarriage. 'If you combine all that together, you can get to a place where you are predicting outcomes with 80 per cent accuracy.' You pay your premium and go to one of Gaia's partner fertility clinics for treatment, who send the bills to Gaia.

If you end up with a baby – which they define as taking a newborn home from hospital – then Gaia insurance is more expensive than paying upfront for your fertility treatment, because you will have paid the premium in addition to the cost of your treatment. If you have success on the sixth round, you'll be paying Gaia back for a very long time. Nader says they do credit and affordability checks to make sure the people they take on can afford it, but biological parenthood is clearly still a luxury good, albeit one you're now able to pay for in instalments.

'The greatest unique selling proposition is the peace of mind – knowing that you have protection over the amount you're going to pay,' Nader says, leaning back in his chair, his arms folded behind his head. It also means that people will try for longer and have more babies, he adds. Their data showed that last year 1,700 more IVF babies would have been born if people stuck at it for one more round. 'We want people not to stop one IVF round short of success.'

In their first year of business, five babies have been born to Gaia members. 'This is the gist of how powerful it is,' Nader says, leading me out of his office to show me a gift from the same-sex parents of the first Gaia baby. It's a framed photo of a newborn, scrawny, pink and curled up on his side, encircled by a spectrum of rainbow-coloured syringes. 'Those are the needles that were used in the treatment,' Nader beams, flushed with pride. 'They've kept them and they've made a rainbow.'

It's certainly a striking image, but I'm not sure I'd want to see a tiny baby surrounded by needles every time I looked up from my work.

Many of Gaia's 'members' are same-sex couples – including lesbians. Prior to the fertility industry boom over the past three decades, same-sex female couples commonly used the kind of 'at-home' method Nicholas was describing (informally known as the 'turkey baster' technique): find someone – perhaps a friend – willing to donate sperm and get it in the right place at the right time during a woman's cycle. It can work quite well; fresh sperm might even be more effective than frozen in fertilizing an egg. (The studies that say this are decades old, though. While lesbians are as likely as straight and bisexual women to have fertility problems, lesbian conception has been barely studied.) But while this low-tech option is far cheaper than using a sperm bank, let alone IVF, it's legally and emotionally much more complicated: a 'turkey baster' sperm donor has a legal right to parental access, and can be pursued for maintenance payments. Still, this is a path to genetic parenthood where money is not the deciding factor in having a child. Nader should approve.

'At Gaia, we believe that that anyone who wants to have a family should be able to try. This includes queer and lesbian couples,' says the Gaia promotional video explaining their partnership with London Women's Clinic, in lower-case text over stock images of sunflowers and roses. 'Mum 1 uses her eggs to create an embryo. Mum 2 carries the embryo to birth. This allows queer or lesbian couples *to both be mothers*.' (The italics are theirs.)

'Shared motherhood or intra-partner egg donation is now the preferred and most popular treatment option for lesbian couples,' says the London Women's Clinic's website. One of the few pieces of research to look at same-sex female conception found this to be the case across the board. I completely understand why mothers would want to share the biological experience of creating a child, but it's not their only way of being 'able to try' to have a family. It is IVF treatment for fertile people. It's painful and expensive. And yet it's being promoted to same-sex female couples as if it's the thing that 'allows' them '*to both be mothers*'.

'There's an idea of biological parenthood that's being marketed to lesbian couples,' I say to Nader. 'It's being presented as doing things properly, and it might mean having quite expensive treatment, which they don't necessarily need to get pregnant.'

There's a long pause. 'I don't know if there's any pressure. We've supported a lesbian couple where one of the women had nothing to do with it,' he replies. It's the only unsatisfying answer Nader has given me today.

'Shared motherhood' exists because of the shifting emphasis onto biological parenthood in the light of technological possibility, and the changing definition of infertility. Same-sex families are increasingly unremarkable, and infertility is beginning to be redefined as the inability to make a baby with your chosen partner, even if you are both fertile. Men Having Babies has been lobbying the US federal government to recognize 'fertility equality' for same-sex couples, arguing that the 'situational infertility' they face is equivalent to medical infertility. Perhaps 'financial infertility' will one day become part of the same definition.

It's in the spirit of our age to give everyone the right to their own biological children, even if it can't happen naturally, Nader argues. 'In a world where we are pushing agency over anything from identity to gender, it can't come down to something biologically constrained,' he says. 'Who really plays God here? Who decides on what we have? The right should sit within the people to decide whether it's something they want to pursue.'

If we have a right to create a life, then fertility treatment should be considered on a par with any other healthcare. In countries where healthcare is free at the point of delivery, that would mean there would be no need for Gaia, but our taxes would go up. Either we accept that biological parenthood is a luxury available to those who can afford it, or we all have to be prepared to pay for everyone to access it. I don't think I want to live in a world where only the wealthiest get to reproduce.

Creating a life is expensive, even without fertility treatment. There are the costs of housing a family, feeding them, entertaining them, educating them, transporting them and finding someone to look after them while you work to earn all the money you need to pay for them. The total price of raising a child to the age of eighteen varies according to where you are in the world, but in 2022 it was calculated to be £160,000–200,000 in the UK, and around $310,000 in the US. Of course, it's not something the average parent would ever think to tot up. Unlike the too-expensive ice cream, whatever costs you bear from having a child are infinitely outweighed by the fulfilment that a much-wanted child brings you.

But if a life is created as a consequence of medical negligence – a 'wrongful birth' – its price is routinely calculated and paid in compensation to parents who would have preferred their baby never to have been born. These cases are never easy to bring, but they are more common than you might imagine. The NHS paid out just under £70 million in wrongful birth compensation for twelve claims in the 2021/22 financial year – almost double the previous year's total.

Wrongful birth claims tend to fall into two categories. The first is after a failed vasectomy or sterilization procedure, when parents can claim for loss of earnings and the physical and emotional pain of an unwanted pregnancy, but not for the cost of bringing up an unwanted child, so long as the child is born healthy. According to the law in England and Wales, it's impossible to calculate whether the joy a child can bring you is greater than the burden they place on your wallet.

In a striking case from 2018, a man known by the alias ARB lost his high court claim for wrongful birth damages for this very reason. ARB and his partner R were married when they went for fertility treatment together in 2008, resulting in the birth of their son. Five remaining embryos were frozen and stored. By 2010 their marriage had broken down, and R returned to the clinic alone for further treatment, having forged ARB's signature on the consent form. She became pregnant with ARB's second baby, without his knowledge or consent, and gave birth to their daughter in 2011. ARB had been seeking over £1 million in damages from the private clinic to cover the costs of raising his unwanted daughter – but, as the judge said, she was 'by all accounts, a lovely, healthy girl', so he couldn't be awarded anything.

The other – and more common – kind of wrongful birth claim is when a baby is born with disabilities that should have been detected during pregnancy and, had they been discovered, would have led the parents to have a termination. Most cases involve children born with conditions like Down syndrome or spina bifida, and the damages awarded reflect both the costs of caring for a child with often very complex needs and the resulting trauma. The level of damages varies, but can be substantial: in 2022, the parents of a boy born with a chromosomal abnormality and the most severe form of spina bifida won a settlement of £19.5 million from Liverpool Women's NHS Foundation Trust after a locum sonographer failed to detect any problem at the twenty-week antenatal scan.

Most of these cases are settled before they go to trial, so the claimants remain anonymous. If they make it to court, parents must stand up in public and say they wish their son or daughter had never been born in order to win damages to cover their care. When Edyta Mordel won a six-figure sum from Royal Berkshire Hospital NHS Trust in 2019 following the birth of her son, Aleksander, she made national headlines as 'Mum who would have aborted baby with Down's syndrome'.

Edyta's medical notes say that she and her partner were '. . . very upset to the point of irrationality' shortly after Aleksander's birth. They believed they had agreed to Down's screening and thought their baby had sailed through it, but the hospital had recorded that Edyta had declined it and he had never been screened. The judge ruled that when the sonographer asked Edyta, whose native language is Polish, if she wanted screening, Edyta hadn't understood the question, and her reflex response was to say 'no'. 'I would not have wanted a disabled child,' she said in her witness statement. 'I would not have continued my pregnancy.'

Edyta is clearly proud to be Aleksander's mother. Her Facebook page is full of images of her golden-haired little boy: posing in a football shirt, larking about on the beach in a sailor's hat, doing aeroplanes suspended on his dad's feet, grinning in a Christmas jumper. In place of a bio on her Facebook page, she has simply written '47,XY,+21♥'.

47,XY,+21 is the set of chromosomes that are expressed as Down's.

'This was never about whether or not they loved their son,' Edyta's lawyer said after the judgement. 'It was always about getting an admission and answers about the failures in Edyta's care to find out what had gone wrong and to ensure that no one else would suffer from similar failings in the future.' The price Edyta paid to get the answers, admission and compensation was for it to be forever on public record that she would have preferred his life to never have been created. Perhaps Aleksander will never see it. But even so, it's an incredibly harsh burden for a mother to have to bear.

The price of creating a life is a heavy one. It's expensive and often overwhelming, full of responsibility as well as reward. And the biological parenthood that so many of us seek is a special kind of lottery that we're not necessarily aware we're playing: if we are winners, we are scarcely aware that we've won.

PART FOUR

SAVING A LIFE

CHAPTER SEVEN
$2,000–3,000

Silicon Valley philanthropy

On the walls of the Open Philanthropy Project meeting room, there's a triptych of framed prints, each bearing a single definition above harmonious geometric shapes.

'Skepticism. The method of practicing doubt when regarding what is held as knowledge,' says the one on the left.

'Altruism. The practice and principle of using actions to benefit others, expecting nothing in return,' reads the middle frame.

'Utilitarianism. The school of ethics that strives towards the maximization of welfare for the maximum number of people,' says the one on the right.

There's little else here, apart from a recycling bin. The deliberate understatement might make this office look humble, were it not for the spectacular view of the San Francisco Bay several storeys below us. The people who work here might not want me to dwell on it too much, but the man who bankrolls all this is very wealthy indeed.

Dustin Moskowitz was nineteen in 2004 when his roommate, Mark Zuckerberg, came up with the idea of Facebook in their Harvard dorm. By the time he was twenty-six he was the youngest self-made billionaire in America (but only because

Zuckerberg is eight days older than him). Moskowitz left Facebook in 2008 to launch the workflow software company Asana, but most of his wealth still comes from his stake in what's now Meta. In 2016 he was ranked number two on *Forbes*' 'America's Richest Entrepreneurs Under 40' list, second only to his old roommate. It's now 2019 and he's the richest person living in the city of San Francisco, and far too important to grant me an audience today.

But I've read enough about him to know that Moskowitz is no ordinary Silicon Valley billionaire. Instead of spending his wealth on jets, yachts, space rockets and apocalypse-proof bunkers, he and his wife, the former *Wall Street Journal* reporter Cari Tuna, are giving his money away. The forty or so millennials who work here at OpenPhil (as they like to call it) are tasked with deciding who gets $11 billion of his fortune.

'Dustin and Cari don't seek accolades for themselves. They are most interested in maximizing the impact of their giving,' Mike Levine, OpenPhil's communications officer, is telling me from across the meeting room table. They plan to give most of their money away before they die, he adds. 'The idea is that it can do the most good sooner: there's an opportunity to lift people out of poverty, and then those people can improve the life of others. It perpetuates and grows.'

I can see a few tattoos inside the sleeves of Mike's mustard V-neck, but that's as playful as things get around here. He takes all this very seriously. I guess I shouldn't be surprised that a PR officer wants to tell me how virtuous the people who employ him are, but there's an earnest logic to all of this that I can tell Mike truly believes.

Behind the thick frames of his glasses, he looks me straight in the eye and says, 'They are trying to do as much good as they can and help as many people as deeply as they can. They've tried really hard to remove their own personal experiences from the equation, and to ask in an almost scientific way, "What can we do that would do the most good?" They've hired experts to help them find the most cost-effective opportunities. They're treating it as a really serious responsibility.'

There's a name for this kind of thinking. 'Effective altruism' (EA) takes the emotion out of the question of how best to do good in the world, and replaces it with empirical data and cold-headed logic. We have a moral obligation to get the most out of our charitable time and money, effective altruists say: we must give as well as we can. Instead of relying on our feelings, intuitions, lived experiences and personal connections to decide which causes to support, we should use cost–benefit analysis to get the maximum return for our investment.

Don't be led astray by shivering orphans in television appeals for disaster relief, they say; don't be tempted to support a breast cancer charity just because that's what killed your mother. Money donated to the families of those killed in terrorist attacks might buy the donor a sense of personal participation in having done something to make an unthinkable tragedy a little more tolerable, but it could make more difference to the human good if spent elsewhere. Emotional giving is ineffective altruism. Give with your head, not your heart; give to maximize the good you can do for the greatest possible number. Strangers overseas matter as much as our neighbours, future generations are just as important as people already alive today, and the lives of sentient animals are valued equally to human lives. Spend as much as you can, to save as many lives as possible, and the good that you do can be objectively measured. And bettered.

The grandfather of the EA approach is the utilitarian philosopher Peter Singer. His 1975 book, *Animal Liberation,* says that we should care equally about any being that has the capacity to suffer, even if we can't see them, even if they are not human. His 1972 essay, *Famine, Affluence, and Morality*, argues that failing to donate to help children dying in the developing world is the same as failing to dive in and rescue a child drowning before your eyes for fear of ruining expensive clothes; if we spend money on things beyond our basic survival, we are essentially walking on by while others die. His brand of utilitarianism has been massively influential on the EA movement. Cari Tuna was motivated to give away her and Moskovitz's fortune after reading Singer's 2009 book, *The Life You Can Save.*

EA applies scientific methods to doing good, reducing it to data-driven calculation. And that makes it appeal to a particular kind of mindset, a mathsiness that has served the latest generation of tech entrepreneurs so well. Now powered by the rocket fuel of Silicon Valley billions, it's gaining traction wherever people who are interested in philosophy, maths and computing gather, both as a set of ideas and as a social movement. It's the product of an era when data became more valuable than oil. Dustin Moskowitz made his enormous fortune out of Facebook's unrivalled ability to accumulate data. Now he's using data to give almost all of it away. He's determined to both build and spend his fortune using the same mindset. I'm hoping the team at OpenPhil can explain it to me.

I had my first taste of how important numbers are to effective altruists when I got in touch with Mike, the communications officer, to arrange my visit to OpenPhil. He agreed to have a meeting using a webconferencing platform called Dialpad, during which he asked me all about my metrics. How big was my audience? How many people read my writing? Was I more interested in focusing on Cari's and Dustin's personalities or the facts of their philanthropy? When it was all over I got an email from Dialpad with a summary breakdown of how long each of us had been speaking during the call: in our twenty-three-minute conversation I'd talked for fifteen minutes and Mike had spoken for eight. It's as if the content of what we said to each other didn't matter: the value of our relative inputs could be measured by time spent speaking alone.

These are brainy people and, interview granted, I'm very aware of the need to know my stuff before I open my mouth in front of them. On the flight over, I listen to a podcast featuring a researcher from the most powerful charity evaluator on the planet, GiveWell, which focuses exclusively on causes in sub-Saharan Africa. GiveWell's reputation for finding the most effective charities is so strong that OpenPhil doesn't have a global health and development department – they just give to whichever causes GiveWell recommends.

'We search for the charities that save or improve lives the most per dollar,' shouts the first thing you see on the GiveWell homepage. For every $2,000–3,000 you give to their recommended charities in 2019, GiveWell says, you will save one life: an African life, because these are the least expensive. Anything donated elsewhere is money wasted, money that could have gone further saving the cheapest lives on the planet.

On the podcast,* GiveWell researcher James Snowden ruminates on the optimum age to save a person's life. Is it worse when a newborn dies, or a ten-year-old, or a grown adult supporting a family? He explains his maths.

'You take the number of expected years of life left, and you multiply it by this pretty subjective factor which accounts for: does this person have cognitive function? Can they make plans

* Episode 37 of the *80,000 Hours* podcast, which is funded by the Centre for Effective Altruism, which, in turn, is largely funded by Moskovitz and Tuna's money.

like a functioning agent in the world? You multiply those things together, you end up with a roughly log-normal distribution over age,' he explains. I can just about work out what this means: if you plot it on a graph, with age on the X axis, it would look like a bell curve, or a wave, or a big drop rollercoaster, squashed up near the Y axis. 'The death of a very young child is something I would value less over . . . I think my peak value is the death of an eight-year-old.'

This makes me catch my breath. Do I really want to fly across the world to meet people who are able to use logic as cold as this? Who on earth are they?

In person, Mike is only slightly less intense than he was in the Dialpad meeting. 'One way that we describe this is "hits-based giving". Sort of like a venture capital approach, where you have this portfolio of investments, and it's OK if many of them – even most of them – fail to have an impact, if one of them really hits,' he tells me in the OpenPhil meeting room. 'Philanthropists are uniquely situated in democratic society to take those risks. Government – which does an enormous amount of good – is constrained in its responsibility to voters. Businesses are responsible to shareholders and have quarterly earnings statements. And philanthropists – there's good and bad that comes with this amount of responsibility and power – they have the advantage of being able to take these risks.'

The power America's top philanthropists have is mind-boggling. They regularly give away more money than the GDP of several countries combined. Amazon founder Jeff Bezos alone donates around $10 billion a year, and a significant part of his wealth comes from Amazon's canny ability to avoid paying tax. Mike would never explain it to me like this, but I hear what he's saying: instead of letting democratically elected governments decide how to spend money, the super-rich are using their money to shape the world according to their own priorities and philosophies. Self-made billionaires view their success as empirical evidence of their good judgement; they consider themselves more adept at solving problems than politicians, and more rational because they don't have to worry about appealing to voters, so they are both better off and better placed to decide how to use their wealth to help society.

Mike has arranged for members of OpenPhil's teams to explain their work to me. They file into this bland space to take a seat opposite me one after another, in precisely timed slots for maximum efficiency so I never have to leave my chair. First up is evaluation officer Morgan Davis, who tells me that, in the early days, geomagnetic storms and supervolcanoes were among OpenPhil's potential targets, problems they could hope to solve, but the risk they posed to life was ultimately deemed too small to justify investment.

This is far less thrilling to hear about than you might imagine, because Morgan is telling me about it using the dry language of venture capitalism. 'There was a giant list of problems in the world, and we tried to rank them by what we are calling "importance", "neglectedness" and "tractability", she says. 'Considering those three factors will help us make better bets, that are investments, as far as the expected value of different causes where additional marginal dollars might help the world.' At the time of my visit, the biggest grants that OpenPhil have paid to date are from the Global Catastrophic Risks department, which funds research that might save future populations from being wiped out by bioengineered pandemics, or the unintended consequences of advanced artificial intelligence.

Morgan sets the tone for her colleagues that follow.

OpenPhil's Farm Animal Welfare team focuses on poultry and fish rather than cows because of the brute numbers of lives saved: a single cow can produce enough meat for 1,500 quarter pounders, whereas twelve sardines have to die to fill a can. 'We're seeking to maximize the number of individuals we impact,' programme officer Lewis Bollard explains earnestly; he clearly knows how strange these ideas sound to new ears like mine, and he has a kind expression on his face, as if he hopes I will one day understand it all. 'We are working on vertebrate animals because we feel most confident in their ability to think and suffer.' It's a lot to take in.

The final person to take a seat opposite me is OpenPhil's managing director, Alexander Berger. He's younger than me; his brown hoodie and youthful face give him the demeanour of an excited child, but he speaks like a philosophy professor. 'Philanthropy – I'm going to butcher the Greek or Latin root, but it means love of humanity. Right now, very little of philanthropy is explicitly, self-consciously aimed not at the self-actualization of the donor but at maximally helping a very wide class of recipients,' he tells me, swivelling from side to side in his chair as I take feverish notes like an undergraduate at my first lecture. 'We're trying to help shift the focus from the donor's personal and idiosyncratic preferences toward an ethos that's truly serving people as much as possible. You need to be able to take the abstract or intellectual leap from the particular needs to the more general human needs.'

I'm sure Alexander doesn't mean it to come across this way, but there's a whiff of superiority in this: effective altruists are more sophisticated and enlightened than people who donate money because they've been handed a charity leaflet with an abandoned puppy on it; they believe they are better equipped to save the world.

I think about how much this approach to doing good accepts that capitalism will allow people like Dustin Moskowitz to become extraordinarily rich while others can't afford to eat. In some ways, it relies on it. What if OpenPhil spent Moskowitz's money tackling the root causes of problems like poverty, disease and animal rights, instead of the manifestations of those problems?

I try to find the words to frame this as a question that won't get me thrown out of the office.

'Are corporations and corrupt governments getting a free pass with this approach?' I ask.

Alexander leans back in his chair, relishing the intellectual challenge. 'Yeah. I think that's an interesting question. I have two lines of response. One is, we are trying to answer the question: where can we spend money to make the most impact? And the key to that is: what is changeable? Where can we make progress? We've tried to pick issues where we think it's possible to make progress, not the ones where we're going to be banging our heads against a wall for the next half century.'

Perhaps he can see how utterly bleak this sounds to me, so he changes tack. 'We try not to get involved in the biggest, most salient social fights, because those have highly polarized sides and tend to be less neglected,' he continues. 'We can have a lot of impact by not necessarily having to be in every fight and picking wisely where our money can help people as much as possible.'

Dollar for dollar, OpenPhil might be able to do more good by focusing on the places where other people aren't spending their money. But this deliberately dispassionate approach, cleaved of activism and personal connection, feels incredibly antiseptic to me, in this white, empty room.

I feel like I'm the only person here who hasn't reached the

plane of enlightenment where I can park my empathy, so I try and put it to good use. I place myself in Dustin Moskowitz's shoes: if I had got all this wealth from being in the right dorm at the same time as the right idea, I'd feel uncomfortable with it. Maybe Moskowitz has emotional reasons for doing all this after all.

'Say you had made a lot of money very quickly when you were very young. It might be something that sits uneasily with you,' I suggest. 'Some people might think, "I really deserve this, I'm great." Others might feel a burden of responsibility.'

'That seems totally accurate. Dustin has written publicly before about the feeling of being very lucky and feeling a responsibility or stewardship towards the resources that have accumulated,' Alexander replies with a sage nod. 'Choosing the thing you're passionate about is an abdication of what has been vested in you via this totally lucky process. Just helping the people nearby you is a little bit of a perversion.'

In another white boardroom in another high-rise building on the other side of the Bay, I am sitting opposite another brainy thirtysomething in a hoodie. Elie Hassenfeld is co-founder and Chief Executive Officer of GiveWell, the charity evaluator that has been practising effective altruism since before there was a name for it. As well as receiving OpenPhil's entire global health and development budget, thousands of other bodies and individuals do whatever GiveWell says when it comes to doing good. Most of those who follow their advice are under forty. GiveWell directed $1.5 million to their chosen charities in 2010, and expect that number to be $1 billion a year by 2025. This may well be the future of philanthropy.

Elie is telling me GiveWell's origin story, with the polish and slight weariness of someone who for whom it is well-worn. He'd been working at a hedge fund for a couple of years when he and a few colleagues, including Holden Karonovski, GiveWell's co-founder, decided they were making more money than they needed and should give to charity. They formed a kind of club, where they'd meet every couple of weeks and compare notes on the most deserving causes.

He liked the idea of improving drinking water in Africa, but determining which programmes were delivering it best was almost impossible, Elie continues. He wanted to know how many wells would be created for every $1,000 he donated to water charities, but when he contacted them to ask for metrics, they just sent him leaflets, pictures, campaigning materials. The information he wanted just wasn't available. Elie and Holden started doing their own research about the effectiveness of each charity. 'All of a sudden I'm staying up until three in the morning reading academic papers about diarrhoea.' Elie grins. 'I'd never stayed up until three in the morning reading papers about the bond market.'

They quit their jobs, sourced $300,000 in startup money, and created GiveWell in 2007, taking the hedge-funder mentality with them. 'We were applying that same sort of critical, sceptical eye,' Elie nods. 'It was very similar to what you do when you make any sort of consumer purchase. You go online to buy a cellphone or a laptop, and you expect good information about how effective the different products are, and how to choose between them.'

And I immediately understand the mindset that allowed GiveWell to come up with their $2,000–3,000 price of life figure: one that sees no distinction between saving a life and buying electronics.

'I think $2,000–3,000 is the right way to describe it,' he says, as breezily as if he were valuing a second-hand car. 'We look at all the academic evidence about the size of the effect of a charitable intervention, the organization's costs, context, monitoring, and where they'll spend the next set of money they receive, and that then creates our cost-effectiveness estimate. We use that as the basis for that $2,000–3,000 per life saved.'

Of course, many charities do this kind of maths when trying to get people to part with their money. But Elie says they do it disingenuously, with little basis in fact, and it infuriates him. 'There's a lot of marketing that says things like "Give fifty cents, save a life." This is crazy. This is terrible. It is false, and when we say to someone, "Guess what we found – you can save a life for $2,000–3,000", they think we're giving them a terrible deal!' He shakes his head. 'It's really up to donors to be intelligent consumers of the information they receive.'

Of the seven top charities GiveWell are recommending at the time of my visit, two focus on malaria prevention and three on deworming programmes. All are in Africa.

'Sub-Saharan Africa, relative to other non-US or European countries, is the poorest [region] and has the highest child mortality of anywhere in the world,' Elie explains. 'Health offers the opportunity for a donor to be confident about the types of impacts that they're getting. If you improve someone's health, or if you avert a death, you know that you've improved someone's life from far away.' Compared with school investment, the impact of health is easier to evaluate, he tells me. 'I imagine the educational intervention that would work in Oakland might be different than what would work in New York, never mind what would work overseas. That's what makes it much more challenging to find the programmatic approach.' Plus education is much more expensive than trying to prevent malaria: GiveWell estimates that the same $2,000–3,000 that will save a sub-Saharan

African child's life will only pay for a year and a half of specialist schooling for a low-income student in the United States.

The numbers say that African kids get the money because it's empirically simpler – and better value – to save them from malaria than it is to try to make a difference in the lives of children closer to home.

Elie might approach his subject like a financier, but there is a warmth to him, and an awareness that, to someone like me who is neither utilitarian philosopher nor economist nor hedge-funder, this kind of thinking is jarring.

'This is not a math problem,' he says gently, sensing my unease. 'There is no right answer, and we know that.'

There may not be right answers, but some answers are definitely better than others, and I worry that this approach could lead people to believe that what's measurable matters most. And, as I already know, these people are prepared to consider unthinkable things.

'I listened to this podcast with your researcher, James Snowden. He was talking about some of the' – I can't quite bring myself to say it – 'controversial moral conundrums that you guys have to face.' Elie frowns. 'He was thinking about how you would value the death of a child depending on age,' I say eventually. 'Is this something you really think about at GiveWell?'

He pauses. 'As a staff we do try to talk through this question, because it's highly relevant,' he finally replies. 'Many charitable programmes focus on those very early days of birth and we struggled with the question of how to weigh the impact there, versus the impact of saving an older child, or even saving an adult who may themselves be contributing to the income of an entire family. It's hard. It's *crazy*. I've had staff members ask me questions about how I felt about *my own* kids at different ages, just as a way of engaging in that conversation, and of course it's not a conversation most people ever have. We try to create an environment where people feel comfortable having awkward conversations.'

I try to imagine having chats about my children around the GiveWell water cooler. I can't.

I appreciate that it takes a certain kind of moral courage to be dispassionate enough to have these conversations. Is it a good kind of courage? Can you save more of humanity if you're prepared to have them? Or does this way of thinking require you to deny your own humanity?

San Francisco has both more millionaires and more homeless people per square mile than anywhere else in the US. The homeless are far more visible. I walk away from the philanthropic foundation belonging to San Francisco's richest resident, and within minutes I'm on streets lined with weathered tents, frayed tarpaulins, shopping trolleys, knots of black bin bags, blankets and sleeping bags left out in the elements. Their owners perch on plastic crates or cardboard boxes, keeping a watchful eye on the little that they have in the world. While they are never physically far from their possessions, many of them aren't really here at all. Every year, hundreds of homeless people die on the streets of this city; the leading cause of death is overdose, followed by suicide, homicide and chronic medical conditions.

To use philosopher Peter Singer's analogy, the 'drowning child' in the Bay Area is the woman sleeping rough on the pavement outside your office, and the people who work at OpenPhil and GiveWell walk past her every day. While OpenPhil has an area of focus it calls 'land use reform' – which it says seeks to 'reduce the harms caused by excessively restrictive local land use regulations' that can lead to higher rents

San Francisco homeless tents under the freeway (courtesy of Shannon Badiee).

– it's about making it easier to build properties and promote economic growth, and not helping rough sleepers specifically. 'More permissive policy could contribute to both affordable housing and the continued growth of centers of economic activity,' reads the relevant page on their website, 'allowing more people to access high-wage jobs and encouraging economic growth.' Rough sleeping has never been on OpenPhil's target list. Meanwhile, GiveWell focuses only on Africa, where dollars go furthest.* Saving the lives of the manifestly desperate

* Both OpenPhil and GiveWell publish where they give grants and make donation recommendations on their websites. At the time of writing, neither has funded or recommended charities that specifically look after rough sleepers in the Bay Area.

in front of their noses in the Bay Area would be ineffective altruism.

'You have these really intense visuals of massive wealth right alongside quite destitute people living in the shadows of that affluence,' Jennifer Friedenbach tells me. She's worked for San Francisco's Coalition on Homelessness for the last twenty-eight years, in a brightly painted office building less than ten minutes away from OpenPhil. 'The lifespan of unhoused people is generally around twenty-five years shorter than someone who's housed. A fifty-year-old homeless woman is going to present medically as a seventy-five-year-old. The impact caused by sleep deprivation, the inability to treat chronic disease, is devastating. We shouldn't be just accepting that it's part of our life in San Francisco, but people don't want to think about it.'

The homelessness crisis can only be properly addressed with an approach that tackles structural inequalities in the city, Jennifer says; soup kitchens and shelters are 'a Band-aid.' Unless there's the will to redress the balance between the richest and the poorest in San Francisco, it will forever be engaged in a game of whack-a-mole: take the homeless off the streets in one area, and more will appear in another.

Jennifer has never heard of the term 'effective altruism' but there's a flicker of weary recognition in her eyes when I explain what it means. 'It's a cold calculus. I understand the thinking behind it. But it feels like putting a price tag on lives, and with the amount of resources that a lot of people who are engaged in these conversations have, it really should be a deeper conversation than numbers on a piece of paper.'

'Why do you think the wealthiest San Franciscans would rather save a child in Africa than help out with the rough sleeping problem on their doorstep?' I ask her.

'I think there's a lot of disdain for people who experience

poverty in the United States,' she replies with a sigh. 'There's blaming – "There's something wrong with you", or "You did something wrong."'

And perhaps that's the thing driving all of this, as much as the numbers: it's easier to idealize people in poverty who live far away, to envisage them as unfortunate and worthy of help, *because* you can't see them. The poor person on your street confronts you with the messy reality of poverty, the inequality in your shared community, and perhaps it's easier to overlook them than acknowledge the fundamentally unfair society in which you happen to have won the lottery. The poor kid in Africa is just a set of data points, not a set of uncomfortable truths you need to reckon with.

Of course, many of those who describe themselves as effective altruists may well help those who sleep rough; but if they did, it would go into the category of the things you do to generate warm fuzzy feelings, to make yourself feel better, rather than to save as many lives as possible. As such, it would be selfish, rather than altruistic.

Five thousand miles away from the minimalist boardrooms and ragged tent cities of the Bay Area, Will MacAskill sits in his Oxford University office in front of two enormous and dazzling daylight therapy lamps, to burn away the January blues. In 2015, when Will was twenty-eight, he became an associate professor here, the youngest philosophy professor in the world. His desk is strewn with envelopes, half empty glasses of water and used mugs; on a low table to his left there's a 1,000-piece jigsaw puzzle of the Northern Lights, half-completed. Someone is asleep on the beanbag outside his office door. There is nothing minimalist about this setup.

I've come here to see where the morality of the future began. With his baggy green jumper, scruffy auburn hair and stubble, Will doesn't look like a man whose ideas can spark the movement of billions of dollars, but he was the one who came up with the term 'effective altruism' back in 2010. Within a few years his ideas were being bankrolled by the richest people in the world.

'How do you feel about that?' I ask.

'Er, weird. Number one would be – awkward. I'm only one person of very many who have contributed. But no – good, ultimately. I think it's a good sign for the world, I feel excited.' His Glasgow accent is thick, his speech every bit the millennial professor. 'You would think that the way to reason is "Wow, I've done so much good, now I can just chill out a little bit." But actually, things get even higher stakes. It warms my heart to see such an uptake of these ideas. Normally you have to wait centuries before seeing the impact of philosophical ideas.'

Will is the co-founder and president of the Centre for Effective Altruism – the premier resource for the 10,000-strong effective altruism community – which is largely funded by Cari Tuna and Dustin Moskowitz. He's reluctant to describe the typical effective altruist – 'I worry talking about that might be self-reinforcing' – but he's happy to answer the 'pure, statistical question of what does the median EA look like', ticking off attributes on his fingers.

'It would be well educated, philosophy, STEM, science background. Kind of nerdy people, I guess, is the most common typical collectivization. And we are young.'

The movement began when Will was an eighteen-year-old Cambridge undergraduate and read Singer's *Famine, Affluence, and Morality* essay. He'd already been volunteering for disabled scout groups and in care homes, and was a 'chugger' for Care International in the summer before his postgraduate degree.

He decided to give away 5 per cent of his £9,000-a-year income. But he didn't feel like he was having enough impact. 'I had this period of moral turmoil, where I felt that the life that I was planning – which was to become a philosopher of language, a Wittgenstein scholar or something – was quite out of whack with what I believed morally.'

Then Will tells me about meeting the computer scientist-turned-philosopher Toby Ord, and his eyes sparkle.

'Toby had been thinking for many years about the problem of global poverty. He had planned to give away most of his income, and had been taking the ideas of cost-effectiveness very seriously.' There was an energy and optimism to Toby that drew Will in, he says. 'With Peter Singer, the framing was always obligation – that you are acting wrongly unless you do this. Whereas Toby was very upbeat.'

Will switched to study ethics, and in 2009 he and Toby launched Giving What We Can, a campaign to encourage people to donate at least 10 per cent of their income to charity.

'How many people have signed the Giving What We Can pledge today?' I ask.

'1,492,' he replies, as if I'd just asked Siri.

Will practises what he preaches, and then some. At the moment, he gives away 55 per cent of his income – everything he earns above £26,000. 'There are caveats,' he says. 'If I have some terrible health condition and it means I'm going to die and therefore not do any good in the future unless I use this money, it would just be ridiculous not to.'

And he's decided not to have children, for equally rational cost–benefit reasons. 'Over time, I've developed preferences for wanting to have the most impact,' he says. 'I'm getting this amazing amount of value and rewards out of my life, and having kids would be a distraction.'

No human being is an altruism computational device, an instrument for maximizing good. Is Will for real, or is this part of a schtick?

'Do you make all of your life choices in this way?' I ask.

'No. In general you don't want to be thinking: *Should I kiss my partner now? Would that be maximizing well-being?* There are certain areas of life where we're very attuned to have a good gut understanding of what to do. Relationships are one of them.' A smile plays on his lips as he says this. He's savouring my bemusement.

Whereas Elie had been careful in his arguments, mindful of how they might sound to unfamiliar ears, Will likes to be flamboyant. During a 2015 public debate, the Anglican priest Giles Fraser put a thought experiment to him: if he was in front of a burning building with a Picasso in one room and a child in another, wouldn't his principles demand that he save the Picasso instead of the child because the proceeds of selling it could save the lives of thousands of children? Will was unapologetic: he'd save the Picasso.

The same cold logic is in play when Will gives career advice. In 2011, he founded *80,000 Hours*, a podcast and a careers advice service named after the amount of time a person will spend at work over their lifetime. One of the ideas it promotes is called 'earning to give', which argues that, if you have an appropriate skill set, you will do more good if you choose a career in finance rather than the charity sector, because an investment banker who gives 50 per cent of his or her salary away can cover the cost of several charity workers. Will tells me dozens of people have been inspired by his advice to do exactly this.

As we sit here together today, the most striking example is Sam Bankman-Fried, who met Will in 2012. Back then, Sam was a geeky undergraduate majoring in physics at MIT, and

Will convinced him that he could have the greatest impact if he made a fortune in finance and gave his money away. Sam went on to become one of the richest people in cryptocurrency. By the time he was twenty-nine, *Forbes* estimated his net worth to be $26.5 billion, with nearly all of it earmarked to go to effective causes.

How far is Will prepared to take this 'earning to give' idea, I wonder?

I lean forward in my chair. 'Is it better to be a top-level cosmetic surgeon and give most of your money away, rather than an A&E doctor?' I ask.

'If you're comparing how much good you do with your donations versus how much good you do as a doctor in the US, I'm pretty confident you will do more good with your donations,' he replies with relish.

'Peter Singer's analogy,' I say. 'Is ignoring a leaflet from an effective charity the same as walking past a drowning child?'

'Morally, yes, it is the same,' he replies. 'We have evolved a set of moral intuitions when it was not possible to have action to do something that could be as significant as saving someone's life thousands of miles away.' Will's thinking is that our helping instincts developed at a time when we couldn't have global impact, but now that we can, we're stuck with a myopic view of how to do good. Our morality is primitive. We just need to evolve. For now, only the deep thinkers understand, but one day the rest of the world will wise up and join them.

It's all so simple to Will. But surely a completely rational approach to making decisions as human as how to be good to other people depends on a robotic analysis of data that denies basic facts about human nature, human connections and lived experience. Being human is more than an exercise in maximizing good. Surely life has to be more complicated than this?

'Don't we make decisions according to our personal experiences and relationships in the world?' I ask him.

'There's the question of what we do do, and what we ought to do. Ultimately I'm looking for the change in social norms. Imagine the social norm was that when you give to charity you try and do as much good as possible. And then you say, "No, I'm going to give to the cat shelter because I just really like cats." I think people would follow along with the social norm. I think that would be the more powerful force.' He looks at his phone. 'I have to go in four minutes.'

Effective altruists are largely white millennial men educated at elite universities, who are drawn to the kind of remorseless logic that underpins the concept. They lack humility, and experience of both life and alternative perspectives. And yet they now have the power to redefine what doing good means. Theirs is an approach that allows you to 'measure' the good you are doing, so that altruism itself can be ranked and compared. It gamifies philanthropy. Once lives have a price, being a good person and saving them comes with a score.

The world is not a computer simulation, where optimal outcomes can always be determined. No matter what Will may argue, I'm still convinced that doing good has to be more than an accounting problem. We help others not just to save crude numbers of lives, but to create the world we want to live in. We can't blind ourselves to the needs of the people on our doorstep – literally, in the case of the Bay Area philanthropists – simply because the numbers say others elsewhere might need our help more. I don't want to live in a world where this is what is 'right.' It undermines our responsibilities to the people we encounter every day. It misses what it means to do things for the benefit of fellow humans, as much as humankind.

Perhaps I'm just not smart enough to get it; my view is

insufficiently evolved. But if that's the case, then there's a danger that EA makes philanthropy sound like hard work, something that can only be done properly at the hands of the very clever.

'I think this is going to grow and be an ethical revolution,' Will says, as the final seconds of our remaining minutes tick away. 'If you look at the scientific method, that was just the domain of a bunch of crackpots who sometimes got burned at the stake for several centuries, and then that caught on pretty well. I think the same can happen with taking the scientific mindset and applying it to doing good.' He smiles. 'Most moral progress has gone via ideas that at one time would get you laughed out of the room.'

To Will's mind – and the thousands of people he's inspired – I'm using the logic of a bygone age. Newtonian physics versus quantum mechanics, maybe even flat earthism. And in one respect, at least, they are completely right. The effective altruists were the first to draw philanthropic attention to the threat of artificial intelligence, or bioengineered pandemics. Maybe they could be the most insightful people on the planet after all.

As this book goes to print, GiveWell has revised the cost of saving a life, putting it at $4,500. 'We generally expect the cost to save a life to increase over time,' they explain in a blog post indignantly entitled 'Why Is It So Expensive To Save Lives?'.

Sam Bankman-Fried's crypto empire came crashing down in November 2022, and $8 billion in customer funds evaporated overnight – along with all his philanthropic promises. A year later, he was found guilty of wire fraud, conspiracy to commit securities fraud, conspiracy to commit commodities fraud and conspiracy to commit money laundering. 'Sam Bankman-Fried perpetrated one of the biggest financial frauds in American history,' said Damian Williams, US attorney for the Southern District of New York, after the verdicts were read. With hindsight, it looks like Bankman-Fried had used EA to launder his voracious greed. This is the problem with removing emotion and duty from giving: it can be hijacked by amoral sociopaths who believe the ends justify the means.

Of course, Will has tried to distance himself from Bankman-Fried. Instead, the father of EA wants to look to the future. EA's most generous donors are increasingly diverting their funds from saving the lives of people today towards saving populations yet to be born from the dangers of malevolent AI. This long-termism makes sense if you look at the numbers: saving a tiny proportion of the trillions of people who could one day live on earth is worth millions – even billions – of people dying today. The maths demands you spend your money saving the future you will not see, not the African kids, and certainly not the man sleeping on the pavement outside your office.

CHAPTER EIGHT
£20,000–30,000 per year

The National Health Service

Edward Willis-Hall has just woken up from his nap. He lies on the carpet between the sofa and the TV in his nappy and grubby white vest, a toy pick-up truck held aloft between the pink soles of his feet. His curly blonde hair trails behind him in the thick pile. He gazes at the neon CGI dinosaurs dancing across the TV screen, until he notices his mother, Megan, coming into the room with me. A goofy grin blooms across his face.

The golden ringlets, the huge blue eyes, the plump, pendulous cheeks should make Edward look like a cherub, but there is no chubbiness to his limbs. His legs are long and scrawny, yet to crawl or kick or bear his own weight for long. He has the expressive, inquisitive face of any other sparky toddler, but his shape tells a different story.

Megan pops Edward onto the sofa beside me and puts some books in his lap while she goes to heat up his lunch. He fixes me with those beguiling eyes.

'How old is he now, exactly?' I call out to Megan in the kitchen.

Edward lifts up his index finger to show me he is one.

'Nineteen months,' Megan says, striding back into the living room with frothy coffees in glass mugs. 'He wants to fist bump you.'

Edward has curled his finger in to make a shaky fist. He pushes it towards me to bump.

I'm happy to oblige.

'His cousins, they taught him that on holiday,' she says brightly. 'Are you going to fist bump Mummy?' He holds out his fist to her. 'Thank you.'

At another point in history, or in another country, Edward would be unable to hold up his head, eat without a feeding tube, or breathe without a ventilator. In a different time or place, he would probably have five months left to live. But he is here, pushing buttons on his noisy books, throwing us fist bumps and eyebrow wiggles, thanks to a single dose of a life-saving drug that cost £1.798 million. And Edward got it for free, because NHS England agreed to pay for it.

But Megan had to fight for it. 'From the word go, it's been difficult.' She checks herself. 'It's been the best thing ever. But. I hated every second of being pregnant. I had awful, *awful* sickness. And the birth was in lockdown, so I was completely on my own.' Covid meant Edward's dad, John, wasn't allowed into the hospital when she had her labour induced. 'Edward was five days late, and also he wasn't moving much,' she explains with a sad smile. 'Now I know why.'

Newborn Edward passed the usual hospital checks without a fuss. He fed well, and only woke up two or three times a night. Megan felt lucky to have such an easy baby. But by the time he was four weeks old, she noticed he'd stopped moving his legs as much, and his head seemed floppy. Instead of developing, he seemed to be doing things *less*. 'Also, he had this really rapid breathing . . .' She gets out her phone to play me a video of Edward, seven weeks old, lying on his back. His limbs are completely still – arms pinned by his sides, legs splayed and folded inwards like a frog's – but his belly is moving fast, distending and collapsing with every quickfire breath.

Two days after that video was taken, Edward collapsed. John had taken him to Asda on a Sunday morning, and Edward had been howling in the car seat on the way home, until he just stopped. He went blue; his eyes and mouth were open. 'Just . . . half dead,' Megan tells me, still in disbelief. John pulled over and gave him mouth to mouth, and Edward began breathing again, but by the time they reached Megan at home it had turned into a death rattle.

They raced to A&E, and Edward was resuscitated and put into an induced coma for a week. When the doctors woke him up and took his breathing tube out, he was 'a different baby. He was so floppy.' On her phone at his bedside, Megan put all Edward's symptoms into Google, and there, at the top of the results, was spinal muscular atrophy. 'The first thing I read was 95 per cent of children don't make it to two. And I just *knew* he had it.' She snaps her fingers. 'The penny dropped as soon as I read it.'

SMA is a motor neuron disease, a disorder of the nerve cells in the spinal cord that transmit signals from the brain to the muscles. The cells can't make enough of a vital protein called SMN, so they deteriorate. That means signals from the brain can't get through to the muscles, which become progressively weaker and wither away. These are muscles that are needed for talking, crawling, walking, swallowing and breathing. SMA is the most common genetic cause of death among children younger than two years old.

Babies are born with SMA if both their parents have a faulty or missing SMN1 gene. One in forty people in the UK – around 1.67 million of us – are carriers of SMA. There are different forms of SMA (1, 2, 3 and 4) which vary in severity according to how much SMN protein the body can produce. Worldwide, one in every 10,000 babies is born with SMA, and 60 per cent of them have Type 1, meaning it's both the most severe and the most common form. Symptoms of SMA1 appear before a child is six months old, and include poor head control, a floppy body, a characteristic 'frog-leg' posture when lying down, rapid breathing and a weak cry.

'A *weak cry*. That's the one that did it for me,' Megan nods. 'When he was three or four weeks old, I remember saying to my mum, "I don't know if it's just because he's mine, but his cry really doesn't bother me."' She considered herself a lucky mum, back then.

When the neurology team came to see them, Megan was suffused with cold-blooded practicality. 'So I'm losing him. I'm losing my baby,' she said to them. 'Don't sugar-coat things.'

'You shouldn't google SMA,' the neurologist replied. 'It's very different to what it once was. There is a treatment called gene therapy. It's really effective. Go home. Do your research on that.'

Until 2016, there was no treatment for SMA. Then the US Food and Drug Agency approved the gene therapy Spinraza (the European Drugs Agency followed in May 2017). Spinraza helps the production of the SMN protein, slowing down the progression of SMA, meaning that babies with SMA1 can live longer. It's delivered by injection into the spine – a lumbar puncture – with an initial four doses spaced out over a number of weeks, followed by three doses a year for the rest of the patient's life. It costs $750,000 (around £580,000) for the first year of treatment, and $375,000 (£290,000) every year that follows.

In a country with a national health service, and a limited budget that must be shared among the population, costs like this are hard to justify. The National Institute for Health and Clinical Excellence, better known as NICE, decides which drugs should be made available on the NHS in England. Since it was founded in 1997, the rule has been that if a drug costs £20,000–30,000 or less per additional year of life in good health it provides for a patient, then NICE will give it the green light. English children with SMA had to wait two years longer than their European neighbours, and three years longer than American kids, because NICE approval only came after much deliberation in 2019. With a degenerative condition, every day without treatment takes its toll.

No sooner had NICE come to a decision on Spinraza than the most expensive medicine ever to come on the market was launched in 2019: the gene therapy Onasemnogene abeparvovec, sold by the Swiss pharmaceutical giant Novartis under the brand name Zolgensma. Where Spinraza slows the progression of SMA and requires a lifetime of treatment, Zolgensma stops it in its tracks with a single dose. Its list price – over $2 million – broke all records.

On the homepage of the official zolgensma.com website, family videos play on a loop, with the words 'I'll always remember the day we received the *one-time only dose for SMA*' superimposed over the footage. A toddler with a bow in her hair stands tall, giving the camera a big smile and a thumbs up. A golden-haired baby sits up confidently in a highchair and stuffs handfuls of birthday cake into his face. Celebrations of milestones, birthdays. The sort of images someone who's just learned their baby has SMA would be desperate to see.

'The sooner the treatment is received, the sooner the progression of SMA can be stopped,' says a smiling woman wearing a mushroom-coloured jacket in another video. Speaking in the tone of an enthusiastic primary school teacher, she explains how Zolgensma is made up of a new, fully functioning SMN gene 'that's just waiting to get to work' and a vector – a harmless virus – that delivers it to the motor neuron cells. 'That's pretty cool, right?'

Cool enough to justify the price tag? Novartis thinks so. When the US FDA approved Zolgensma in 2019, CEO Vas Narasimhan declared it to be good value compared with the cost of caring for someone with SMA over a lifetime without it. 'We believe by taking this responsible approach, we will help patients benefit from this transformative medical innovation and generate significant cost savings,' he said.

This silver bullet that promised to solve all Edward's problems wasn't yet approved by NICE, and cost six times the price of their family home. Megan opened new social media accounts, setting herself up as @SMA_mumma on Facebook, Instagram, TikTok and YouTube, connecting with families of kids with SMA and gaining thousands of followers from around the world. She created a JustGiving page to crowdsource funds to take Edward to the US for private treatment. She gave interviews to her local paper, trying to drum up support and donations. She raised tens of thousands of pounds within a couple of months. But despite her effort and energy, and the generosity of so many people, it was a drop in the ocean.

When the news that NICE had approved Zolgensma came in March 2021, the UK was in lockdown and Edward was six months old. 'NHS England has moved mountains to make this treatment available, while successfully negotiating hard behind the scenes to ensure a price that is fair to taxpayers,' NHS England Chief Executive Sir Simon Stevens said at the time.

We will never know what that price is: the terms of the deal the NHS struck with Novartis mean it will remain forever confidential.

'We were absolutely beside ourselves with happiness,' Megan says, her eyes glistening at the memory. 'The whole family was on Zoom, crying with joy.'

But an hour later, her phone buzzed with a message from the mother of another child with SMA, who had been present at the NICE committee meetings. 'She messaged me and said, "FYI, I don't think Edward will be eligible." That's all she put.'

NICE had recommended that Zolgensma be available for children under six months old. Edward was just over the age limit.

'I was beside myself again,' Megan tells me. 'It was like a carrot being held in front of us: we can save your child's life but we're not going to. As a mum, you should be able to fix everything, but I couldn't. I was so completely helpless.'

This seems unbearably cruel. But Megan says she wasn't angry. 'I was frustrated. I'm not so naive to think a drug can just be free for everyone. There has to be a line that you draw. I'd hate to be the people that make the decisions, but they also need to be a bit more human as well. The NHS isn't human, unfortunately. You think it is, until you're deep into the system, and then you realize it's a pure numbers game. I get it, they have to be. I empathize with them. But at the same time, they need to empathize with us.'

Megan's next move was to present Edward to the world as a human being, a child in need of compassion, rather than a figure in an equation. 'What about the rest of us, the ones over six months?' she implored in an urgent interview with ITV News. 'There was this big fanfare when the drug was approved and we were ecstatic but now we feel like it gave us false hope.'

'Edward needs this drug now,' she told the BBC. 'We just feel like we have been abandoned. I can't just sit here and let this happen, I can't fail Edward. This is really cruel.'

'I was trying to embarrass them a little bit,' she says with a cheeky smile. 'I thought, *You need to see the faces that are waiting on your decision*. They don't think about the lives they are affecting; they're just looking at whether it is cost-effective to save this person's life. I wanted to be as annoying as possible so they would just put him through.'

And it worked.

The NHS began to roll out treatment to older children on a case-by-case basis, and Edward got his dose of Zolgensma in August 2021, when he was ten months old, several months before other babies the same age as him. By refusing to let her son be just a number, Megan saved his life.

Megan Willis and her son Edward Willis-Hall (courtesy of Megan Willis).

NICE doesn't make quick decisions. Their press officer tells me they'd be happy to explain their process to me, but it takes seven weeks and fifteen emails for them to determine who the right person to do it will be. Fortunately, I can wait. The right person turns out to be Helen Knight, Programme Director of Medicines, a health economist who joined NICE's technology appraisal programme fifteen years ago. I'd hoped to be able to get a sense of the personality behind NICE's life-or-death decision-making, the people who make up that monolithic institution that had seemed so inhuman to Megan, but when she logs onto our Zoom call she has blurred her background. I get the human face of NICE, but no other clues.

Still, the face is friendly. Helen clearly loves talking about her work. Her blue eyes twinkle with lively enthusiasm behind her glasses, even if the language she uses is very much that of a public body that likes a lot of spreadsheets.

'It's balancing individual patient need, versus allocating scarce resources, to maximize population health. That's the function that we have to look at,' she tells me, nodding with satisfaction at having put NICE's task into such a neat formulation. NICE needs to be dispassionate enough to work out how to deliver maximum health for the population on a fixed budget, she says. 'Patients and clinicians can be *very* personally invested. We do need that – they are the people who can tell us what difference a drug can make – but we need to balance out that there's not anything overly optimistic within the information that we're hearing about a drug.'

NICE was set up in December 1997, in response to reports that individual NHS hospitals had started to ration expensive new medicines, including cancer drugs, antipsychotics and treatments for multiple sclerosis. There was a postcode lottery: you'd get the medicine if you were lucky enough to be under the care of the right hospital. 'In a healthcare system funded by general taxation, individual pharmaceutical products must be available to all or to none,' Professor Sir Michael D. Rawlins, NICE's founding chairman, wrote in a 2015 paper about the history of NICE. NICE's first official act was to say no – to an influenza drug (it didn't reduce complications in high-risk groups, limited the duration of flu symptoms from six to five days only, and would have cost the NHS £100 million if there was a flu epidemic). By March 2020, NICE had appraised 782 technologies, and approved 83 per cent of them.

The process begins with a package of evidence submitted by a pharmaceutical company outlining the benefits of the new drug they are developing, and how much they intend to charge the NHS for it. 'We are looking for treatments that are both clinically and cost effective,' Helen tells me. NICE works in parallel with the medicines regulator, the Medicines and Healthcare products Regulatory Agency, but while the MHRA balances benefits versus safety risks, NICE appraises benefits versus costs.

Next, NICE invites patients' organizations, clinical experts, research bodies, NHS England and others who might have skin in the game to take a look at the pharmaceutical company's evidence package. Then an independent academic group has a look. 'It does become very technical, Jenny,' Helen warns me. 'It's economic modelling, it's statistical, it's numbers, it's mathematical equations to extrapolate the data, to capture all the potential benefits and potential costs.' Finally, an independent appraisal committee made up of twenty-four members – clinicians, nurses, psychiatrists, statisticians and health economists, as well as two lay people per committee, all recruited and paid by NICE – meet up to discuss all the submissions and eventually decide on whether it's cost-effective for the NHS to provide a drug free at the point of delivery.

But there is a golden value, totemic in the world of healthcare economics, that is vital in this decision-making process. The QALY (pronounced *kwally*, short for quality-adjusted life year) is a measure of the goodness of life – of well-being, in a utilitarian sense – over time. One QALY is one year in perfect health; a year lived with a health problem that reduces quality of life would be worth less than one QALY, and the benefit of medicines can be measured in terms of the QALYs they add to a patient's life. 'QALYs are calculated by estimating the years of life remaining for a patient following a particular treatment or intervention and weighting each year with a quality-of-life score (on a 0 to 1 scale). It is often measured in terms of the person's ability to carry out the activities of daily life, and freedom from pain and mental disturbance', NICE's website explains.

As a concept, the QALY has been around in one form or another since at least the late 1960s, but it gained new saliency when NICE enthusiastically grasped it as the key to fairness in healthcare. Its use now goes well beyond health policy: it's through QALYs that the Home Office calculated the cost of physical harm to a murder victim at £2,082,430, based on the number of years that homicide takes away from an average life.

'We have a cost per QALY. If the cost-effectiveness is within this range it's probably a good use of NHS resources, and the committee can recommend it,' Helen tells me. 'We've said £20,000–30,000 per QALY gained is a reasonable demonstration of value. That range has been established pretty much since NICE started. And in all honesty, Jenny, there's no real mathematical calculation that derived it.' She adjusts her glasses. 'I think originally it was around what people would be prepared to pay for dialysis for a patient.'

I was expecting Helen to tell me about the clever formula

the NHS uses to determine the price it's prepared to pay to save a life, a breakdown of numbers like the tally in the Home Office's *Research Report 99*, or the calculations given in the spreadsheets GiveWell publishes to demonstrate their current going rate for saving lives. I thought I was going to be taken through the inputs and outputs from which this £20,000–30,000 value is derived. But instead, she is telling me that this incredibly important figure that determines the fortunes of so many people – an actual life-or-death number – is a convention, not a calculation. It might as well have been plucked out of the air.

'Is that number . . . arbitrary?' I ask, just to make sure.

Helen winces at my wording, so I try again. 'It started at a certain standard and that just . . . stuck?'

'Yup. It stuck. And we haven't changed it. Industry and patient groups feel that we should have changed it. Actually, we believe it's probably the right ballpark at this point.'

I still feel like I need to say it back to her to get my head around this.

'That £20,000–30,000 figure doesn't come from any calculation based on NHS budgets and the number of people using the health service . . . A QALY was measured against the cost of dialysis in the late nineties, and that's worked so far?'

'Yup,' she says matter-of-factly, adjusting her glasses again. 'It was a starting point that everybody felt was reasonable. A QALY is a *tool*. We know it's not perfect. It won't capture everything. But it's useful because it's a generic measure across all disease areas. It's very difficult to compare outcomes for a cancer patient versus somebody that's got multiple sclerosis, but the QALY allows you to at least get some common measure.'

I guess you have to start somewhere. The price of a QALY may seem arbitrary, but the idea is that it applies equally to everyone: every quality-adjusted life year costs the same, no matter who is living it, what disease they may have, what life circumstances they face, or where they live.

Except it doesn't. The value of a QALY varies widely according to which country you happen to be in, the way the healthcare system works there, and how much your healthcare provider, be it the state or a private insurer, is willing to pay to keep you alive in good health for a year. In US dollars, the price of a British life may be around $36,000 a year, but it is currently set at around $41,000 in Japan, $47,000 in Australia, $74,000 in Korea and $77,000 in Taiwan. Surprisingly, health economists have found no relationship between a country's willingness to pay for healthcare and its wealth. Using QALYs means accepting that healthcare will be rationed, but you might get a bigger portion per person depending on where you are.

This is politically toxic in the USA, where 'rationing' in healthcare has become a dirty word. America has resisted using QALYs to dictate willingness to pay for healthcare; Barack Obama banned their use in cost-effectiveness analyses in the Medicare programme (also known as Obamacare) on the grounds that an arbitrary value applied to diseases across the board would discourage innovation into drugs for rare diseases. But even if QALYs are not formally used, there is a limit to the amount insures are prepared to pay for a treatment, which, of course, means there's a price of life calculation. The US Institute for Clinical and Economic Review, the leading independent non-profit which evaluates the cost-effectiveness of drugs, values one QALY in America at $50,000 to $200,000. Perhaps if Americans were more willing to discuss what a QALY could be, there wouldn't be such an enormous discrepancy in what American lives are worth, according to their insurance coverage.

But even within the British healthcare system a QALY isn't actually the same for everyone, or every condition. 'For most of our appraisals, a QALY is a QALY,' Helen tells me. 'We go up to a maximum of £50,000 per QALY for end-of-life treatments. That means we were valuing one QALY by a factor of 1.7 at the end of life.' It will be cold comfort to the terminally ill to know the NHS views each year of their lives as worth 1.7 times more than those of someone who isn't terminally ill.

I'd assumed Zolgensma must have been approved because it cured SMA in babies who would then go on to have dozens of years of good-quality life ahead of them; it would be cost-effective for the NHS, even with a list price of £1.798 million a dose, because the treatment was so effective and the patient population was so young. But, again, things turn out to be more complicated than that. Helen tells me Zolgensma was appraised through NICE's Highly Specialised Technology Programme, which looks at treatments for rare conditions with small patient numbers. 'We don't want to discourage development for those very rare diseases,' she says. The cost-effectiveness level in this programme is up to £100,000 per QALY.

'We have very, very careful consideration about which topics go into that programme because we are giving away more health elsewhere to fund those very few patients,' she says, and I think about Edward on the carpet, and how his life was being weighed up against the conceptual exercise of 'giving away health' to some other people elsewhere. This kind of thinking takes a particular kind of disengaged brain, one I don't have.

'It's for those very rare conditions we *know* companies may not look to invest in. We want to encourage innovation and research in those areas,' Helen continues. In those circumstances, NICE is happy to change how it does things, approve more expensive drugs. 'We'd be willing to accept that taking that approach is, in a way, an inequity because those groups are getting that bit more. But we're comfortable with that.'

It's reassuring to hear that the healthcare decisions NICE makes aren't always based on a utilitarian ideal of justice, providing the greatest good to the greatest number; that it is prepared to tip the balance so that companies might sometimes have an incentive to provide the greatest good to the smallest number. It invites the pharma industry to view rare diseases as commercial opportunities. And in those circumstances, companies will always charge eye-watering prices for drugs like Zolgensma: because they can. It is a game, a dance between NICE and the pharmaceutical companies, who will adjust their prices according to what the NHS will pay.

Fairness, according to NICE, doesn't necessarily mean equality; it may mean putting a higher price on some lives than others. But it is still a numbers game, as Megan identified. As the mother of a child with a wasting disease, she is all too aware that budgets are finite, and they have to draw a line somewhere. There will always be people like Edward whose circumstances put them right on the cusp of those boundaries.

Is it right that babies with a degenerative condition and campaigning parents can get treatment earlier than those whose families sit back quietly and accept whatever edict NICE might make?

'It's very difficult for us to cater for every individual person that has that condition in a piece of guidance,' Helen says. 'There has to be a level of judgement applied, in a way.'

Like Will MacAskill, Helen is good at presenting herself as a device for maximizing good. I wonder if she'll tell me what it's like to be a human being amid all this cost–benefit analysis.

'Is it daunting making decisions like this, which are truly life-or-death decisions?' I ask.

'We recognize it's a really important job. It's quite highly pressured,' she replies, in full corporate machine mode. 'Patient groups can lobby, they'll go to ministers and MPs, and that's fine, that's part of what they do. But we could do with explaining a little bit more what the impact would be if we were to say yes to everything.'

NICE was under particular pressure to say a quick yes to Zolgensma because of how long they had taken to recommend Spinraza. 'We are the last developed nation to license this; that is unthinkable,' Professor Kevin Talbot told *The Times* newspaper in 2018. 'One way or another we need to find a way to give it to patients.'

Talbot is a consultant neurologist, professor of Motor Neuron Biology and head of Oxford University's Nuffield Department of Clinical Neurosciences. He's also a former trustee and current senior advisor to Spinal Muscular Atrophy UK, the leading British information and support group for families and health professionals. So he knows his stuff. But when he made those comments, some people wished he'd stayed quiet.

'I got backlash from a quarter that I hadn't expected, which was patients and some trustees,' he tells me, leaning back in his chair in his sparse Oxford office. 'They had been led to believe they had to be very nice to NICE. And that this was all going to be OK if everyone did it according to NICE's way: you accept that it's going to take ages, and you don't upset anybody. They thought I was going to somehow sabotage it by being rude. I was simply just saying something factual.'

Talbot does not shy away from uncomfortable facts. He treats patients with motor neuron disorders, including motor neuron disease and adults with SMA2, 3 and 4. Ninety per cent of his patients are dead within five years of first seeing him.

'I have been to a NICE committee hearing. I think the people who go into that game are very different sorts of characters to the sort of people who sit in front of patients. Maybe that's the way it has to be – if they were thinking, on an emotional level, as a treating physician, perhaps they would take the wrong decisions – but they are much more comfortable with actuarial decision-making. And that isn't applicable here. There were babies who died while NICE were scratching their heads about this. That's unforgivable.'

That's the point of all of this, I guess: this is not a philosophical puzzle or a thought experiment. There are real-world consequences for taking your time wondering what the 'right' move might be.

NICE's existence has led us to believe that the right answers to life-or-death questions can be reached with the right method. But medicine isn't just about what's clinically effective and cost-effective – it's about doing the right thing for patients, and it is an art as well as a science. In Talbot's neurology clinic, he says it's not unusual for a patient who has endured a severe headache for the last five years to tell him she wants to kill herself, while someone with advanced MND might not be able to move a muscle but is very happy to be alive. By reducing the 'quality' part of a QALY to a number, something is always lost.

'QALYs and the like – it's a very dry, academic way of working out these things. The problem really is that there are lots of diseases like SMA that will come along that could be treated. If you take an individual disease, you can always make the argument, but then you've got a hundred other diseases. That's why, ultimately, we need to reformulate the relationship between pharma and healthcare systems, because it's not sustainable.'

And Talbot is right. No sooner had the eye-watering Spinraza been superseded by the even more exorbitant Zolgensma, than

Libmeldy, a gene therapy for the rare and fatal degenerative condition metachromatic leukodystrophy, took the record for the most expensive drug ever developed, with a whopping list price of £2.8 million. NICE approved Libmeldy in February 2022, this time only two months after it was approved for use by the European regulator.

As long as pharmaceutical companies are run for profit there will be a price on life. But we have no other model for health-care innovation, and it's easy for Talbot to argue against exploitative capitalism in the pharma industry from his office inside Oxford University, his salary paid with public money.

There is a cheaper way to stop SMA. The NHS has rejected the idea of routine screening for SMA in newborns, even though early detection and treatment would save lives. Talbot says we could go back further: screening every pregnant woman in the antenatal clinic for the SMN gene mutation. If they had it, you'd screen their partner too. If both parents were carriers you could test the foetus for SMA in the womb. 'You could terminate the foetus and SMA could be eliminated. That's perfectly possible. You could prevent most SMA children from ever being born,' he declares with jarring straightforwardness; he can somehow be as pragmatic as the number crunchers when it comes to his own field. 'Why aren't we doing that?'

This is a horrible question, but worth asking. Over 3,000 babies a year are aborted in England and Wales because of a risk of serious mental or physical disability. Babies with Down's syndrome make up a significant proportion of that number, and their lives would be arguably less short and marked by disability than babies born with SMA1.

'The reason that it's not happening, I think, is because the song and dance about new treatments has created a sense that SMA is a curable problem. I don't think it's necessarily as simple as that. I think that some of these children who are doing so well now in infancy may later on develop a disabling disorder. The sense of disappointment they are going to feel is going to be very huge.'

'Even with Zolgensma?' I ask.

He nods. 'Yes. I think it's at least a possibility.'

I can't believe I'm hearing this. 'Isn't Zolgensma a cure?'

'Type 1 almost certainly begins in utero,' Talbot explains. 'People with SMA1 are apparently normal at birth in as much as we can tell, but actually some of their neuromuscular connections may not have formed properly. That is only going to manifest itself in puberty or adulthood. These people might develop a late form of SMA.'

I think about how Megan's labour had to be induced partly because Edward wasn't moving around much inside her belly. Even if he had been given Zolgensma at birth, SMA could have harmed him before he was born.

'We simply do not know that these kids treated with 1.8 million quid's worth of gene therapy aren't going to pitch up in my clinic in early adulthood with a progressive disorder. Not so severe and probably not life-limiting – but these are kids who have walked and played football. They may lose that, and be more like my motor neuron disease patients.'

It took an hour for the drip to deliver the dose of Zolgensma into ten-month-old Edward's veins. 'I just felt like, *finally* it's over, he's got it, I can stop fighting,' Megan says.

The difference was visible the next day. 'He could never bend his knees to hold them up from off the floor. And one leg came up. I screamed at John – it was amazing.' She places Edward on the rug and begins changing him into a clean vest. He reaches out to gather a beaker of water and pops it into his mouth. 'Since then, he's different in every way imaginable. He can speak, he can sit up, he can roll, he can eat, he can bear weight on his legs and his arms, he can stand.' The £170,000 raised from Edward's Crowdfunder campaign is being spent on private physiotherapy. Megan's social media accounts, once filled with images of Edward with breathing tubes, now show him taking his first wobbly steps.

'He's getting stronger all the time. Will he walk like me or you? No, I don't think he ever will. Will he ever be able to walk with a stroller? Yes, I think so. But we don't know. I'm never going to say never. For a child with SMA, Edward is doing extraordinarily well.' She beams down at him. 'He's got a personality now. He's cheeky. Naughty.' He wiggles his eyebrows back at her. 'Cute. Intelligent – *so* smart. Funny. He's just a *joy.* I just enjoy him so much now. And he *has a future.* It's really bright. He can be whatever he wants to be.'

Megan doesn't yet know whether she and John will have more children. There is still a one in four chance any baby they have will have SMA; and some children have natural immunity to the viral vector, which means they can't be given Zolgensma. 'It's a big risk,' she says.

There will still be battles ahead for Edward. Megan has read new studies that suggest children with SMA should have an initial treatment of Zolgensma, followed by an ongoing course of Risdiplam or Spinraza. 'Say there was a big water tank, with a split in it: Zolgensma fixes the split, but it won't replace the water that was lost. Risdiplam or Spinraza will start filling the tank back up,' she explains.

Spinraza costs over £300,000 a year; Risdiplam is taken once a day in a syrup, each daily dose costs £8,000. 'We've got a second fight on our hands now trying to get the dual treatment.

I appreciate that there isn't a never-ending supply of money, but when it's your child . . .'

Zolgensma is now approved and available in over forty countries, including the UK, France, Germany, Australia, Brazil and Japan. It's covered by all the major health insurance companies in the US, as well as Medicaid. Every year, Novartis gives away a hundred free doses of Zolgensma to lucky babies in countries where it isn't available in a lottery-style draw that's been dubbed a 'real-life hunger games'. Children in India, Pakistan, Mexico and Vietnam have been among the winners so far. But across the world, there are thousands of babies born every year with SMA1 who will never have a hope of getting Zolgensma.

When Megan gets messages from those families, she doesn't reply. 'I can't.' She looks me dead in the eye. 'They have to watch their child deteriorate. I can't even think about it. I don't think I've got the emotional capacity to talk to them right now. It's so raw.'

She lifts Edward up and holds him close. 'We're so lucky that we live in a country like England where we do have the NHS. With all its faults, we are incredibly lucky to have it.'

CHAPTER NINE
£180,000 per year

Covid lockdown

It is illegal for more than two people to meet up in England on Saturday, 28 November 2020 under section 5 of *The Health Protection (Coronavirus, Restrictions) (England) (No. 4) Regulations 2020*. But the genteel streets of Mayfair are thronging with thousands of defiantly unmasked faces, male and female, young and old, black, white and brown; Barbour jackets rub shoulders with bare tattooed arms. The crowd is marching towards Claridge's Hotel shouting 'We do not consent!' while bemused residents of elegant town houses peer down at the din from behind their Georgian windowpanes.

This isn't how I'd choose to spend a Saturday morning in the middle of the UK's second wave of the Covid-19 pandemic, but it's unexpectedly thrilling to be here. This is the first time in nine months that I have been truly among people – throngs of strangers, a real, proper crowd – and it feels wonderful. The tambourines and whistles give it a carnival atmosphere, and the air is thick with a fug of skunk. But if this is a kind of street party, it's a genuinely dangerous one: no one outside a clinical trial has received a Covid-19 vaccine anywhere in the world yet; 16,975 people are in British hospitals with Covid today and

451 people died with it yesterday. Plus, some of the people here are really very angry indeed.

'Shame, shame, shame on you!' a scowling woman with bright lipstick and a tight blonde ponytail shouts at the dozens of masked police officers walking parallel to the protest on the pavement. She is holding hands with a little girl wearing pink boots and ear defenders. 'I'm just doing my job is not a defence!' she spits, her face contorted with disgust. 'Look at the Nuremberg trials!'

The placards, painted on cardboard or printed from home computers, have slogans that range from the rabble rousing (*People have the power/It stops when the people say no*) to the depressing (*Another lockdown – jobs will be deleted*) to the disturbing (*THINK* – reads one, over a picture of a smirking Bill Gates – *THE SAME PERSON THAT THINKS THE EARTH IS OVERPOPULATED WANTS TO 'SAVE' YOUR LIFE WITH A VACCINE!*). Many are peppered with hashtags directing people to go down conspiracy rabbit holes like *#TheNewWorldOrder* (the belief that authoritarian globalist elites are conspiring to take over the word) and *#TheGreatReset* (the belief that authoritarian socialist globalist capitalists are using the World Economic Forum to take over the world). Piers Corbyn, brother of former Labour Party leader Jeremy, who believes Covid-19 is a hoax and somehow connected to 5G, is here somewhere. But for every committed conspiracy theorist, there is someone else who is just fed up with lockdown and frustrated that there is no way to call it into question.

A woman in a belted trenchcoat is about to meet up and march with her parents, both in their seventies, both vulnerable. 'This is not just hippies thinking they don't want state control. This is every generation saying this is bullshit,' she tells me. 'We're calling the government out on lies and manipulation and statistics that, on their own website, don't add up.'

I am scanning the faces in the crowd, trying to spot Louise Creffield, but she's keeping a low profile – for now. Louise is a thirty-four-year-old single mother of four, and this protest is her baby, the fourth national march against lockdown that has been convened through her organization, Save Our Rights UK. It didn't exist six months ago, but now 40,000 people have signed up to its Facebook page.

The protest was made on and for social media: its location was disclosed on Facebook at the last minute to stop the police from shutting it down before it began, and everyone here is filming on their phones, taking selfies, or trying to get noticed. There's a man in a full Santa suit, a green sack slung over his shoulder, a garland of fairy lights hanging from his neck. His placard reads *All we want for Christmas is our freedom back!*

Santa and the elves at the anti-lockdown march, 28 November 2020.

He's flanked by two elves – boys who look eight or nine, with fingers jammed in their ears. A few paces behind Santa, a woman in striped tights and a pointy hat pushes a pram containing a toddler in an elf suit.

'I'm here because the numbers don't add up,' another woman tells me. 'The government are manipulating, using numbers like people *always* use numbers. You can mould statistics to make them say whatever you want them to say.'

The government *is* being dishonest, of course. Nobody here will know it until the story breaks a year later, but the evening before this march, there was a secret party in Downing Street. Two weeks earlier, there was a gathering in Prime Minister Boris Johnson's own flat – one of dozens of parties that will ultimately come to light. But no one knows about this yet. It is still a time when most of us would feel sheepish if we sat on a park bench with our grandparents, because this would be breaking the law.

Santa gets arrested near Grosvenor Square and the elves scatter. I hear that Louise Creffield has knocked down a plastic barrier near Regent Street and has been taken into custody; she's ultimately charged with criminal damage, obstruction of the highway and breaching Coronavirus regulations by organizing a gathering of more than two people. By the end of the day, more than 150 protesters have been arrested.

I spoke to Louise over Zoom two weeks before the march. (All of my conversations on the subject of lockdowns in this chapter are on Zoom, appropriately enough.) She was at home in Brighton, her mantelpiece heaving with cards because three of her four children (then aged fourteen, nine, eight and six) had a birthday that month. Her strong eyebrows and multiple piercings, in her nose and upper lip, make her look like a force to be reckoned with, but there was a softness to her as she hugged her knees into her chest in her chair. Before the pandemic, Louise worked in the constituency office of her local Labour MP, Lloyd Russell-Moyle. Her former boss told Brighton's newspaper, *The Argus*, that he thought what Louise was doing was 'tantamount to bonkers'.

When Boris Johnson gave his sombre televised address on 23 March 2020 committing the nation to lockdown, Louise supported the idea. 'I could *tolerate* it,' she explained to me. 'We didn't know about the virus. Three weeks was tolerable.' But at the end of those three weeks, lockdown was extended. 'Sir Patrick Vallance said – live on TV – that it was worth remembering that the ONS [Office for National Statistics] data comes from people that have got Covid-19 on their death certificate, but it doesn't necessarily mean they're infected, because many of them weren't tested. And I went, "Hold up, now."' She put her fingers to her temples. '"Did you just say that you're making up the death figures?"'

That was when it all began to crumble for Louise. We'd put our faith in the government to save us and the NHS, in the face of terrifying numbers; now the numbers were officially dodgy.

There were other numbers she couldn't put out of her mind. Louise is a domestic abuse survivor. What about all the other women stuck at home with violent partners? A woman and her young children were murdered not far from Louise's home. 'The thought of women locked up with their abusers – I just couldn't bear the thought of it.' Her eyes brimmed as she told me this. 'I just can't imagine how those women must have been feeling, watching the lockdown coming and knowing what was going to come to them.' She shuddered. 'I hate it.'

Louise searched Facebook to find groups she could join that were prepared to challenge the government's approach, and when she discovered there wasn't one, she set up her own. Her first protest was 'me and six people on Brighton beach' in May 2020. While the press characterized the Save Our Rights protestors as anarchists, conspiracy theorists and extremists, Louise was keen for me to know she was simply fighting for rights at a time when those in charge barely felt the impact of the restrictions they were imposing. 'If you can work from home, and you've got a garden for your kids to play in, or you can survive on furlough – on 80 per cent of your wages – you're OK. Who doesn't need 20 per cent of their wages? Fairly well-off people. If you're just making ends meet, losing 20 per cent is a big deal.'

She told me she believed the poor were being sacrificed, and businesses were being forced to go under, in order to protect people who only had a few years left to live. It was hard to argue with her about this then – and even harder since, given all we have come to learn about Covid-19. But I wouldn't want to argue for the alternative, either. Would it be right for old people to die so those with more years left don't suffer?

Perhaps Louise also believed there was a murky authoritarian global conspiracy to microchip people with enforced vaccination too, but if so, she wasn't letting on in our Zoom chat. Occasionally, there were hints of conspiracy thinking: when she talked about how she'd seen evidence that positive PCR tests don't mean you have Covid, that the newly announced vaccine wasn't going to improve anyone's chances of surviving it, that the pandemic itself 'isn't real.' And she certainly had sympathy for those that did believe dark forces were at work behind the global lockdowns. 'You can understand why people end up down these rabbit holes,' she said, shifting in her chair. 'The government have been misleading, disingenuous and outright inflating numbers. Once trust is broken, why would you trust the rest?'

*

So what were the real Covid-19 numbers? And what was the true human cost of lockdown?

First: deaths. It is hard to be precise about the total number of lives taken by Covid-19 during the pandemic, because different countries counted deaths in different ways, and some barely counted them at all. Many who died from the virus wouldn't have been tested for it, many who died *with it* didn't die *from it,* and many will have died as a result of Covid disruption (such as cancer patients unable to get a diagnosis early enough for their disease to be survivable) but not from Covid-19 itself. The general consensus is that excess deaths – the increase in fatalities during a given time period compared with the average number of deaths expected during that period – is the best measure of the true Covid death toll. *The Economist*'s extensive analysis of international data sets concluded that, from January 2020 to November 2021, there were around 22 million excess deaths worldwide – three and a half times the official global Covid death figures.

When you look at excess deaths within individual countries, there are some surprises. The United States had 1.2 to 1.3 million excess deaths to November 2021, 20 per cent more than the 1,026,951 officially recorded Covid deaths. Russia's 1.2 to 1.3 million excess deaths are around 200 per cent more than the official death toll, and India's are 1,100 per cent more. But Britain reported *fewer* excess deaths than the official Covid death numbers, with 160,000 to 170,000 versus 182,912 reported deaths – around a 10 per cent decrease. In Germany and France, the excess death toll was lower too – about 7 per cent lower in Germany (130,000 to 140,000 excess deaths versus 143,177 official Covid deaths) and 20 per cent lower in France (110,000 to 130,000 excess deaths versus 151,419 official Covid deaths). This wasn't the case across the board in Europe – Spain and

Italy both experienced higher excess deaths than official Covid figures – and hundreds of thousands of extra deaths is a staggering loss of life, however you look at it. But it does seem that – in some European countries at least – things may have been slightly less bad than the official numbers suggested.

Next: lockdowns. On 24 January 2020, when the Chinese government first imposed restrictions in Wuhan's Hubei province, compelling people to stay at home seemed inconceivable elsewhere. This strategy might work in authoritarian regimes, went the thinking, but citizens of Western liberal democracies simply wouldn't abide it. Yet as bodies filled hospital corridors across Italy and Spain, the idea of lockdown became contagious. By early April, over four billion people – more than half the population of the earth – had been asked or ordered to stay at home. In the absence of a vaccine, we agreed that the best way to stop the virus was to keep away from each other.

Lockdown didn't eliminate the virus; it mitigated it, slowed it down, while throwing as many as 115 million people into extreme poverty, according to the World Bank. A team of health economists at the University of Michigan conducted a cost–benefit analysis of US lockdowns during the first six months of the pandemic and found they were likely to have saved between 913,762 and 2,046,322 American lives from Covid, but may have cost 84,000 to 514,800 lives because of the economic downturn caused by shutting the economy down. The enormous range in numbers here makes them pretty useless for estimating how many people were saved or killed by lockdown, but the difference between the figures is stark, even at the low end: at least ten times as many lives were saved by the US's spring and summer 2020 lockdown than were taken due to the economic harm caused by it.

But lockdown didn't just kill people by throwing them into

poverty. In the UK alone, 8,974 people died as a direct result of alcohol misuse in 2020 – an 18.6 per cent increase compared with 2019, and an NHS-commissioned report has warned that there could be over 25,000 excess deaths in the twenty years following the pandemic linked to excessive drinking during lockdown. Between April 2020 and February 2021, the National Domestic Abuse Helpline reported a 61 per cent increase in calls and contacts, and the Counting Dead Women project identified sixteen domestic abuse murders in the first three weeks of lockdown alone – 70 per cent more than the ten-year average of the same calendar period. The number of children reported to have been killed or seriously harmed following abuse or neglect rose by 27 per cent from April to September 2020 compared with the same period in 2019. This is just the direct physical harm that can be measured in the immediate aftermath of pandemic restrictions; the psychological and developmental damage may take years to emerge.

Finally: the price we paid to save lives with lockdown. Politicians around the world recognized that the decision to impose lockdowns was a cost–benefit decision. On 5 May 2020, New York Governor Andrew Cuomo was under pressure to relax restrictions. 'The faster we reopen, the lower the economic cost, but the higher the human cost because the more lives lost. That, my friends, is the decision we are really making,' he said in a televised address. 'The question comes back to how much is a human life worth. That's the real discussion that no one is admitting openly or freely, but we should. To me, I say, the cost of a human life – a human life is priceless, period.'

The British government held the same view. In his public statement on 17 March 2020, Rishi Sunak, then Chancellor of the Exchequer, promised to do 'whatever it takes' to see the UK through the crisis. 'We will support jobs, we will support incomes, we will support businesses, and we will help you protect your loved ones. We will do whatever it takes,' he said. He repeated 'whatever it takes' *six times* in this single address, and it became a kind of catchphrase for him during the pandemic, a mantra. A country with a national health service that assiduously rations healthcare, that will only pay for medical interventions if they cost less than £30,000 per quality-adjusted life year, was now prepared to pay *whatever it took* to support the non-medical interventions that kept the pandemic at bay.

But 'whatever it takes' has a price tag, and you don't need to be a maths professor to work it out – even though it was Simon Wood, professor of statistics at Edinburgh University, who did, in an October 2020 article for *The Spectator*. Divide the amount of money spent on lockdown (£550 billion in extra borrowing, according to figures from the Office for Budget Responsibility) by the number of life years it saved (three million, according to the Department of Health and Social Care's analysis) and you get £180,000 per life year. That's six or seven times what NICE is prepared to pay to save your life from almost every other condition. This level of spending, he argued, would only be in line with the usual NICE threshold if we had faced a loss of 20 million life years.

'Statistics is about the honest interpretation of data,' Professor Simon Wood says on his University of Edinburgh webpage. 'It's not always a popular subject: honest interpretation of data is difficult, and much less appealing than less honest interpretation.' This statement is right at the top of his biography, underneath a photo of him grinning broadly, and an animation of a dancing penguin wearing sunglasses. I imagine there must be a dark and intriguing story behind these words, and I'm determined to hear it.

'An awful lot of science has the tendency to slip into this adversarial mode, a bit like being in court. You'd think scientists wouldn't do this, but there's quite a lot of cherry-picking – "I have my theory and I wish to find the evidence to support my theory", he explains to me from his Edinburgh University office, in front of a whiteboard covered in scrawls. 'It's appealing, right?'

I feel a pang of recognition. 'Journalism is quite a lot like that, isn't it? We pick the data that academics like you generate to make an argument,' I say. 'But I guess that's OK, because we're not claiming to be scientists.'

'Well . . .' He cocks his head to the side. Smile lines erupt behind his frameless glasses, and he looks out of the window, in search of a way to disagree politely. 'I think it's really difficult. We all have those psychological tendencies to look for what supports us. I've got no idea how you get over it.'

Simon decided to calculate the price of using lockdowns to save lives from Covid because of what he saw in two very different sets of data released in the first few months of 2020. First, there was early information from Wuhan about the level of risk that Covid represented. 'It's not like it wasn't a serious, unpleasant new disease, but we seemed to be going absolutely berserk in response,' he says.

Then there was Professor Sir Michael Marmot's landmark report on the effect of economic deprivation on health, updated in February 2020 to show that the already huge gap in life expectancy between those living in the richest and poorest parts of the UK had increased since 2010. The wealthiest British people can expect to live at least ten years longer than the poorest.

It should be possible for those at the bottom of the income distribution to live as long as those at the top, Simon says. Their early deaths could be avoided if there was the necessary political will. And it looked, at the beginning of 2020, as if both Labour and the Conservatives wanted to mitigate inequality: the Tories' 'levelling up' agenda had been a big part of the manifesto that had just won them a general election, promising to redress the balance between rich and poor parts of the country through government intervention and public spending. But, Simon argues, the Conservative government – unopposed by the opposition – ultimately chose to spend billions on saving people from Covid instead of poverty.

The figure of £180,000 per life year saved is 'absolutely at the lower end,' he says. The indicator Simon used to estimate the cost of lockdown was only government borrowing figures; if you include the loss in GDP, 'it's really quite a large figure, relative to the usual NICE threshold. You can do the maths – it's £300,000 per life year saved, at least.'

While lockdown restrictions applied to everyone equally (even though some may have felt them less keenly, as Louise says, and those who devised them may have taken them less seriously than most of the rest of us), the risk did not. Children aged five to fourteen had a 1 in 660,000 chance of dying with Covid-19 in England and Wales in the year from 14 March 2020, whereas adults aged fifty-five to sixty-four had a 1 in 730 chance, and those over ninety had a 1 in 19 chance. With schools closed, teachers and older relatives of students may have been protected, but the young experienced a blunt instrument of lockdown measures that was completely disproportional to their individual risk of harm. 'I think you should manage a disease in relation to the risk profile,' Simon shrugs. 'In the case of Covid you've got these risk factors that differ by a factor of ten thousand or a hundred thousand, but we chose to treat everybody the same. That does seem odd.'

But we had to, didn't we?

'Wouldn't it have been completely impossible to entirely isolate the most at risk? They would need carers; they would need people coming and going from them,' I say.

'That is definitely the argument made. I'm not sure to what extent it's true. The measures we took were *extreme*.' His eyes narrow. In the Second World War, we evacuated children from cities and placed them with families in the countryside to keep them safe, he says – why couldn't we move older people in multigenerational households to empty hotel rooms? 'You had so many people volunteering to help the NHS that they just stopped asking. So it wasn't really necessary to have the same carer going from person to person to person representing a transmission risk.'

And then he says something that sounds like heresy.

'Actually, if you look at the evidence that the full, hard lockdowns, the stay-at-home orders, really were necessary, it does seem very, very tenuous. There's a lot of statistical evidence that infections were coming down *before* the lockdowns.' Early on in the pandemic, Simon looked at five separate official data sources and found they all showed that infections were waning at the time stay-at-home lockdowns were imposed, even though deaths were still rising. 'It isn't clear that the lockdowns were actually necessary to do what was claimed for them.'

'You know how outrageous that sounds,' I say.

'The possibility that the drastic, enormous move of locking everyone down might not have been necessary – that's a horrendous thing to entertain. A giant political mistake. Even if it was at some level understandable: it's just really hard for policymakers to sit it out when the deaths are going up. Some big measure that says, "We're really hammering this thing that we can't really control" is politically popular. And people were absolutely clamouring for it at the time.'

'But lockdowns must have worked. We couldn't have infected each other if we kept away from each other.'

'The numbers bear out that lockdowns reduce infection rates. It's not that they weren't doing *anything*. It's just that they weren't *necessary* in order to turn the waves of infection around,' Simon replies. In his view, what people were *already* doing before the full lockdowns were called appears to have been sufficient. The full lockdowns were excessive. 'It's a sledgehammer to crack a nut. All the modelling will say, "If you use a sledgehammer it will crack the nut", but no one was asking, "How small a hammer do you need?"'

'So should we have let more older people die?'

'Well. Yes,' he says, shrugging once more. He must be aware of how this must sound, and is visibly uncomfortable saying it. 'It's all about whose life gets shortened in the end. The alternative is that you tolerate more people dying of Covid in order to prevent more life being lost from other things.'

But this was not an alternative that was openly on the table at the time. It's a strategy that ignores all that we didn't know when lockdowns were imposed: the risk of dying from Covid, and for whom. I think about how Kevin Talbot said the deaths of the babies who died while NICE were 'scratching their heads' deciding whether to approve Spinraza were 'inexcusable'. Governments had to make big decisions without having the right numbers to determine the price of saving a life from Covid.

'Putting a lot of effort and resources into protecting the elderly and people with comorbidities is the right thing to do, but *not* at a level that you are not prepared to spend on any other health condition,' Simon continues, looking out of the window again. 'Otherwise you have a hierarchy of the vulnerable. And the underserving vulnerable appear to be all the ones that die early as a result of miserable life circumstances related to economic inequality.'

When I first read about Simon, I wasn't expecting him to come from such a left-wing perspective. Sure, his article outlining how he came to his £180,000 per life year price tag mentioned poverty and inequality, but it was in *The Spectator* – a politically conservative, right-leaning magazine. He tells me it was a 'big wrench' to talk to *The Spectator* at all, but the left-wing outlets he approached didn't want to publish his articles questioning the wisdom of lockdown. He was flummoxed. Even more so when academic journals didn't want to publish his May 2020 research into how Covid infections were falling before lockdown was imposed. It takes a quarter of an hour for Simon to talk me through all the rejections his paper received, his brow furrowed in bewilderment. There were no criticisms of his methods, nothing apparently wrong in his analysis, but editor after editor refused it. His paper went to five journals before it was finally published in September 2021, by which time no one cared much about the wisdom of locking down, because lockdowns were essentially over.

I have some sympathy with the journal editors who rejected Simon's paper. For every person holding a placard with an unhinged slogan at the anti-lockdown march, there were thousands more who spent every moment they had stuck at home in front of their keyboards, searching for anything that would back up their feelings of injustice and conspiracy. A paper from a maths professor like Simon would be perfect fuel for people questioning much more than just the wisdom of lockdown.

'A lot of anti-lockdown campaigning was tied to a particular world view,' I say. 'Do you feel that if you ask questions that deviate from the consensus, you're being tarred with the same brush as anti-vax people would be?'

'Yes, I think that's right. There's a tendency to lump everybody who disagrees into the same bin, essentially. And the most extreme voices on both sides are the ones that get heard, often because they've got a very clear message. If reality is more complicated than that, it gets lost.'

Public faith in science relies on journals not refusing to publish well-researched papers without good reason. Otherwise conspiracy theorists are completely justified in refusing to listen to scientific consensus, even when it's backed up with overwhelming evidence. Why should anyone believe in the benefits of vaccination or the dangers of climate change if they know that journal editors refuse to publish research that might be politically dangerous?

I had been nervous about speaking to Simon. In the same way that I couldn't quite place Louise, I didn't know if he subscribed to the full range of weird and wonderful scepticism that existed at the protest. But beyond his lockdown scepticism, Simon has very little in common with the people marching through Mayfair that November morning. He is anti-lockdown but pro-vaccination ('you'd sort of have to be nuts to be anti-vaccine,' he tells me). He believes in man-made climate change ('the climate modellers have spent decades measuring, checking, refining'). But he is living and working in an age when we are all being asked to pick sides, and being led by the data means he doesn't belong anywhere.

There was another reason for my nerves: I worried our conversation might be a blizzard of mathematics that went over my head. But I understood everything he said, because none of this is about statistics after all: it's about the lines of inquiry we are not allowed to take – the questions that are deemed too dangerous to ask, even if they are maths problems.

And sometimes you do have to ask difficult questions, like how much does it cost to save a life. A question that seemed so cold and inhuman to me when posed by the effective altruists suddenly makes sense, because the price of saving a life is about justice and fairness, as much as value. If you aren't prepared to ask it – if you say human life is priceless, and you will do whatever it takes to save it – you might create a scenario that ends up undermining itself: more people might lose their lives in the future as a result of the unlimited measures taken to save lives now. Or you might end up making choices you never intended to, like paying for one more year of life in good health for someone with Covid instead of six more years for anyone needing treatment for almost anything else under the NHS. Uncosted solutions and unlimited spending – in the form of lockdowns, or the F-35 weapons system programme – can end up taking us places we never intended to go.

Simon Wood is done with asking questions about Covid. 'I'm trying not to do any more on it if I possibly can, because the culture wars aspect of it is just a bit disturbing. I've turned myself into something of an outsider to some of my colleagues. I'm fairly sure there's a fair number who look a bit askance at me, like I'm a bit of a loony, just from having followed the data and done this.' But then the smile lines erupt behind his glasses again. 'I would have felt much worse having looked at the data and decided that in order to stay on the right side of everyone I just wouldn't say anything.'

The city of Melbourne in Australia holds the record for the longest lockdown in the world: 262 days in total. Restrictions were only relaxed for good once 70 per cent of the population were fully vaccinated, on 22 October 2021. There were 1,590 recorded Covid deaths in the whole of the country by that date, demonstrating that, while Australia's 'Zero Covid' policy didn't mean zero deaths, it fared far better than most.

One of Melbourne's most influential residents is Peter Singer, the utilitarian philosopher who has inspired millions of vegans and billions in philanthropic donations. Singer is an uncompromising, polarizing figure, happy to use cold calculus in the most emotionally febrile circumstances. After seeing the impact his ideas have had on the effective altruists, I feel it's finally time to ask him for his take on how humanity handled the greatest existential threat it's faced in more than a generation.

When Singer was made Professor of Bioethics at Princeton University in 1999, wheelchair users blocked the main university building in protest against the arguments he made in his 1979 book, *Practical Ethics*, that concluded that parents of disabled newborns should be allowed to end their child's life. Well before the likes of Will MacAskill and Elie Hassenfeld, any approach that puts prices on lives in order to save them probably owes a debt to Singer. So when he agrees to speak to me from the home where he had once been confined for 262 days, I'm expecting him to tell me he's a critic of lockdown. The brand of utilitarianism that he believes in – consequentialism – encourages people like the GiveWell researcher on the podcast to calculate the worst age to die, after all. Surely he would find it troubling that so many young people made enormous sacrifices to save the very old?

'No, I don't think lockdowns were a mistake,' he says. 'I think it's still arguable that Australian lockdowns generally saved a sufficient number of lives to be worth the inconvenience and the hardships that that caused. It's still a defensible position.'

'Was it justifiable to lock down so many young people when

they were so much less likely to die?' I ask. 'They were effectively staying at home to save the old.'

He nods slowly. 'That's certainly something to consider, that most of those who would have died without lockdown will be people that have lived a full life already. It depends on how great a hardship the lockdowns are on the younger people,' he says. That hardship is more difficult to calculate, he continues: it's easier to determine the number of life years lost to a disease than the long-term cost to children of missing a year or more of schooling.

I see what he means. The harm of lockdown is certainly more difficult to quantify than the number of Covid deaths. Death is easier to measure than suffering, and measuring the damage lockdown did, who suffered most from it, and whether it is better, worse or equal to a Covid death, isn't a simple thing.

As I mull this over I realize how the more I investigate the price of saving a life, the more comfortable I am with questions that initially repelled me. It's likely Will MacAskill would see this as moral progress, but I'm not sure it is.

Whatever his views on lockdown, Singer thinks a policy of doing 'whatever it takes,' of saying life is priceless – the policy adopted by the British government and the Governor of New York during the pandemic – is morally wrong. 'I think it's unethical for a policymaker not to try to put a price on life at some point,' he tells me. 'It's good to be able to put figures so that you don't get swayed by the intuitive appeal of the person who is evident to you because they are there, identifiable.'

'Doesn't Covid demonstrate something about human nature – that we just *do* get swayed by the intuitive appeal? When faced with real lives at risk of ending before our eyes, when our feelings are engaged, we don't care about numbers – we *want* to do whatever it takes,' I say.

'We certainly have that tendency to do that,' he says dryly. 'The identifiable victim makes a visceral appeal to us that the statistical victim doesn't, but we can try to combat that if we are aware of it, we can try and resist it. And maybe to some extent we do fight it off successfully, but maybe not 100 per cent. So I think it helps to be aware of the danger and to know that we're particularly susceptible to that.'

If using the price of life to save lives involves a mindset that sees our empathy as 'dangerous', that requires us to 'resist' any 'visceral appeal' from those around us, to 'fight off' our instincts to help, then surely it is potentially more dangerous than wasting money that could be spent saving lives. If doing good for humanity means rejecting our humanity, what good can it be?

'Removing a personal connection has a cost as well, doesn't it?' I ask. 'We're denying our own empathy.'

'That's true, but maybe this empathy, if it leads us to be too partial towards those who we find affective, is not a good thing, right?' Singer replies.

Lockdowns saved lives precisely *because* we are too partial towards those we find affective. Lockdowns worked because we consented to them, and we consented to them because we love each other. The thought of our grandparents dying, of accidentally killing our neighbours or friends because we left our homes when we didn't really need to, made us comply. It was a price we were prepared to pay to keep each other alive. The protesters were right to say *It stops when the people say no*, but we said yes, over and over again, even in the face of changing numbers and hypocritical politicians, because saving life is about our connection to other human beings and our consciences. It is easier for us to live with ourselves if we make huge sacrifices to avert the threat to life in front of us, even if it might harm more of us in the long run. Given the choice again, even given what we know now, I'm sure many of us would still stay at home.

PART FIVE

A HUMAN BEING

CHAPTER TEN

$368,901

The average ransom demand

'We were up in bed, just above here,' Chris says, pointing at the ceiling. 'Just before seven, on a Friday morning . . .'

'The phone went . . .' says Stephen.

'. . . and it was Steve's youngest sister, Sarah. I *knew* it was something important because Sarah hardly ever rings us . . .'

'We are not a close family at all.'

Stephen and Chris Collett, on the other hand, are close enough to finish off each other's sentences. Married for forty-three years, they are very much a team. Stephen used to be a farmer, and Chris did everything else, taking care of the accounts, their home and their two children. We are sitting at the kitchen table of the Suffolk house they bought after they sold the farm. It's the kind of place you'd dream of retiring to. Their garden tumbles down to a river, with a swimming pool, a greenhouse and a huge climbing frame for their grandson. A black pheasant is strutting around the trunk of a magnolia tree in full bloom.

They'd only been living here a year on Friday, 23 October 2009, that morning when the phone rang far too early. Sarah was calling because the emergency beacon on the *Lynn Rival*

– the yacht belonging to their sister Rachel and her husband Paul – had been activated. Paul and Rachel Chandler, then aged fifty-eight and fifty-five, had taken early retirement and were sailing around the world; they were due to be somewhere near the Seychelles. Sarah had been trying to work out what had happened but couldn't get hold of the Chandlers.

'She'd been up all night,' Stephen continues. 'So I said, "I'll take over."'

They had chatted about the alarm in September, when the Chandlers were back in the UK for Chris and Stephen's daughter's wedding. 'We actually discussed the risks, and they said there were very little,' Stephen tells me. 'They laughed it off. Their biggest concern was being run down in the night by one of those tankers on autopilot.'

Sarah wasn't at the wedding, and neither was their eldest brother, Aubrey. The four siblings tended to only see each other at weddings and funerals, and even then it was never guaranteed that they'd all make the effort to attend; they'd never fallen out, but they had little in common.

'They're just very different people,' Chris shrugs. 'Aubrey was an accountant, Steve a farmer . . .'

'. . . Rachel moved to London, went to the LSE, got a job in government,' Stephen adds. 'My mother died young and, once she had gone, I think the family broke up.'

Stephen and Rachel were the middle siblings, three years apart. They kept in touch, Chris says. 'But then we got married, and Rachel and Paul got married. We're country people. We had children.' The Chandlers, who had been married nearly thirty years by 2009, chose not to have kids. They moved to Tunbridge Wells, bought a share in a yacht, and began spending more and more time renovating it, saving up so they could one day buy it outright and sail around the world. The Colletts were spending seven days a week keeping the farm going, growing potatoes, onions and vast quantities of parsley. 'We lived different lives.'

So Stephen took over the job of trying to find the sister he barely saw. He checked Rachel and Paul's blog, but they hadn't posted anything new. Their satellite phone was off. He rang the British High Commission in the Seychelles, who reckoned the Chandlers must have activated the beacon by accident, because it had only gone off for about twenty minutes, but promised to send out an air and sea search for the *Lynn Rival* all the same. Stephen left some posts on yachting forums asking Rachel and Paul to get in touch. Later that day, someone from the Foreign Office's family division contacted them: the search had found nothing, he said, but they shouldn't worry; in all likelihood, the Chandlers were simply on their way to Tanzania as planned, out of the range of their satellite phone in the blissful waters of the Indian Ocean, oblivious to all the fuss back home.

But the following Monday, the Foreign Office rang again. An ITN television crew were outside Paul's ninety-eight-year-old father's house, they said, poised to break the news that the Chandlers had been kidnapped by Somali pirates.

Tens of thousands of people are kidnapped every year. When they are kidnapped for ransom (rather than used as human shields by bank robbers, or as political bargaining chips by terrorists), they are being sold in a transaction, and a price is put on their lives. Only 3 per cent of kidnaps for ransom worldwide involve foreign nationals, but hostages from overseas can be the most expensive. Kidnapping thrives wherever there's weak governance, scrappy law enforcement and a huge gulf between rich and poor. Hotspots change, depending on the political and security climate in any given region. In 2009, the epicentre of the kidnap for ransom industry was Somalia.

'The Foreign Office never said, "Don't speak to the press",' Stephen says, placing his glasses on the tablecloth. 'I thought, *you can't have them doorstepping a ninety-eight-year-old man – he might collapse*.' So he rang ITN, and they explained they'd had a tip from someone in Somalia that a British couple had been taken hostage on their yacht, and they'd worked out it had to be the Chandlers from the online chatter on yachting forums about the missing couple. Before he had time to process the information, Stephen offered himself up for interview in Paul's father's place. ITN sent a taxi to take him to London, all the way from the outskirts of Bury St Edmunds.

'In these studios, you're suddenly in another, totally different world, a world of glitz, of glamour.' Famous newsreaders – household names – stopped by to offer Stephen their sympathy. 'There are all these computer screens. They're sifting through everything, trying to get information as fast as they can.' It was like he was a character in some kind of Hollywood disaster movie starring a retired parsley farmer.

The ITN team managed to get through to Paul and Rachel on the phone. 'I found that *very* hard to handle,' says Stephen. His eyes brim at the memory. 'They were obviously terrified, and they didn't know what was happening, and they were surrounded by guards. There were tears. I was in tears too.'

'His hands were shaking at the time,' Chris adds, and at first I think, *How can she possibly know this, given that she was here in Suffolk when he was making the call from London?* But then I realize: she saw it on the news. Stephen was being filmed. His phone call with his distraught sister was a spectacle captured on camera, engineered to make the top of the nightly bulletin.

No demands were made in that first call. There wasn't even any conversation between Stephen and the people holding the

Chandlers hostage. But the situation was obviously very grave. Somali pirates had been responsible for 164 kidnappings at sea from January to September 2009, and ransom payments had become enormous: a Saudi-owned supertanker had been released a few months earlier after Somali pirates received a reported $3 million in cash. It was lucrative enough for pirates to sail as far away as the Seychelles in search of fresh hostages.

Paul and Rachel were no oil barons. They lived frugally, pouring most of what they had into their yacht. They didn't have kidnap insurance. 'They turned it down, I believe, for the sake of about £15,' Stephen tells me, his mouth agape. Stephen was determined to get the message out that the pirates had targeted the wrong people. Within a few hours he'd given interviews to the BBC, Sky and Channel 4 News. But he was soon told that this was a terrible mistake.

A firm of solicitors specializing in maritime law asked him for a meeting.

'They gave us *vast* amounts of pro bono help.' Stephen looks me dead in the eyes and nods slowly, as if there's so much he would like to tell me but is honour-bound to keep secret. 'They emphasized that it was *so* critical to shut up. Not to speak to *anybody*.'

Raising Paul and Rachel's public profile had increased the price of their lives, the solicitors warned. The negotiation would need to be carefully managed. 'They also introduced us to a gentleman who gave us *a lot of help*,' he adds, nodding even more while saying even less.

'An *expert*,' Chris interjects from the kitchen island, where she's making coleslaw for lunch. 'We'll call them *experts*.'

'Our expert, the same negotiator, he'd previously been working on this Esso oil carrier. It was worth 350 million quid, including its cargo!' Stephen blinks in disbelief.

'Why do you think all these very knowledgeable people were happy to work for you for free?' I ask.

He shrugs. 'They could see that we were trapped in a situation way beyond our control, and it wasn't helped by the fact that they'd been paying ransoms in the past.'

I'm not sure I share Stephen's faith in the depth of social responsibility felt by solicitors and kidnap negotiators normally employed by the oil industry, but the help was clearly welcome. The solicitors said the family needed to appoint one person to act as negotiator, and form a family committee to decide how much ransom money was available.

Stephen said he didn't mind being the negotiator, but he was only prepared to negotiate in terms of the money that he knew he had. 'That led to quite a problem, because I'd got quite a bit of money,' he tells me, suddenly sheepish. 'I had just sold the farm a year earlier, and for an awful lot.'

Chris stops chopping cabbage and looks up. 'Well, to *us* it was a lot of money,' she interjects. 'It wasn't *millions*.'

Stephen shoots her a look. 'It was!' he laughs. 'We probably made double what we were expecting.'

Chris and Stephen had spent their adult lives working seven days a week, never taking holidays, struggling with a huge mortgage, only to retire with a fortune. Rachel and Paul had been kidnapped at the one time in Stephen's life when he had both the time to negotiate and the money to pay a serious ransom. But this was supposed to be their nest egg.

'I wouldn't have liked to have had to sell my house,' says Chris. 'I wouldn't have wanted it to go that far.'

Some family members were dead against paying anything at all. 'There was resentment from all sides of the family to some degree that they had put themselves in this situation,' Stephen says carefully. And it's British government policy to have nothing to do with ransom payments.

The 'expert' recommended Stephen work alongside the authorities at first. Two Metropolitan Police officers drove up to Suffolk to give him a voice recorder and advice on what to say when the kidnappers called. 'The training was . . .' He trails off into a deep chuckle. 'We would sit in chairs not facing each other, and one of them would be doing a gruff African accent – I can't begin to replicate it – role playing how there should be absolutely *no* payment of ransom. I should emphasize these were innocent, poor sailors who got caught up in a situation which was far beyond them; I was just a poor farmer, and so forth.'

His home office became the negotiation nerve centre. He stuck Post-it notes around his computer monitor telling him what to say, in what order, and reminding him to press record whenever the calls came in.

It was very slow going in those first few weeks. The contact in Somalia – Omar – was supposed to speak English, but barely did. He called most days. Sometimes the phone rang when Stephen was away from his desk. He answered a call while he was driving once; it was around Christmas time, and snow covered the ground. 'We were on our way back from the butchers in Walsham,' Chris remembers. 'Steve's got hands-free. And *Paul* came on the line. I just had to sit there and be as quiet as a mouse. Paul was saying he and Rachel had been split up: "I don't know what to do and I don't know where Rachel is." He kept saying how hot it was. And I was sitting there in the car, shivering.'

Whenever Omar put Paul or Rachel on the line, they begged Stephen to sell their Tunbridge Wells home, raid their bank accounts, do anything to come up with cash to set them free.

Stephen told them that wasn't possible: they were under duress, so the banks wouldn't release any of their money. After the kidnappers split them up, they became very depressed. Paul was running out of contact lens solution and was worried he would soon be unable to see. Rachel lost a tooth after one of the gangsters smacked her in the face with a rifle butt.

A video of the Chandlers came in to Channel 4 News: topless guards with defiantly uncovered faces point AK-47s at Paul's and Rachel's heads.

'We ask our government and the people of Britain and our family to do whatever they can to enter into negotiations with these people to buy back our lives,' Rachel implores the camera.

'I have no doubt they will not hesitate to kill us within a week or so if there is no response,' says Paul.

If this was supposed to spur the family into action, it had the opposite effect. Although obviously distressed in the video, the Chandlers looked clean, fed and physically very well. Their family had been told at the beginning that the kidnappers would put Rachel's and Paul's needs before their own. 'They'd kill a goat every day and Paul and Rachel would get given the liver, which was considered the best bit.' Stephen grimaces. 'Obviously, if they die, they are worth nothing.'

Even the police conceded that some kind of ransom was inevitable. 'They told us at the beginning, "You won't get away with not paying *something* to these sorts of people."' But they warned that as soon as money was discussed, they'd have to withdraw. 'That was their absolute rule. Eventually, it came to a point where the police said, "You'll just have to make up your mind about paying."'

Then they bowed out, and the 'expert' took over.

The family thought they might 'get away' with paying $100,000 for Rachel and Paul, but they were prepared to aim for a figure as high as $400,000 if they had to, Stephen says. His initial offer was $20,000, 'to cover expenses.' This was not an appropriate opening gambit for Omar. The price of Rachel's and Paul's lives was $10 million, he said. Following the expert's guidance to the letter, Stephen stuck at $20,000. The price went down to $6 million. Stephen moved to $90,000.

The transcripts Stephen made of these discussions make for desperate reading.

'We cannot negotiate in millions. We must negotiate in thousands. Do you understand this? There is no insurance, there is no government, just me and the money that I can get for you,' he said in one mid-January call. 'I'm offering you $90,000 to make a quick finish. Do you understand?'

Omar didn't really understand. By late January, he'd been replaced by a man called Ali, a former New York taxi driver with English to match. They began to make progress.

Ali went down to $500,000.

Stephen went up to $165,000.

Ali went back up to $800,000.

Then $1.5 million.

Then $2 million.

Stephen stood firm at $165,000.

Ali went down to $750,000.

Stephen went up to $235,000.

$650,000?

$350,000.

$580,000?

$350,000.

$520,000?

$380,000.

'It would go in stages, and suddenly you'd lose contact for a fortnight or more. You'd think, *What's going on?*'

I look straight into Stephen's warm and earnest face, and try to imagine him playing hardball. I really can't.

'Had you done a lot of negotiating before?' I ask.

'No. Well, I'd negotiated on sales. Crops and cattle.'

'Did you feel like you were negotiating for your sister's life?'

Stephen ponders this enormous question for a moment. 'It becomes like throwing numbers around. You have to be quite brave in your language and say, "Well, if they die, they die", that sort of thing.'

We tuck into lunch. Chris has made a perfect bacon and cheese quiche: golden on top, with flaky, hand-made pastry. I think of her pottering around this cheerful kitchen, while her husband was across the hall, haggling over the price of her in-laws.

'What was all of this like for you?' I ask her.

'Well,' she says, taking a deep breath. 'Steve was told not to tell *anybody* else what was discussed. We had farmed together all those years. Been a couple together all those years. And he used to say, "I can't tell you anything."' She glances across the table at him. 'In the first few weeks, we had more arguments than we'd ever had in our entire lives together.'

But she got used to it. 'I took on my role. I stopped asking him questions.'

After eight months of captivity, the price of Paul and Rachel Chandler's lives was finally settled at $440,000. The initial plan was for Chris to collect the cash in carrier bags from Barclays bank in Bury St Edmunds, but then they realized it would be tricky to send such vast wodges of banknotes over to Africa, so they transferred it to a bank in Nairobi, and hired two security guards to fly over – first class – to withdraw it. The guards chartered a plane and pilot in Nairobi, put the cash in a holdall they were confident would withstand the impact of being dropped from the air, and readied themselves for the handover, on 14 June 2010.

'Ali agreed he would sit at the end of the runway of Adado airport, an old Russian-built airport in Western Somalia,' Stephen says.

'We all got up at four o'clock that morning,' adds Chris.

'First thing in the morning, their time.'

'The expert was staying here, then. While they were doing the drop, I was sitting on the stairs, listening to them in the office. It was a bit surreal, really. I thought, *Oh great, it's going to be over*.' She throws her hands up. 'But of course it wasn't.'

Ali had promised that Rachel and Paul would be released once the pirates had counted the money, but after the drop, his phone went dead. Five days later, Stephen received a text:

> You know well they are not taking 440 and you refuse an other deel so this is not real money pelas pay money now quik.
>
> The pracy refuse to take that money now so they say we need 1,000,000 $

Stephen still finds it hard to talk about that text. He shakes his head, despair etched across his face.

'It was *horrible* after that,' Chris says. 'What more could you do?'

'Did you offer more money?' I ask.

'No,' says Stephen. 'Ali contacted us once every fortnight for months. We said, "We haven't got any more."'

In the end, it all came down to a former minicab driver from Leytonstone, a man who didn't seem to care about money at all. Dahir Abdullahi Kadiye got in touch with Stephen through the Foreign Office. He was in Somalia, he said. Originally from Adado, Dahir was granted asylum in the UK in 1997. His children had told him they were ashamed to go to school after they'd seen the Chandlers' appeal for help on the news. He wanted to put things right, and he didn't want payment.

Just over a year after Rachel and Paul were taken captive, Dahir travelled to Adado. 'We spoke once or twice, but he didn't want to speak too often – I think he was afraid of people overhearing. Then he rang and said he was hoping to get them out the next morning.' Stephen's voice suddenly falters, and his eyes fill with tears. '*And he did*.'

At 2.50 a.m. on 14 November 2010 – first light in Somalia – Stephen was woken up by a call from Dahir's phone. It was Rachel, who was in the back of a car with Paul and Dahir, on her way to Nairobi.

'Thank you, thank you,' she managed to say.

To this day, no one knows exactly what Dahir did to secure the Chandlers' release. There's no doubt that keeping two people in captivity for 388 days was an expensive business: there was rice, spaghetti, goats, tea and sugar to pay for; guards to watch them; and khat to keep the guards happy. Paul later estimated it must have cost the gang nearly £12,000 a month to hold them hostage. Reports abounded at the time that the kidnappers had received more money; that the Somali community in the UK must have made a contribution, or that an extra payment might have come from the UK's development budget.

'That's rubbish,' Chris says when I bring it up.

'Nothing came from the government?'

'No. No. And it would *never* be allowed,' says Stephen.

'We didn't expect anything from the government either,' Chris adds. 'Why should the hard-up taxpayer pay for a well-off couple who'd taken early retirement? We were always prepared to pay.'

Stephen is mopping his eyes with a hanky. His emotions are so close to the surface. I wonder how he managed to hold his nerve for over a year, and throw around lines like, *if they die, they die.*

'Do you think the fact that you and Rachel were not close may have made you a better negotiator?' I ask.

'I don't think I was a very good negotiator at all, to be honest,' Stephen replies, with a sniff.

'You can see now, he still gets upset about it,' Chris says, smiling gently at her husband. 'I think probably Steve is too caring to be a negotiator.'

Kidnap for ransom is a harrowing, traumatizing and remarkably safe crime to fall victim to: 97 per cent of kidnap victims will return home alive when professional crisis responders are involved in negotiations, and the 3 per cent that don't either have existing medical conditions or have bungled attempts at escape. On balance, the Chandlers were very unlucky: most negotiations are typically resolved in far less time than the 388 days Paul and Rachel endured.

Somalia is no longer the global hotspot (ransom payments grew to such enormous sums that oil tankers started routinely hiring onboard private security, and the pirates were largely out of business by 2015), but sub-Saharan Africa still has the highest rates of kidnap in the world, with Nigeria, South Africa and Mozambique leading the way. The Americas come in a close second, largely driven by high rates in Mexico. Europe sees less than 1 per cent of the world's kidnaps for ransom. Overall, kidnap rates are on the rise, and so are ransom demands. The average global demand in 2021 was $368,901, 43 per cent higher than the pre-pandemic average recorded in 2019. The highest recorded single demand in 2021 was a whopping $77.3 million.

I know this because of data published by Control Risks, the

crisis response consultancy firm retained by Hiscox, the market leader for kidnap and ransom (K&R) insurance, and – reluctantly – the most famous 'expert' negotiators out there. Control Risks are very careful about what they make public – while they are prepared to reveal the figure for the highest ransom demand, they won't disclose who it was for or where – and their average global demand figure is likely to be on the low side: they won't put anything on their website that will give the enemy a useful going rate.

Control Risks have a press office, but they don't talk to the press. I emailed to ask if anyone would be happy to tell me anything at all, and eventually received the most charming rejection message I think I've ever had. 'We can't be associated with a book that looks at the dynamics of putting a price on life, however intelligently and objectively I'm sure you would do that. Just not a space we want to be entering I'm afraid,' wrote a member of the communications team, despite the fact that it's a space they've effectively owned since 1975: they put prices on lives every day. 'We try to keep any insight that criminals might find useful out of the public domain where at all possible thus are very low profile,' she added.

Ransoms have been demanded for millennia, but the process of negotiating them became formalized in the twentieth century, with the advent of K&R policies and the rise of specialist negotiators. More than three quarters of Fortune 500 companies now have K&R insurance. But this is a very special form of coverage: it only works if the policy is kept secret. Every negotiation backed by an insurance company is conducted to mimic a situation where the hostage has the insurance status of Rachel and Paul Chandler, and the negotiator has the expertise of Stephen Collett.

*

In a cafe a short walk from her office, Anja Shortland is eating a hot cross bun and telling me how she became an authority in doing business with baddies. She's Professor of Political Economy at King's College London – and she looks the part, in her black cardigan, lanyards and glasses – but her job title doesn't really do her justice. Anja studies how economics works when the rules do not apply.

'*Tricky* markets,' she explains, a trace of her German accent barely discernible. 'Markets where one party is a legal entity and the other is either underworld or strongly connected to the underworld. Transactions that take place in a very low trust environment.' Kidnaps, stolen art, antiquities and ransomware (malicious software that holds your computer or network hostage until you pay up) are her stock in trade. There's normally a fear of future reputational damage in dealmaking that incentivizes both parties to play fair, and a state that will enforce contracts if they don't. 'I am asking, how do you make a contract with someone you inherently distrust, that you tend to be in a one-off relationship with?'

When it comes to kidnap for ransom, the answer, Anja says, lies with K&R insurance itself. Policies are taken out by people and organizations who have reason to make repeated trips to dangerous places, which means an extra-legal set of norms between potential kidnapper and potential victim has been established. 'The time horizon is not in the current relationship, it's in the long-run relationship with all insured companies.' That's why it's in the interest of kidnappers to release hostages alive, even if they could go on to give evidence against them. Kidnaps are generally avoided when people have to think through the risks in order to qualify for a K&R policy. They occur when people don't know about the risks: they don't realize they are going into a hostile environment, or are unaware of how they should be behaving, and who they need to ask for protection.

As Anja talks through all the kinds of people who have to go to areas of weak governance – extraction companies, NGO staff, journalists – my mind suddenly races back over a decade, to the dry, dull, endless forms I once had to fill in before I went on exciting adventures as a foreign correspondent on a TV series called *Unreported World*.

'I was a reporter in hostile environments, in places like Afghanistan, Nigeria and Honduras,' I tell her. 'Every time, I'd have to fill in this Hiscox form.' She nods. 'But I never really knew what it meant.'

'That's right, yes. If you know that you're insured and what you're insured for, and you tell your kidnapper, then you've just invalidated your insurance.'

'The less the insured person knows, the safer they'll be?'

'Absolutely.'

I would have been very safe, it seems, because I was more or less oblivious. So much for the investigative journalist.

'What kind of person is most likely to be a target?' I ask.

'People like you,' Anja replies, with a mischievous smile. 'People in a white Toyota Landcruiser. The kidnappers have *no idea* who's going to hop out of it. Kidnapping is mostly not targeted.'

No matter where we were, my crew and I had to keep a low profile and travel in whatever beaten-up car our local driver used. 'I thought that's because our bosses cared for us, but I guess it was to qualify for the insurance, so they wouldn't be out of pocket if anything happened to us.'

'You're using almost the right word – it's a *duty* of care. They would not fulfil their duty of care if they let you stand out.'

I was a foreign correspondent at the same time as Paul and Rachel were being held in the desert. Somalia was the one place that was out of bounds to me. 'I thought it was because it was too dangerous,' I say, 'but it was because they couldn't get insurance to cover the price of my life there.'

'It's the same thing!' she says with a laugh. 'Some things are just not a good idea. A missing market is not a market failure here – it's a sign of the market working well.'

You'd think the existence of K&R insurance in general would incentivize hostage-taking, but it doesn't work that way, Anja says. The insured are 'the hardest targets there are,' because in order to qualify for a policy you need to be taking all necessary steps to avoid kidnap. Plus, if an insured person is taken hostage and the experts get called in, the kidnappers are very unlikely to make a profit from the ransom. 'Those involved in the negotiation are driving the price down to the point where the kidnappers have held the hostage for such a long period of time, with so much manpower and so much capital and social investment, that $1 million will look like nothing.'

Determining the price of a hostage starts with a number the kidnapper will have plucked out of thin air, Anja says, a figure beyond their wildest dreams. 'It gives you an insight into who you're talking to, that person's mindset and what a huge amount of money is for them. If someone asks for a thousand dollars, you know you're talking to a kid,' she says, with another grin. 'If it sounds like not very much money at all, and you say, "That's fine, I'm quite happy to pay that", then they double it.'

Of course, if you can afford it, your instinct would be to accept the first offer: you want the person you love home, now. The kidnappers are selling you something that has no price ceiling for you. It's just like the price elasticity Nader AlSalim at Gaia was talking about, and the price of hope in fertility treatment: you'd be prepared to pay whatever it takes when the life of someone you love is at stake.

'You'll go as far as you can go, in theory, won't you?' I say.

'Yes. But they don't know how far that is. It depends on who they think they're negotiating with. It's squeezing the towel dry.' She clenches her delicate hands into fists and makes a wringing motion. 'If you're managing that process, you've got some control over which towel you are handing them. Are you handing them the husband towel? The King's College London towel? Or the Lloyds of London towel?'

'Or the British government towel,' I add, delighted with this metaphor.

'That's not a great one, actually. But the German one, in my case, would be. At which point we're really squeezing a bath sheet, rather than just a damp rag.'

Escalating threats of violence are actually a good sign, she says, because they mean the hostage is close to being freed; it's a final twist of the towel. You will only resist if you really don't have any extra money to buy back your loved one's life; or if you're being advised by a crisis negotiator to act as if you don't.

The reason why the Chandlers weren't freed after the $440,000 ransom payment is probably because, despite all his efforts to appear the poor retired parsley farmer, the Somali kidnappers realized Stephen's towel was still soaking wet. A few days before the drop, Stephen had asked Mohamed Aden, the Mayor of Adado, for permission to use the airfield. Aden had demanded a 'security fee' of $20,000, which Stephen haggled down to $18,000. Stephen thinks Aden then told the pirates there was money to spare, and they needed to ask for more. (In 2016, a Belgian court sentenced Mohamed Aden to five years in prison for his role in facilitating piracy in Somalia.)

Anja is convinced Paul and Rachel's kidnappers would have regretted taking them hostage: they were guarded around the clock by dozens of people for over a year. 'Everyone was in debt to everyone else, because they had borrowed a gun or they'd bought khat on credit. At the end, they would have come up with a rational consideration – was that fun? Did we actually make any money? What did we actually gain? They would have been disappointed. That would have been exactly the point. Nobody comes out going, "Yay! Again!"'

Successful ransom negotiations require a kind of perversity. You must turn against your instincts, your nature, your rationality, your humanity. Urgency leads to delay, expressions of love and concern result in further pain and harm. To get your loved one back safe as soon as possible, you have to be prepared to wait, to turn down offers of fundraising; you have to resist the siren call of both your head and your heart. You must block your ears, shut your eyes and hold your nerve.

If you are not disciplined and overpay, you not only put future hostages at further risk, but you might be endangering the rest of your family. Anja points to the oil millionaire John Paul Getty, whose grandson, John Paul Getty III, was kidnapped by the Mafia in Rome in 1973 for an initial ransom demand of $17 million. Getty's first response to pleas from his abducted grandson was to say, 'If I pay one penny now, I will have fourteen kidnapped grandchildren.'

'Even if he was a disappointing grandfather for young Paul Getty,' she remarks, 'he kept the rest of his family safe.' (Getty eventually paid a $2.2 million ransom after his grandson's severed ear was sent to a Roman newspaper. John Paul III was released after five months of captivity.)

'If you're not insured and you don't have experts telling you what the going rate is, how do you find out what to offer, so you don't overpay?' I ask.

Anja drains the last of her coffee. 'In a case like the Chandlers,' they weren't insured, but it was very clear to insurers that this was something that could move markets,' she says. 'So there was pro bono practice.' And suddenly it becomes obvious: Stephen had access to the experts because without them he might do something silly and mess up the market price of life, causing real problems for the insurance companies. The generosity of those corporates was actually a by-product of their self-interest.

In another example of how black is white in the world of ransom negotiation, Anja argues that the American and British policy of refusing to pay ransoms puts British and American lives at risk. 'If you have anomalies where you have some hostages that could fetch a very high price and some where the government claims to wash their hands of them, and you can double the price of a French hostage by killing an American or a British hostage, then that's worth doing,' she says.

'Wouldn't it make British hostages more attractive to kidnappers if the British government had a reputation for paying out?' I ask.

'Yes. But how can you tell if someone's British when they're inside the Toyota Landcruiser?'

It's one more thing that makes intuitive sense but is totally wrong in the world of kidnap and ransom: kidnappers won't know if they've got someone from a ransom-paying country like France or Germany until after they've captured them. You couldn't tell Anja had a German passport from her accent. British people don't go around foreign countries singing 'Rule, Britannia' and waving Union Jack flags. Or at least most of us don't.

The price of life in kidnap for ransom differs according to nationality, of course, and not just of the hostage. Kidnappers have different expenses to cover depending on their location. 'If a week in the Niger Delta costs you $10,000 and in Mexico it costs you $100,000, it just gives you some idea of how much it costs to hold a hostage,' Anja says. Control Risks will have geolocated data of the going rate and average duration of kidnap in every part of the world, and how that has changed over time, but they can never make it public. It is the opacity of all of this that makes it work; if the numbers were explicit, they would evaporate.

But is hostage negotiation really about numbers? Or is it a craft – the art of making a deal – that relies on emotional intelligence as much as data? The charismatic expert who so impressed Stephen and Chris, the crisis management consultants from Control Risks who so elegantly turned down my interview request . . . how much is all of this about charm?

'I think it's *hugely* important. The crisis responder has to project their charisma via another person,' Anja says, wide-eyed. 'They will wisely choose the person with the best attributes for running the negotiation. It might not be your dad, it might not be your husband, it might be an uncle – someone a little bit removed. They obviously did the right thing for the Chandlers.'

'People imagine that when the hostage is freed the trauma must be over,' I say, as Chris loads the dishwasher. 'Has it had a lasting impact on you both?'

Stephen looks down at the table. 'I think it would be fair to say yes, it has,' he replies.

'I was afraid that Steve might have a stroke at one point, because he was under so much pressure,' Chris says. 'He was very difficult to live with, I can tell you. He wasn't the Steve I knew. He was impatient, he was angry. We were *both* angry.'

For many years, Stephen was furious with the Foreign Office: he's convinced they knew from day one that the Chandlers had been kidnapped but never told the family, and didn't warn them away from the media in those crucial first few days. They are both still angry with journalists, who camped out in front of their home, published their daughter's wedding photographs and broadcast hurtful rumours that the family wasn't prepared to pay up. 'You can't say anything. You can't comment,' Chris says. 'It's like the Royal Family.'

Rachel and Paul eventually sold their story to the *Daily Mail* and got a book deal. They used the money to pay Stephen back. 'At the end of the day, we weren't far out of pocket,' he says.

The Royal Navy found the *Lynn Rival* and returned it to the UK; the Chandlers told the *Daily Mail* that restoring their yacht was the only therapy they needed to get over their trauma. 'After a long enforced interlude we have now "ticked off" Somalia and will soon resume normal service,' they wrote on their blog on 15 November 2010. As soon as it was shipshape, they set off again.

In August 2012, a Kenyan court sentenced seven of the pirates who kidnapped Rachel and Paul to twenty years in jail for another crime, when they tried to raid a French trawler. To date, none of the thirty-strong gang who took the Chandlers hostage has ever been brought to justice for what they did to Paul and Rachel.

When I ask what Stephen's relationship with Rachel and Paul is like now, he throws his head back and roars with laughter.

'They've joined the anti-vax crowd,' he says, once he's caught his breath.

I knew this already; I've read their blog, and it's full of posts about the dangers of the 'experimental vaccines', with titles like 'Be On The Right Side Of History'.

'They got held up in the Caribbean during lockdown,' he adds. 'I think the sun affected them, because they came out with all of this afterwards.'

'We can't relate to this anti-vax.' Chris frowns, and it makes Stephen crack up again. 'I couldn't *wait* for us to get the jab.'

It's all about a different understanding of what it means to be free, I guess.

They both shake their heads.

'We're just very different people,' Chris says.

CHAPTER ELEVEN

From $400

A slave

He seems a little overwhelmed as the crowd pulls at his shoulders to spin him around to face their phone cameras, but Aliyu Na Idris is smiling in the video. Perhaps he's glad to finally have some attention; by the time the footage was shot, he had been walking the streets of Nigeria's second largest city, Kano, for five days. Aliyu's black beanie and Arsenal shirt are dusty, the cardboard sandwich board is battered and the string holding it over his shoulders is frayed, but the message on it is unmissable – capitalized, in black marker, the same words on both front and back panels:

THIS MAN IS
FOR SALE
20,000,000 N

Twenty million Nigerian naira was around £36,000, or $48,000, in late October 2021. Aliyu's name and phone number are there, along with his bank account details, in case someone might be ready to make an immediate transfer; this is a transaction designed for the digital age. Aliyu's sales pitch went viral – of course it did – and the twenty-six-year-old tailor from Kaduna state was very briefly famous.

'The decision to sell myself was due to poverty. I learnt a trade, but I don't have capital, so I've not been successful,' he told the rolling news channel Trust TV on 26 October, seated on a sofa in an unidentified living room, still wearing the sandwich board. 'I plan to give my family 10 million naira [$24,000; £18,000] when I eventually get a buyer, pay five million naira [$12,000; £9,000] in tax to the government, give two million naira [$5,000; £4,000] to anyone who helped me get a buyer and the remaining three million will be retained by my owner for my daily upkeep.' His attempts to sell himself in Kaduna had come to nothing so he had moved on to Kano, he said, home to some of the wealthiest men in northern Nigeria. He had already received offers, but they were below his asking price, so he was keeping himself on the market.

Perhaps this was just a stunt: the sign was written in English, after all, the universal language of online fame, rather than Hausa, the language of Kano and Kaduna and the one Aliyu is speaking in the interview. But there's an urgency and an earnestness to his answers, and a level of detail to his plans, that make me think he's genuine. He'd even taken the trouble to include a trafficking fee in his breakdown of costs.

Aliyu might not have used the word, but he was trying to sell himself as a slave.

A day after the Trust TV interview, the Islamic police in Kano state arrested him and returned him to his family. 'What he did is forbidden in Islam,' Commander Harun Ibn Sina told the BBC at the time. 'You can't try to sell yourself, no matter your condition or situation.' Aliyu disappeared as quickly as his name had started to trend on Nigerian social media. The phone number on the placard no longer works, and no journalist has bothered to follow up on his life back home in Kaduna. Everyday poverty is not a news story.

Forget what religious, domestic or international human rights laws say. Human beings are routinely bought and sold: by traffickers and slave traders; by family members; sometimes they sell themselves. Like sex work and kidnap for ransom – the world's other oldest enterprises – the trade in human beings refuses to wither away, no matter what legislation may be in place to ban it. It thrives wherever there is a disparity between rich and poor, and there are power differentials to exploit across borders, races and genders.

In the days when people bid for slaves in open public auctions, no one was coy about putting prices on human beings. This was merchandise for the wealthy: male slaves in ancient Egypt cost approximately £25,000 in today's money; a gladiator in the Roman Empire was £1,600; a 'prime male field hand' in the southern states of America could be bought for around £31,000. Slavery began to be outlawed in the nineteenth century – by France, Sweden, Portugal and the Netherlands between 1810 and 1820, by the UK in 1833, and by the US in 1865. The UN General Assembly adopted the Universal Declaration of Human Rights in 1948, with Article 4 explicitly stating that 'slavery and the slave trade should be prohibited in all their forms.' We no longer buy and sell people in the street, but human beings have always remained on sale.

In 2017, an undercover CNN crew managed to secretly film twelve migrants from Niger being sold at a secret auction outside Tripoli in Libya, fetching as little as $400 apiece. But the slave trade has morphed and adapted for the modern age, and the vast majority of human beings traded today are not sold in manacles at auctions. They go willingly, facilitated by traffickers and sometimes their own families, motivated by the promise of a better life for themselves and their loved ones. When they are traded across borders, they often pay upfront for their journey to enslavement, with loans they promise to pay back with whatever they earn when they arrive. When they leave home, they have no idea that their freedom has been sold.

Sometimes it's those who love you the most who sell you. The same week that Aliyu was walking on the streets of Kano wearing his sandwich board, hundreds of families across Afghanistan were selling their daughters for around $500 each. Many were babies, sold into marriage by their starving parents at a time when only 5 per cent of Afghans had enough to eat. By February 2022, in the remote village of Qadis in the north of the country, Sky News reported that it was hard to find a family who *hadn't* sold one of their daughters. The payments are supposed to be dowries, but the little girls are expected to move into their new households as soon as they can begin domestic work – in some cases, as soon as they can walk. They are child brides, and also slaves.

The buying and selling of people may be most visible in the poorest countries in the world, but human beings are trafficked and exploited everywhere. In the UK alone, 16,938 potential victims of modern slavery were referred to the Home Office in 2022. Worldwide, 50 million people were estimated to be living as slaves on any given day in 2021, 10 million more than in 2016, according to the International Labour Organization. Of those, 28 million were in forced labour and 22 million were trapped in forced marriage. Women and girls made up over 60 per cent of trafficking victims detected globally in 2020. (This is down from 72 per cent in 2016, a decline that may partly be due to a fall in the reporting of sex trafficking during the pandemic.)

Modern slavery is not restricted by gender, but the price of a human being is more often than not the price of a woman. And while prices vary widely according to who is being sold, where, and to whom, they are much cheaper than those paid in Ancient Rome or antebellum America. A Home Office report based on interviews conducted in 2006 found the average sale value of a female trafficking victim in the UK was £3,000–£4,000.

Aliyu's mistake was to set the price of his life too high, and make its sale too public. If he had been prepared to settle for less, more quietly, it's likely he would have found a buyer. And if he had been a woman, he wouldn't have had to look very long for one.

'Sit,' says the man in the face mask and cap by the front door. 'Pick colour.'

A ceramic lucky cat on the counter waves me towards the racks of tiny bottles on the wall above the chairs. Every shade imaginable is there, from *Malaga Wine* to *Lincoln Park After Dark* to *I'm Not Really a Waitress*. Happy names, happy colours. I can't decide between *Orange You a Rock Star?* and *Cajun Shrimp*.

I like getting pedicures. I love looking down at brightly coloured toes in the summertime, neat and sandal-ready. A foot massage, an hour or so of peace, followed by pretty feet for weeks. Pure indulgence. This place is one of several local to me, and it's been in my London neighbourhood at least as long as I have. I first came here when the more upmarket salon on the high street couldn't fit me in. The Google reviews were decent enough. It had an ugly neon sign and steel grilles across the windows, but the pedicure was good. And it was *cheap* – a whole £5 cheaper than the other place. So I kept coming back, again and again. Until 2020, when I stopped.

On 23 October 2019, thirty-nine Vietnamese people – thirty-one male, eight female – were found dead inside the trailer of an articulated lorry in an industrial park in Essex. Ten of them were teenagers: the youngest were two fifteen-year-old boys. They had suffocated in searing heat and pitch darkness, after at least twelve hours locked inside the airtight unit. The driver discovered them dead at 1.15 a.m. They were packed closely together; one couple died in each other's arms. The lorry's cargo had been described on the customs papers as a shipment of Vietnamese biscuits.

In their final moments on the ferry journey across the North Sea, some of the people tried in vain to ring 113, the number for the emergency services in Vietnam. Twenty-six-year-old Pham Thi Tra My texted from the back of the lorry two hours before it arrived in Purfleet from Zeebrugge. 'I am really, really sorry, Mum and Dad, my trip to a foreign land has failed,' My wrote. 'I am dying, I can't breathe. I love you very much Mum and Dad. I am sorry, Mother.'

My's parents had mortgaged their land to raise the £19,000 they needed to buy her journey to Britain. They believed she would pay back all their debts with money earned in the UK. 'Her goal was to make enough money to fix the house for Mum and Dad,' her mother, Nguyen Thi Phong, told Sky News. My was going to work in the beauty industry. Nineteen-year-old Anna Bui Thi Nhung's family clubbed together to come up with the £8,000 she paid to come here. She had been travelling to the UK to work in a nail bar. That was twenty-year-old Nguyen Dinh Luong's plan too.

Every year for the past decade, Vietnamese nationals have been among the most likely to be referred to the Home Office as suspected victims of trafficking, and they generally come to work either on cannabis farms or in nail salons. As the number of Vietnamese people trafficked to the UK has grown, so have the number of nail bars. There were over 3,500 nail salons in Britain in 2019 – up 56 per cent over the previous five years – and in some parts of London, it's now unremarkable to see four nail bars within minutes' walk of each other on a short stretch of high street.*

At the time of writing, ten people have been convicted in the UK, and nineteen in Belgium, for their role in the Essex lorry tragedy, on charges ranging from people smuggling to manslaughter. But this is cold comfort for the families in Vietnam. As well as having to endure the horror of losing their loved ones in the most appalling circumstances, many are still saddled with the debts they took on to pay for the journey that killed them. The British Home Secretary at the time, Priti Patel, may have tweeted that she was 'Shocked & saddened by this utterly tragic incident', but neither the UK nor the Vietnamese governments agreed to cover the costs of repatriating the bodies from England. And, of course, there is no compensation to claim for their loss.

In the weeks that followed, there was a wave of soul-searching on Britain's high streets. Everyone, from the Gangmasters and Labour Abuse Authority and anti-trafficking charities to the British Beauty Council and *Stylist* magazine (the sort of glossy you might have on your lap during a treatment) published helpful bulleted guides on how to spot slavery in your local salon. We read and we nodded, and then directed our gaze back down to our hands and feet, away from the masked faces of those giving us impossibly cheap beauty treatments. Nail bars remain as popular as ever.

* In London, for example, Finchley Road in Swiss Cottage and Walworth Road in Southwark.

I went back to the Vietnamese place near me after the lorry tragedy. Just once, when salons were reopening after the first lockdown. It had been here for so long, right on the main road, minutes away from the police station; surely there couldn't be trafficked slaves working here? I should be supporting local businesses in the aftermath of the pandemic, I told myself. It turned out the nail bar didn't need my support – it was rammed. But when I came to pay, they wanted only cash, at a time when the world had gone contactless. It just felt wrong. Was my affordable luxury the product of modern slavery? It has niggled at me ever since. So I have come back determined to look and actually see this time, with a comprehensive checklist of all the signs we've been told to spot, saved in the notes app on my phone.

An acrid smell hits me as soon as I walk through the door (*Does the salon reek of chemicals?*) but within five minutes I'm used to it. After the man in the mask and cap confirms my booking and orders me to sit (*Is there a domineering man at the door?*) I see the framed certificates on the wall above the racks of polish, which look legitimate. (*Do the staff seem properly trained?*) But some of them were issued fifteen years ago, and the Vietnamese names on them could belong to anyone. The price list is in a gold frame: £3 for upper lip threading, £4 for eyebrows. A manicure starts at £10, a pedicure is on offer from £23, and both together from £30. (*Are the prices too good to be true?*)

The phone rings constantly. 'We are fully booked today. Have to be next week,' says the woman in charge of picking it up. Every chair is taken, even though they are open 10 a.m. to 7 p.m. seven days a week. (*Is the salon always open?*) The ringing is the only sound here, apart from the whizz of electric nail files and the whirr of hot air hand dryers; there is no music, no conversation. (*Are the staff reluctant to engage with clients?*) There are white flakes of someone's feet all over the floor near the pedicure chairs. (*Is hygiene a priority?*)

When my turn comes, the woman who's been answering the phone gestures for me to go over to a black massage chair, and sprinkles some blue bath salts in the basin of water sitting at its base. Rips in the chair's fake leather have been covered over with black gaffer tape. She presses my knee in a gesture intended to convey warmth. 'My friend come to you in one minute,' she says. (*Are the instructions given through a third party? Are you told: sit here, and that person will do your nails?*) She points to a woman in a white pinafore who is finishing up with another client. (*Is anyone taking breaks?*) The woman goes over to a sink to rinse a file that's white with the previous customer's nail dust. (*Do files come fresh out of a wrapper? Is hygiene a priority?*) I had never noticed any of this before.

The phone-answering lady moves on to a woman in burgundy yoga pants next to me. 'How are you today?' she asks, with a smile. 'You going away later?' (*Are the staff reluctant to engage with clients?*) The customer looks up from her phone for a moment. Her partner is looking after the baby while she takes some time to pamper herself, she says. I can hear someone walking around on the floor above us. (*Are people living in the salon?*)

The woman serving me comes over with her rinsed tools in a little plastic basket. She doesn't introduce herself, or say hello; she just switches on the massage part of my chair, which thrusts my ribcage forward suddenly and not altogether comfortably. I look at her weary eyes, above her blue mask, behind her thick glasses. (*Do the staff seem tired?*) There are streaks of grey in her hair. She could be my age. (*Do they look younger than you would expect?*) I realize that I recognize both women: they've

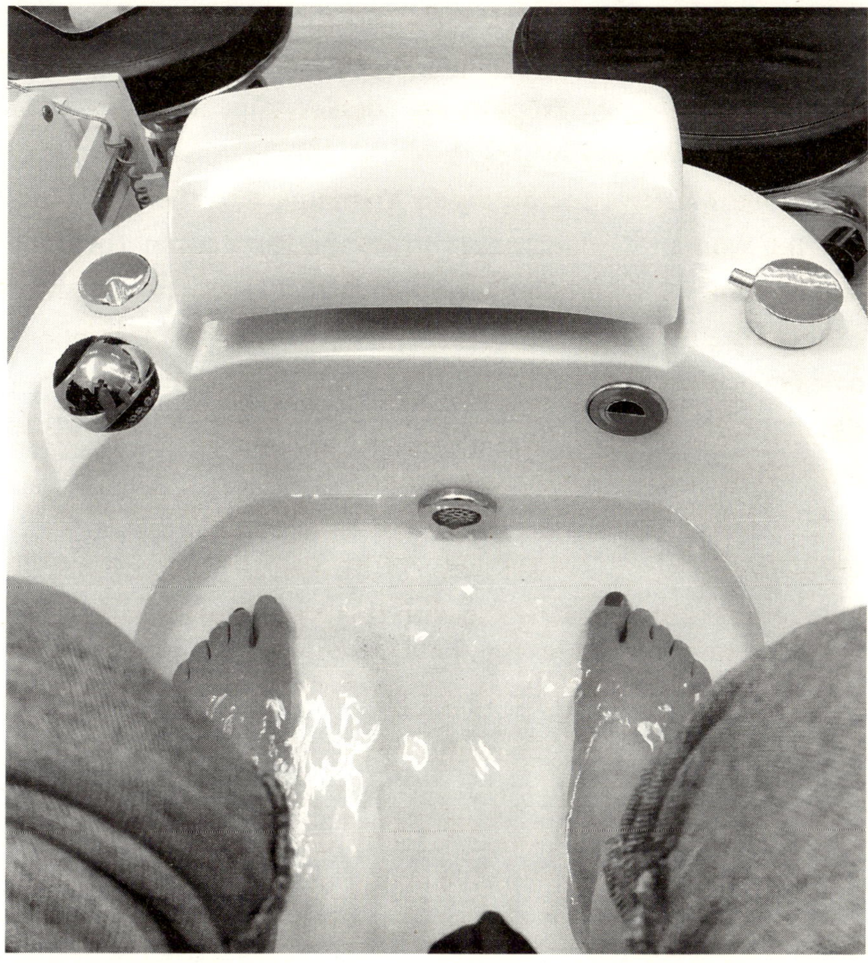

My £23 pedicure.

both done my nails in the past. They must have been here for years. (*Is there high staff turnover?*)

My nail technician pulls on white latex gloves. 'How are you today?' she asks. 'You going away later?' Maybe there is some kind of script the staff are told to follow – a few words to suggest friendliness, then nothing. None of the clients are talking to the people doing their nails; even those who can't justify their silence with phone-scrolling because their hands are occupied. They stare out of the window onto the grey road. A police car rolls by.

She taps my left knee to signal that I should take that foot out of the water and place it on the purple towel, and then gets to work on my feet. She snips at my cuticles, clips my nails, drags a dirty file across my big toe, buffs, scrapes, scrubs. Every once in a while, she says something in Vietnamese to the phone-answering woman working next to her, and the man by the door. (*Do they engage with other team members?*) He is chatting away easily to them both, sometimes making them laugh. (*Are the staff on edge around the manager?*) I can't tell who the manager is – the man? The woman who answers the phone? I wonder if they are talking about us, laughing at our gross feet.

She takes a mounted blade out of the plastic basket (*Are the tools sterilized?*), grabs the arch of my foot firmly in a gloved hand and begins to hack away at the dead skin on my heel. Her neck is bent almost to ninety degrees. 'Very hard skin,' she frowns. (*Does the worker carry on in silence?*) I feel bad for being so ticklish, for having to fight the instinct to withdraw my feet from her hands, and for having such thick callouses. She smears lotion on my calves and gives me a half-hearted massage; she is clearly much happier cutting away bits of my foot. The basin beneath me burps and gurgles as she drains the water, and then she paints my toes, in tiny, deliberate strokes.

I've been getting pedicures for over twenty years, but this is the first time I've thought about *how* exactly my nails are done, and by whom, and I don't know what to think. There are so many boxes unchecked on my list, so many factors that won't conform to the signs I've been told to look out for. It is possible to not be a slave but still be exploited: this £23 pedicure has taken seventy-five minutes. Does £23 adequately cover her time, and the manager's time, plus the materials, the London rent, the energy bills? I'd never thought to do the maths before.

'Lovely colour,' she says, and I know that's my signal to get out of the hellish massage chair and waddle back to the waiting area. There, she puts my toes in the air dryer before moving directly on to the next client. The phone-answering woman comes over to ask for payment; no, they still don't take cards. I go over to my technician and tip her directly, and she says something to the phone-answering woman in Vietnamese. (*Does the manager let their staff handle money?*)

Perhaps we don't want to know when we use slaves; we want permission to look away while something too cheap to be legal, but from which we benefit, takes place in front of us. Perhaps the line between slavery and very low-paid work is so blurred that it's almost impossible to make out. Whose responsibility is it to check? Is it me, the council, the police? Is it racist to think people must be trafficked simply because they happen to be Vietnamese and working in a cheap nail bar? Or is slavery such an accepted part of modern life that we just can't see it when it's at our fingertips?

I leave with no answers, and lovely feet.

When the family Gigi worked for spent their summers in their four-storey London holiday home overlooking Hyde Park, Gigi's bed was the laundry room floor. 'It was carpeted,' she says, with disarming generosity. 'Still. This is not a proper place to sleep.'

The house, on Bayswater Road, was directly in front of the park, but Gigi wasn't allowed outside the door. 'Every morning, I stared at the window when I woke up. It was beautiful, in Hyde Park.'

Gigi never thought she would be a domestic worker. She was studying psychology in Manila, and only left the Philippines because her parents and grandparents needed her to. The Philippines' economy depends on people like Gigi working overseas: 10 per cent of GDP comes from the money people send home to support their families. The agency said it would be an admin assistant job, but when she arrived in Saudi Arabia she found herself working as a cashier. After three months, she was told the shop's owner – a venture capitalist who advised the Saudi royal family – needed a new nanny for his eleven-year-old daughter, and she was sent to work in his home. 'I didn't know that the job also included household work, domestic work, everything.' The hours were 6 a.m. until 2 a.m. 'You don't sleep.' They paid her 900 riyals a month – around £190.

The family came to the UK for six or eight weeks every year. They brought Gigi with them for the first time in 2009, on a domestic worker visa. As soon as her passport had been stamped, they took it away from her. She wasn't paid anything while she was in the UK, but she worked seven days a week, cooking, cleaning that huge house, sleeping next to the ironing board. She ate the family's leftovers.

'They were a rich family. They owned thirteen cars! Range Rovers, the best you can imagine.'

'But they weren't paying you?' I ask.

'Yes!' Gigi replies indignantly. 'This was the sad thing, you know. They had the money, but they don't pay.'

We're talking in a meeting room at the London headquarters of Unite, the union, where the Voice of Domestic Workers meets every Sunday. While human rights organizations, immigration lawyers and government bodies speak *for* victims of modern slavery, the Voice is run by and for people who have lived experience of it. Having spent weeks trying to find someone who will tell me what being a slave today is like, I find myself in a place packed with people who have first-hand knowledge of how it exists all around me, in my home town, an unremarkable and tacitly accepted part of modern life.

The Voice is open to all, but pretty much everyone who comes here is a woman originally from the Philippines, like its founder, Marissa Begonia. They gather to learn about their rights from each other, but the Voice is also a social group, and every Sunday is a big get-together for the thirty or so women who come regularly. Gigi has come dressed in her Sunday best, in a glamorous purple velvet devoré top, glittery eyeshadow and deep red lipstick. She hugs a fake fur-trimmed black coat to her chest as she tells me about how the family she worked for – adults and children alike – spoke to her.

'It's really like you're not human. "You're an animal," they say. "You're a poo poo." The thing is, I learned how to speak Arabic fluently, so I understood.'

The Voice of Domestic Workers.

Everything changed for Gigi in 2013, the year her boss's brother joined them on holiday, and Gigi had to look after his three kids in addition to her usual duties. This time, she was expected to take them to the Diana Memorial Playground, in Hyde Park, after lunch every day. The brother bought her a mobile phone so he could keep tabs on her. And in the late afternoons, she took the kids to the Queensway Bowling Centre, just around the corner.

'That's where I meet these Filipina ladies,' she says, with a nod. 'We had conversations. I told them about my situation. Somebody said, "Oh, you need to leave them." I was scared. I didn't know anything about this country. I honestly didn't know anyone here, how I could survive? But I couldn't take it any more. So I left them.'

But Gigi's story does not have a happy ending. While she escaped from the Saudi family – sneaking away one day when they were out for lunch – the woman from the playground she rang for help took her jewellery before passing her on to another Filipina domestic worker, who threatened to report Gigi to the police unless she worked alongside her, unpaid, for weeks. Gigi managed to escape from there, too – with the help of the woman she'd met at the bowling centre – and found paid work. First with a family of five in Golders Green for £300 a week, until her employers got nervous about her immigration status and fired her, and then with another family, in Camden, and finally with a family in Kensington.

The axe that Gigi always felt was above her head finally fell in 2018, when officers from Immigration and Border Control turned up at the home she shared with a few other Filipina women. 'I hid in the toilet for almost thirty minutes,' she says, tears making tracks in her make-up. To this day, Gigi has no idea who reported her. The officers interviewed her, and then passed her on to the

National Referral Mechanism, the system that assesses potential victims of trafficking. 'After five years of waiting, I'm still under the National Referral Mechanism,' she says.

I must have misunderstood. 'Five years of waiting to see whether or not they think you're a victim of trafficking?' I ask.

'Yes,' she replies. 'Imagine! You're not allowed to work. The agony of waiting. The uncertainty. For five years. They give me £35 weekly allowance. Five pounds a day.' She laughs. 'Imagine that!'

I can't imagine it. I'm lost for words.

'You know, I have to ask you this, Gigi,' I begin. 'Did the Home Office offer to send you back to the Philippines?'

'Yes.'

'Why didn't you go?'

'How can I start my life there? I don't have anything. My family rely on me. My parents are very sick, the hospital is expensive. Even though I want to go back, what kind of life could I have there? That's the thing.'

Gigi never stopped sending money back home to her family. She's been in the same job for nearly a decade, working – secretly and illegally, which is why she doesn't want me to know her last name – as a live-out nanny-housekeeper to the family of six in Kensington, near the Natural History Museum.

'My boss is a banker. He's nice.' She smiles. 'He understands my situation, even when I got arrested.' She works 8 a.m. to 6 p.m., five days a week, and gets £600 a week. 'They wanted to take me to work on holiday with them, but they can't because I don't have papers. But the good thing is, even though they are away, they still pay me!'

Gigi smiles broadly at this. She is grateful to have holiday pay, at her rate of £12 an hour after ten years of continuous service, in the wealthiest borough of one of the world's most expensive cities. She knows they value her, she says, because the demand for domestic workers outstrips supply in London. 'I've seen it. The demand is *high*. If you go through agencies and do it properly, it's £20 an hour.' Which a London banker should be able to afford, of course.

When I ask if she thinks of herself as a slave, Gigi hugs her fur-trimmed coat closer. 'It's *modern-day* slavery. It happens in these places where all the rich people are living. I want to be recognized as a worker. I'm here to work to earn a living.' Her anger is saved for the immigration system that leaves her open to exploitation, rather than the people who choose to exploit her. 'We're helping families,' she says. 'It's decent work.'

There are peals of laughter from the women in the rowdy English class taking place in the boardroom next door to us. 'We're all in the same situation,' Gigi says. 'The good thing about this is, you meet your friends. You have chit-chat. Computer class, English class, things like that. I don't know what would have happened to me if I didn't join this group. I'm a victim of modern slavery and nobody knew about it. I didn't know.' She laughs in disbelief. 'The only thing I knew was that I was working.'

Perhaps it was in everybody else's interest for Gigi not to know.

'Every Sunday, I come here,' Lyn Caballero tells me. She too has dressed up for today's get-together, with a fresh turquoise manicure and sunglasses purposefully tucked into the neck of her black and white striped dress. 'I don't know anyone in the UK. The Voice of Domestic Workers is my family here.'

Lyn hasn't seen her family in the Philippines for eight years. The youngest of her three children was eight months old when she left Daet, in Camarines Norte. 'I'm forty-one now, she is *nine*,' she tells me, wide-eyed at the idea they've been apart for so long. Like Gigi, Lyn came to the UK via the Middle East.

Every penny of her salary – 1,500 Saudi riyals a month, around £320 – was sent directly back to the Philippines.

Her Saudi employer brought her to the UK when the family moved to York so the three children could attend British private schools. Lyn's working day began at 6 a.m.: making breakfast, laying out the kids' clothes, taking them to school, buying groceries, cleaning the four-storey house, making the beds, picking the kids up, cooking the meals, brushing their teeth. The youngest child – a five-year-old girl – expected Lyn to accompany her to the toilet throughout the night. She was never off duty; she had no day off.

'Sometimes they kicked me. They pushed me. The small one spat at me when she didn't get what she wanted. The children spoke to me like I was the same age as them.' Her voice begins to falter. 'I don't know how many times I said to them, "Please respect me, because I'm here looking after you instead of my own children. My children know that I am a good mother. I am sending money for them, for their education, to support them, but I'm looking after *you* instead of them."'

There's another burst of laughter from the class next door as Lyn and I sit for a moment in silence, both of us in tears.

The children Lyn worked for were openly contemptuous of her in public, drawing stares at the school gates when she dropped them off. Lyn kept quiet. Her employers had withheld her passport and a month's salary; they threatened to report her to the police or sell her on to another family if she caused them any trouble. But sometimes there were unexpected bonuses. They would set her tasks and give her rewards if she completed them: *teach the five-year old to ride a bike and we'll give you £50.* After three months, she'd managed to gather almost £100 together – money she was determined to get to her children.

After dropping the kids off one day, Lyn approached one of

the British mums just outside the school to ask if she could send Lyn's money back home on her behalf, because she didn't have her own ID. 'She told me, "If you've got a passport, you can send it yourself." That must be how she got the idea that all my documents were not with me.'

A week later, two police officers approached Lyn outside the school gates. 'And I'm scared, because this is the first time someone is talking to me like this, and it's in the street,' she says, twisting a tissue in her hands. She told the officers her employer was waiting for her and she wasn't allowed to talk to anyone else. They showed her their badges. 'It was like . . .' she draws a whirlwind with her finger above her head.

It took only five days for Lyn to get a positive decision from the National Referral Mechanism, meaning she was eligible for discretionary leave to remain in the UK. She was legally allowed to work, but she didn't yet have her paperwork. The first job she took – a live-in, seven-day-a-week job as a carer for a disabled woman – was still slave labour. 'She paid me £250 for two weeks. I had to leave – I couldn't stay with that amount of salary and no day off.' Livid that Lyn had left her, the woman reported her to HMRC for working without a National Insurance number. Lyn's next job – as a carer for a ninety-two-year-old man in London's High Street Kensington – was little better. When the pandemic came, she was forbidden to leave the house. Sometimes he refused to pay her. 'I was scared. It was hard to look for another job. So I stayed with him, taking my salary when he decided to pay me, for seven days a week.'

Now Lyn works as a nanny-housekeeper in Fulham, looking after a family of five from 10 a.m. to 7 p.m., five days a week. Everything is above board – she gets a decent salary, holiday pay and sick pay, she pays tax and National Insurance – and it's too good to be true, because it's all coming to an end in a few months, when her visa expires, and she becomes undocumented once again.

'I can't look for another job in the Philippines. I'm already *old.* And the salaries in the Philippines can't meet the needs of my family. I'm the only breadwinner. This is for them.'

'Do you want to go back?' I ask.

'I *want*,' she says, her eyes full of longing. 'But the problem is the policy, the system here. Once you go back, you can never come back.'

Lyn speaks to her children every morning, before she takes care of other people's children. Sometimes they send messages, sometimes it's video calls. 'But sometimes, especially my youngest . . . In December I cried. I tried to talk to her, and . . .' Lyn whips her shoulder away and turns her back to me, mimicking a child in a temper. 'She was expecting me to go to the Philippines. And then she said, "You make promises, promises, promises." She didn't want to talk to me.' She sighs. 'I try to explain to her. Little by little, she understands.'

The English class next to us is coming to an end; we can hear chairs being dragged across the floor as everyone gets ready for Sunday lunch. Lyn stands up, smooths the skirt of her dress, and gives me a hug.

'I'm so sorry,' I say.

'It's OK,' she replies. 'To tell my story again is – *ouch*. But I know it can help other people if I share it. It can open people's minds. It's *happening*. That's the reality here in the UK.'

Family-sized buckets of KFC and enormous bottles of Coke and Fanta are spread out across the boardroom table. Mimi Jalmasco hands me a paper plate lunch of salad, chips and glass noodles. She's one of Gigi's best friends, and is just as glamorous, with mahogany hair and wearing a black trouser suit.

'Sometimes I can understand why there are employers who

prefer to hire someone not from an agency or who don't have legal papers,' Mimi says. 'It happened to me.' She had a job with a family in Edgware, she explains, but they fired her when she got her visa because they said they couldn't pay her tax. 'Maybe they just weren't rich enough to hire someone and pay them properly.' She pauses. 'But I can't even say that they didn't have money, because they could afford to get someone who helps them around the house.'

Cheap nails, car washes and taxi rides, cheap help around the home: things you could do yourself but would rather not, indulgences you wish cost just that little bit less. If you feel entitled to it, you will pay for it, even if you know it's a little too cheap. Before the nineteenth century, when slavery was legal, it was the wealthiest in society who benefited from it; now it's those of us who want affordable luxuries.

'They want something, but they don't want to pay the proper price for it,' I say.

'Exactly. But we also want domestic workers to have work, to find jobs.'

'Did you ever find it difficult to find work?'

Mimi cocks her head at me, like this is a very stupid question indeed. 'There's *always* a big demand for domestic workers.'

The arc of Mimi's story is already so familiar now: sent by an unscrupulous employment agency in the Philippines to wealthy employers in the Middle East; abuse, threats and exploitation, her passport taken from her on a trip the UK; escape, followed by further exploitation in London; then recognition as a victim of trafficking, but perpetual fear of the next visa decision. And she also stops short of criticizing the British people who paid her slave wages.

'They are good people. Even the ones who didn't pay my tax gave me bank holidays off.'

'You shouldn't feel grateful for that.'

'I'm grateful because I know what an abusive employer is like.' Abuse, of course, exists on a continuum.

The people who Mimi, Gigi and Lyn have worked for could afford to pay them properly, if they were willing to tailor the hours they were offering to their budgets. But this is about more than money: people have slaves because they want total control and absolute power. A slave is their owner's property and lives to do their owner's bidding. Their lack of autonomy is a large part of their appeal.

Once you have been sold, can you ever get yourself back? Lyn isn't sure.

'I lost my dignity and confidence. You follow what they say. They are the gods. Sometimes I was asking myself, "Am I an animal?" But for the sake of the future of your children, and for your safety as well, you just accept it.'

Even though she has escaped slavery, Mimi says she is still being victimized by it. She tells me about an event she went to in parliament, where everyone was referring to her as a 'survivor' of trafficking. 'Am I really a survivor? A survivor that has no proper support? A survivor that can't even visit my family? They call me a survivor, but the anxiety, the trauma, the fear of what will happen to my next application – it's still there. I'm a survivor that's in limbo.' She stiffens. 'That's why I told them, "Don't call me a survivor."'

PART SIX

A HUMAN BODY

CHAPTER TWELVE

$5,000 – excluding shipping

A cadaver

In a vanilla-coloured single-storey building, five minutes' drive from Phoenix Sky Harbor International Airport, Garland Shreves is ushering a group of retired people into an enormous freezer. They've come dressed for Arizona weather, in shorts, polo shirts and vest tops, so their shoulders are hunched and their arms are crossed over their chests and bellies against the chill. All around them are racks of steel shelving, each stacked high with packages wrapped in polythene.

By this point in the promotional video, there's little doubt what those packages contain. 'One of the things that we really emphasize with families when they come to the tour is that they have the ability to ask questions,' Garland explains, seated in front of a potted palm, in a gently crumpled suit and tie, with silver hair and an earnest, slightly weathered face. 'They get to see how human tissue looks when it's been wrapped and labelled.'

Garland is in the business of dead bodies. He buries and cremates them in his funeral homes, and he sells them through his tissue banking company. The men and women on the tour, and the intended audience for this video, are people considering leaving their own bodies – or the bodies of their nearest and dearest – to Research For Life to sell on, whole or in pieces, after death.

Over a bed of euphoric synth arpeggios, the camera shot tracks the dozen or so tour group members as they shuffle down a narrow corridor. 'I'm going to explain real quick a little of what they're doing,' Garland says, holding open a door to a bright space where six people in blue surgical scrubs, hairnets, disposable overshoes and face masks are peering over a pixelated something on a gurney. 'They're actually doing a procedure on a shoulder!' he exclaims in wonderment. In another windowless room, Garland's audience is seated behind desks with cookies and coffee while he gives them a presentation. 'You don't pay us *anything*. We're a *no cost* programme. There's *no charge* for what we do,' he says, arms spread, palms down, shaking his head, as if he can't believe how good the deal he's offering is.

It's a pretty simple deal: donors (and their families) give Garland's company permission to dismember their body and trade the individual parts to other organizations for a profit, and in return their families won't have to pay any burial or cremation costs. It's a deal plenty of people take up: Research For Life's website says they have 'served more than 10,000 families' since they opened their doors in 2009.

'Open houses are important to me because it shows that we care and we're transparent,' says Garland's voiceover. 'We think the public deserves to come and see what a tissue bank is about.'

Garland is under no obligation to be transparent. America's tissue banking industry is almost entirely unregulated, existing in – and perhaps exploiting – a legal black hole. While it's illegal to sell organs for transplant in the USA, cadavers and body parts can be supplied for profit by pretty much anyone, regardless of training or expertise, without breaking any federal laws.

Body donation is by definition an altruistic act: if you do it, you will not be around to reap the benefit. Almost everywhere else in the world, profiting from dead bodies is illegal – even with the express permission of their owners. In an age where virtual reality and 3D imaging make almost anything possible in simulation, medical schools still consider that hands-on experience of the human body is vital in understanding how it works. Cadavers are cut open on a daily basis by anatomy students across the world, and the dissecting table is often where first-year medical students get their first glimpse of a dead body. When people donate their body to medical schools, no one – in theory – should be making a profit from it.

But cadavers are needed in medical and military research, in training and product innovation, as well as anatomical education. The international demand for dead human flesh is growing, and can't be met by bequests to medical schools and university anatomy offices. American entrepreneurs like Garland step up to meet this need. They are the facilitators, the middlemen between donor and dissector, in the commercial world. Some people call them 'body brokers'.

How far are they prepared to go to get hold of the bodies? How do they put prices on them? How much money do they make out of them? And what kind of person dedicates their life to selling the dead?

No one has any idea how big this industry is. The American Association of Tissue Banks – the body that acts as the lone arbiter of respectability in the American cadaver trade – has given accreditation to only seven companies, one of which is

Garland's, and four of which are in Arizona (where as many as 7 per cent of the those who die each year – around 4,000 people – are donors.) A 2017 Reuters investigation (perhaps the only time anyone outside the sector has taken a comprehensive look at it) identified thirty-four private tissue banks in the US, and revealed that the industry leader, Phoenix-based Science Care, is owned by a billion-dollar private equity firm and generates $27 million a year in revenue. Science Care don't operate tours of their facility, and rarely speak to journalists: after emailing them three times I eventually receive a one-line reply saying they are 'not interested in participating' in this book. But for every multimillion-dollar enterprise there are dozens of small-time independent body brokers in suburban warehouses and lock-ups across the US. While legal, these companies tend to operate in the shadows, shrinking from scrutiny like vampires from daylight.

Garland is an outlier for opening his doors to the public. Pre-Covid, he ran the tours four times a year. But on the day I contact him, Garland *has* Covid, and is stuck at home. It turns out to be a piece of luck for me: he's bored, and happy to speak on the phone for as long as I like. We talk for almost two hours, and he is prepared to answer (almost) any question I have for him. On one condition: I must not call him a body broker.

'If you refer to me as a body broker, I'm going to refer to you as a prostitute,' he declares, thirty seconds into our conversation.

I did not see this coming. 'Explain your thinking there,' I say.

'I will,' he replies. 'I hate that term for the same reason a female journalist would hate the term "prostitute". You're being paid to do a job. You'll say, "I'm a professional and I'm a journalist and it is insulting to me that you would associate me with a prostitute." When you refer to me as a body broker, you would like me to consent to the fact that it isn't worthy of the professionalism that we bring to it, or the skill, or the tools to do it correctly. You want to diminish that, and make it like we're some dark, evil people.'

It's a pretty wild way to start things, and I worry Garland might be delirious from Covid and too unwell to give an interview, but then I remember what I've read about him online; this is just how Garland talks. He ran an unsuccessful bid as a Republican candidate for the state senate in 2020, and got into trouble after he said the Arizona Advocacy Network and Foundation were 'certified shitbags' for expressing solidarity with Black communities protesting police violence. 'I'm always going to be who I am. You can tell I grew up in the 'hood, because if you piss me off I tell you,' he told reporters at the time. 'I speak freely, I speak passionately, and I believe in what I am doing. We lack that in politics.'

Garland assures me he's fine – he tested positive a week ago, and he's had all his vaccinations. 'A lot of drug people made a lot of damn money off of the crisis,' he sniffs. Even though Research For Life deals in dead bodies, the pandemic was a financial disaster for the company. 'Our donation rate went from a hundred a month to almost nothing because everybody had Covid, and nobody wanted to take a Covid donor.' He says they lost over $2 million in the first year of the pandemic. 'That's a ton of a lot of money.'

It's a family-run business, with close to fifty employees, including his wife, Laurie, and three of Garland's four children. 'My wife and I own the company. My kids have grown up in the death-care industry and have been with Research For Life since its inception.' Garland suddenly lowers his voice. 'You're focused on this business, but I just wanted to tell you, you *really* don't know what I do in real life. I don't know that I want you to mention it too much because you don't see it in public view.'

'OK . . .' I say, my pen poised over my notepad. 'Tell me what you're able to tell me.'

'Well, it's going to help you understand why I know so much about this industry.'

'OK.'

'I'm number three in the prosecutor's office. Did you know that?'

I did know that. It's on his LinkedIn profile. 'I saw that online,' I say.

'Did you really? Oh. I will just say that . . . I have a lot of government agencies that call me periodically. They're like, "Hey, Garland, you and your wife own a tissue bank, can you help us with some insight on this case?" I'm asked questions by various government entities, on a regular basis.'

'That's intriguing,' I say. 'You can tell me more about that if you want to.'

'Let's stick to tissue banking,' Garland replies, almost in a whisper. 'But I wanted you to know that I'm a little more multi-faceted than you thought.'

Facets flaunted, Garland walks me through the journey a human body takes as it becomes tissue. It goes like this. Within two or three hours of notification of a death, Research For Life has transported the body to their premises in an inconspicuous white van. It's placed in a holding cooler, and lab staff then make a physical assessment of the body, noting its condition, any scars, tattoos or bruising. They draw a blood sample and test the cadaver for infectious diseases like HIV and hepatitis, which would preclude it from being used in most research settings. Laurie and the family services team contact the next of kin to take down what they call a 'medical social history' that will inform how the cadaver might best be used. All of this is logged in a database. A lab supervisor will look at what their customers are seeking to purchase (it's sometimes whole cadavers but mostly specific body parts) and come up with a 'cut plan' for how that body will be sold. It's divided up accordingly, and then sent on to Garland's customers – the 'end users'.

Every piece of tissue is identified with a unique number to make it traceable. 'End users are not permitted to remove these tags from the specimens. They are not allowed to what is called 'resect'. They're not allowed to provide it to third parties,' Garland says. They have to keep the tissue in a secure, locked place, where only trained people will handle it. 'If it's not going to be disposed of on their premises – which they have to provide proof of – they have to send it back to us. If they send it back to us, we don't charge a fee for disposal. Because we *like* to do it. That way, I know it's done.'

Garland knows a lot more about disposal than he does about scientific research. He began in the funeral industry four decades ago, when he was sixteen years old. He opened his first funeral home in his early twenties. His family now owns four of them.

'People think there's so much money to be made in whole-body donation, just shit loads of money just rolling off the hill. But if you're doing it right, I can tell you right now, that's just not the case. My wife and I have the lifestyle we do because my government job pays six figures. My funeral homes make more profit than my fricking tissue bank. And that's pretty pathetic.'

Why would anyone who isn't a scientist do this, if not for money?

Out of a desire to do things right, to change the industry from within, Garland assures me. 'I felt that families were not very well served by whole-body donor organizations. I just felt there could be a higher degree of service to those families.

Because of my background in funeral service, I thought – I could do that.'

Garland sees no conflict of interest between his two businesses. 'I never allowed my tissue bank to operate within the funeral home,' he declares. 'I never, *ever*, mention body donation to families in my funeral home. You won't find marketing material in my funeral homes. There's no law that bars us from doing it, but I don't think it's appropriate.' There's a righteousness in his voice that suggests he feels a higher sense of moral responsibility is behind this, rather than an instinctive revulsion at the idea of soliciting corpses from bereaved families. 'I don't think it's right for a tissue bank to operate inside a funeral home,' he continues. 'I don't think you should be dissecting human bodies at the funeral home.'

It's amazing that this needs to be said.

But Garland is right to position himself on a kind of moral high ground. America's most notorious body brokers also work in the funeral industry. Megan Hess was sentenced to twenty years for fraud in January 2023 after the Colorado funeral home she ran with her mother, Shirley Koch, was found to have charged families $1,000 for cremations that never happened because the corpses had secretly been sold off in pieces for profit. Licensed funeral director Arthur Rathburn was sentenced to nine years in prison in 2018 for defrauding customers and violating hazardous shipping laws: his tissue bank shipped picnic coolers full of severed human heads preserved in red Listerine mouthwash, as well as whole cadavers infected with HIV and hepatitis. Southern Nevada Donor Services shared premises with Valley Cremation and Burial just outside Las Vegas; when health inspectors visited the warehouse in 2015, they found a man trying to thaw out a human torso with a hose in the back courtyard, spraying tissue and blood into gutters that washed down local streets. A funeral home employee who helped prepare body parts for the donor services company was slapped with a minor pollution charge.

Even in the most grotesque of cases, body brokers can only be charged with fraud or breaking environmental protection and health regulations. The investigation into Arthur Rathburn led the FBI to raid one of his suppliers, the Phoenix-based Biological Resource Center, where special agents reported seeing a cooler filled with penises, as well as a 'large torso with the head removed and replaced with a smaller head sewn together in a Frankenstein manner'. BRC's owner, Stephen Gore (yes, that's his name), pleaded guilty to selling infected body parts and deceiving families about how their loved ones' bodies would be used. 'I could have been more open about the process of donation on the brochure,' he said at the time.

The National Funeral Directors Association is trying to introduce a 'Body Broker Bill' that they say will ensure donor families are no longer 'unknowingly contributing to a for-profit industry in which the body of their loved one could be traded as raw material in a largely unregulated national market.' But Garland says the funeral industry only wants to regulate companies like Research For Life because they see them as competition.

'They have vested interests. They don't like the fact that when a donor goes to a whole-body donation organization like us, it won't go to that local funeral home for cremation, you see. I want people to have a *choice*. Some families find a lot of comfort and peace in their loved one being able to serve, in death, a greater purpose. The reality is the funeral industry wants to cremate and bury all future medical hope.'

Some families may find comfort and peace in there being no bill for their loved one's cremation too. Surely Garland can recognize that could incentivize poor donors and their families?

'In the US, you can get a cheap cremation now for $495, $550,' he says dismissively. 'It's bullshit that it's poor families who donate their loved ones. We keep track of the demographics – you're more likely to be a donor the more educated and affluent you are. Our company does not take indigent donors – did you know that? We don't have a deal or a contract worked out with any governmental or fiduciary public county burial system.'

Once again, Garland is taking the moral high ground above some almost unfathomable depths. Many counties across the US have discovered they can make hefty savings by giving up on pauper burials, instead donating the corpses of homeless and destitute people to a tissue bank. Sullivan County, in Tennessee, has been giving its impoverished dead to a company with the unfortunate name of Restore Life USA since 2011.

To be fair to Garland, university programmes and other non-profit donor organizations will also regularly offer to cremate donor remains for free. But they don't have marketing budgets to solicit donations in the way that for-profit tissue banks do.

'Do you want to bury or cremate the hope of future medicine?' Garland says, repeating the phrase like a mantra. Now he's on some kind of crusade, spurred by the optimism of all future medical hope. 'If you were going to have brain surgery on a tumour, would you like yours to be the first brain that doctor ever looked inside and started waddling around in with a new device?'

'Not at all,' I say.

'That's why the value of what we do is so important. And that's why we can no longer continue to allow the funeral industry or others – university programmes – to undermine and diminish the important role that companies like mine play in bringing innovative technologies to the American people and the world.'

The innovative technologies Garland is talking about are new surgical techniques and instruments. Companies that engineer medical devices use the tissue he sells to develop their products, get them through clinical trials and train surgeons in how they should be implemented. 'We didn't just wake up today and have all the marvels of medicine that we do. It's a combination of donors helping engineers, donors helping doctors learn,' Garland effuses. 'If you broke your hip in 1973, you'd be dead in three weeks. Now we have you up walking around, usually in the same day, with a double hip transplant. And that's because *donors* made that medicine happen.'

This would all be very worthy were it not for the fact that the consent form on the Research For Life website – which I've got in front of me as we speak – appears to give Garland permission to sell donated cadavers to anyone he likes.

'On your form it says you may supply donated tissue to "*universities, hospitals, medical device organizations, researchers, other tissue banks, bio-skill facilities, intermediaries, or others deemed appropriate at the sole discretion of RFL*". That's pretty broad, isn't it?' I say.

'It sure is.'

'Can anyone buy from you?'

'No,' he replies, suddenly laconic.

'Who do you turn down?'

'If you don't fall into the category of medical education and research, you're going to be turned down.' He pauses. 'I like the fact that you're on my website looking at this form. The funeral industry says, "They don't really inform the consumer." Well, that's bunk, and I'm going to debunk that today with you.'

He takes a deep breath.

'The first thing the funeral industry will tell families, our Congress, our legislators, is "They act like they are the ones doing the research! The donors think it's being done at that facility!" Bullshit.' He's shouting now. 'What do I do in line one? In bold? "*RFL does not perform research or medical education but acts as a bridge between authorized and permissible users.*"'

'Yes. But then in number eight, Garland, you say, "*RFL reserves the right to make changes to, modify, suspend, discontinue or otherwise alter its services without notice.*" Doesn't that mean you can do whatever you like?'

'I can't modify your consent. Let me give you an example. Can I use this authorization for the purposes of military testing? The answer is no, I cannot. I can't use it for ballistics testing. For blowing them up.'

My head is in my hands.

'I have veterans calling me all the time saying, "Garland, I'm getting ready to die and I want to help my brethren that are fighting battles for the US. I want to donate my body. I want it to go to the military and they can test, shoot me, blow me up, save my comrades,"' he continues. 'Now, I think it's awesome to do that, and it's perfectly legit, but the name of my company is Research For *Life*, not Research For *Death*. I don't do that. Besides that, my consent form would not allow me to do that. Some companies do.'

One of those companies is Science Care, the titan of tissue banking, whose consent form makes Garland's look like the children's menu at Pizza Express. Point twenty on their form says tissue may be exposed to 'simulated injury, trauma, impact, crash, ballistic, or blast exposure' and could be used in 'development of protective equipment for transportation, military, sports, or law enforcement purposes' and 'training in the performance of procedures intended to improve or correct superficial, aesthetic, or cosmetic anatomical deficiencies'. If you donate your corpse to Science Care, you might become a crash-test dummy or a nose-job guinea pig.

I think I'd rather be blown up.

Garland may have certain standards when it comes to the use of the tissue he sells, but he has little way of ensuring that the 'end users' do, beyond getting them to sign contracts.

'We do the best due diligence that we can,' he says. 'Here's the cool thing that *you* should be happy with, because you're worried about me doing whatever I want with the tissue: number thirteen on the form. I bold it up. "*It is further agreed that RFL shall be held harmless for any and all acts of third parties in connection with this donation.*" Do you know why that's a good thing? I'm being totally transparent with the consumer. Any tissue bank that tells you that they know exactly what that end user is going to do, if they're not standing by them, babysitting them, is full of shit. You don't know how the hell the donor will be used.'

Transparency is clearly a major part of Garland's schtick, the bit of his sales pitch that marks out the Research For Life brand. Emboldened by this openness, I ask him the question I rang him up for in the first place.

'How much does a human body cost, Garland?'

'I'm going to answer your question, but let me ask you a question first. Why do reporters think money is the most important part of this? Why is that?'

I consider this for a moment. 'Well, people feel a kind of shock at the idea that you can put a price on bodies, or on body parts, and I'm trying to understand the thinking that goes behind the price.'

'Why in the hell is it *shocking* that a tissue bank who has to pay the electric bill, who has to pay their staff, give them benefits, retirement, pay for vans and gas and training and insurance and liabilities – which costs millions of dollars, by the way – why is it *shocking* that the end user would have to pay a fee in order to attain those specimens? Why is that *shocking*?' He's shouting again. 'I charge end users because nobody gives me shit for free. You cannot run a business or have a mission that is going to be successful and have impact if you cannot generate the income that will allow you to do so.'

He pauses for breath. 'So. Please ask your question regarding money.'

'OK. Can you give me an indication of costs?'

'Here's the thing I will say. Everyone wants to know, "Well, how much is a head? How much is a foot? How much is a hand? How much is a finger? How much is a piece of this? How much is a piece of that?"' This is a rant now. 'I am *disgusted* with that. I find it *offensive* that the thing some people think is really titillating and sensational about this is that we charge a fee for human body parts. There's no way to operate or function unless there's a fee recovery system. That's all there is to it.'

'Yes – but do you have to make a profit out of it, Garland?' I want to ask. But I don't. I give up – or maybe I chicken out. This question will not go down well, and Garland is in no mood to answer it anyway, just like he isn't in the mood to share his price list.

'You're very passionate about this, Garland, aren't you?' I say instead.

'Can you tell?' he replies.

Prices are out there, of course; even Garland's prices. In 2015, he told them to some radio reporters: $500 for a fresh frozen head, $200 for a foot, $1,500–1,800 for a torso, a little over $300 for a knee, $125 for a hand. Everything being perfect, the whole body will generate $2,000–3,000, he said at the time. A 2013 price list from the Biological Resource Center was submitted to court in a civil action against Stephen Gore. It revealed that a whole body without shoulders or a head went for $2,900; a torso with a head was $2,400; a whole leg was $1,100. In 2017, Reuters came up with average sums charged, by comparing lists, quotes and sales from seven separate brokers: a head is $500; a hand is $250; a leg is $1,300; and an entire cadaver is $5,000 – excluding shipping.

These are market-driven prices, and they will change according to supply and demand. It's always more lucrative to sell a dismembered body than a whole cadaver. All bodies cost the same – male, female, black, white, young or old; so long as they were healthy, who the person was has no bearing on the value of their constituent parts. Death truly is the leveller.

Organs from the living are much more valuable than body parts from the dead. The organ trade is illegal almost everywhere, except for Iran, where a government foundation matches up kidney sellers and buyers for a fixed price of around $4,600 per organ. A black market in kidneys exists wherever people are desperate enough to sell them. In 2021, the Afghan news channel Tolo News quoted figures from the Afghan Ministry of Public Health showing that 1,000 people in the western province of Herat had sold their kidneys over the previous five years. The average rate for a kidney was $3,800; those who sold them were otherwise earning little over a dollar a day. With altruistic donation making up only 10 per cent of organ transplant need, the black market is estimated to be worth up to $1.7 billion a year, and human beings are regularly trafficked for their kidneys, livers and corneas. If they are paid at all, they can receive between $500 and $10,000 per organ, according to the United Nations Office on Drugs and Crime.

When it comes to 'naturally replenishable' tissue, the legal line becomes more blurred – and the internet comes into its own – particularly in America. Bone marrow can be sold in the USA for $3,000 a time on moremarrowdonors.org. Depending on the condition and length of your hair, you might be able to sell it for up to $800 on websites like OnlineHairAffair.com. Breastmilk goes for a dollar an ounce on onlythebreast.com. Every donation of blood plasma can earn you $30 to $50 in the US (an offer that has attracted desperate Americans, including drug addicts, and led to the contaminated blood scandal of the 1970s and 80s where thousands of British haemophiliacs were infected with HIV and hepatitis from blood products imported from the US). Rates vary widely, but women can expect to make a hundred times as much as men when they sell their gametes in the US. As a fertile woman in good health, if I was determined enough I could make well over $60,000 in a year from my tissue in America, without having to die.*

It's easy to feel as though everything has its price in the land of the free, but the trade in cadavers goes way beyond the US. Even countries with strict laws against selling body parts aren't averse to buying them. Science Care alone ships to over fifty countries worldwide, including the UK. When there aren't enough domestic donors to go around, British institutions are

* This is based on a very crude calculation of being able to donate six cycles of eggs, priced at $10,000 a cycle, a bit of bone marrow and lots of blood.

willing to hold their nose, pull out their chequebook and call America for dead bodies.

I meet Laura Arnold next to a metal table covered in very old pickled brains. The anatomy room at Brighton and Sussex Medical School (BSMS) is usually strictly off limits to casual visitors, but Professor Claire Smith has thrown the doors open to the public on the night of her inaugural lecture. We have fifteen minutes to inspect the different stations set up for us around the very bright lab, and it's not enough to take it all in.

There's a huge, distended uterus that was removed during a caesarean section. There's a polycystic kidney, riddled with tumours and so impossibly large that it looks like a lung. 'These are all historically obtained specimens,' the earnest anatomist behind the kidney table explains. 'These days it's very, very hard to find any pathological specimens that aren't stolen.' Discoloured by age and formaldehyde, most of the body parts on display don't look real, until something unmistakeably human – the inward curvature of fingers on a hand, a clipped fingernail – reminds you what they really are.

Laura is the anatomy administrator. That's her title, at least. 'It doesn't really explain what I do,' she says with a smile. When the lab isn't in use by undergraduate and postgraduate anatomy students, local surgeons or medical device companies can use the space for training. It's Laura's job to organize the courses – and obtain the tissue for them.

She talks me through how the process works in a video call a few days later, and manages to make it sound as unremarkable as if she were coordinating an evening life drawing class. 'The initial email or call will come to me. They will fill in our proforma with all of the details of the course they want to run, which specimens they'll need, any other facilities they'll need. If we're happy to run the course I'll find them a date that they can come into the lab, and then I'll give them an initial budget of how much that's going to cost them.'

Then Laura orders the necessary tissue, either from the London Anatomy Office (on the rare occasions when an entire cadaver is required), the Nottingham Repository (for both whole cadavers and individual body parts), or from Science Care (for body parts only). In line with guidelines from the Human Tissue Authority, bodies donated in the UK can't be provided for profit, and BSMS makes no profit from the tissue they get from Science Care – they simply pass on the cost to the course provider, who can't buy it directly because they aren't licensed by the HTA.

Laura says they only use Science Care when they need lots of specimens quickly. 'They are able to source donors from different parts of the US, so they have a larger pool – it's as simple as that. But we tend to only use Science Care if we really need to. The people running the courses prefer to use Nottingham because it's a lot cheaper. And it's easier for us. I can't ring the US as easily – it's in the middle of the night over there, usually.'

She sounds almost apologetic when she talks about shipping from the US.

'Do you have more confidence in who the donors are, and why they've donated, when it's in the UK?' I ask.

There's a very long pause. 'Probably yes. In this country we have self-consenting donors. Donors have to have signed the paperwork themselves. I know in the US it's done a little bit differently.'

Out of the fifty-four external courses BSMS has run over the past eighteen months, only five of them used Science Care tissue. 'We spent around $70,000 importing tissue from

America,' she says, glancing down at her calculator; the money went on upper and lower limbs, and a lot of heads. 'This may be the impact of Covid, but we've had a lot of ENT [ear, nose and throat] courses – they require head specimens.'

'How much does a head, a lower limb and upper limb cost?' I still can't believe I'm asking people questions like this – particularly warm, approachable Laura, with her stripy top and her neat eyebrows.

But Laura doesn't flinch at all. 'For a head, it's usually between $600 and $650. Lower limbs, upper limbs, are a little bit less – between $400 and $500. But the thing that increases the cost is the shipping fees,' she replies breezily. 'Say we needed fifteen heads – they're getting their specimens from all over the US to one place where they can be packaged and sent on to us, so it depends where all the specimens are going to come from.'

The increasing cost of living has affected the cost of the dead, Laura tells me. She got an email from Science Care only yesterday telling her they're putting their prices up due to rising fuel costs. The transatlantic part of shipping alone added an extra $2,000 to their last order of heads. I try to imagine the text updates from the courier pinging onto her phone.

'It arrives in a big box, with everything packaged in ice packs,' she tells me. 'It's like the weirdest delivery ever.'

Delivery day can be stressful, Laura says. The courses they run are generally for top surgeons trying out cutting-edge techniques, and they are paying a lot of money for the specimens. Nothing has gone missing so far, but she usually makes sure she gets the tissue in a few weeks early. 'Just to give you that buffer in case the flight got cancelled, or it got held up at customs for some reason.'

If these American tissue banks, run for profit, didn't exist, Laura reckons the courses would either not run, or would take place without enough specimens to go round. 'Is everybody getting their full experience if they're having to share one specimen between four or five?' she asks. 'I wouldn't want them practising on me first.' Anatomists, medical students, surgeons and medical engineers in the UK who want to use British donors depend on the altruism and resourcefulness of those who are determined to leave their bodies to medical research and education. There are never enough of them. 'Ideally, we'd have a lot more people donating in the UK,' Laura nods.

Garland has no plans to donate his own body in the name of future medical hope.

'I want to be buried at my cattle ranch in north-eastern Arizona. I have Black Angus cows. I love cows,' he declares, revelling in his own contrariness. 'Am I going to be a whole-body donor? No, because my family works at our donor company, and I think it would be very, very difficult for them to take care of that.' It doesn't occur to him to leave his body to another tissue bank. 'Would I be an organ donor? Would I give my heart or something that would help somebody live? Absolutely.'

Garland isn't shouting any more. He asks me about the other prices put on human lives that I've uncovered, and I tell him about the cost of creating a baby, of hiring a hitman, criminal injury compensation and healthcare. 'How do you put a price on a cancer treatment that could save a child's life? How do you do that?' he asks me.

'Pharmaceutical companies do,' I say. 'The NHS decides whether or not to pay for it.'

'Why would it be any different for me? I hope that you can help people understand that comparison. Some people say,

"These families make no money off these bodies!" That's right, but that type of inducement would be not healthy: you'd have family members who want to *profit* off the death of their loved ones. I don't think the cremation in and of itself is going to be sufficient enough to be the driving factor in the majority of donations. In some cases it is, but in the vast majority it's not.'

I can see the point he's making. There's a squeamishness around what body donation might entail, yet there's a reverence for scientific experimentation and medical advancement, even though so much of medicine relies on cadavers. And in the US, where medicine is a business run for profit, it seems hypocritical to laud medical innovation while denigrating the legitimate businesses that provide the raw materials it depends on. In a country where people can get rich from treating cancer, why shouldn't they be able to earn a living selling dead bodies? Both kinds of business are legal and flourishing in the US, after all. It's just the way things are done there.

Towards the end of the Research For Life promotional video, Garland stops to draw the tour group's attention to a sign on an internal door, that reads: "*To all staff. We, at Research For Life, have been granted a very special privilege: to be allowed to contribute our donors' bodies to the future of science. Our first priority is and shall always be to treat them with the utmost dignity and respect.*"

'Every time my employees close that door, I want them to remember what has been entrusted to us, because I may not be there,' Garland explains to me. 'I think there's a higher power that watches over all of us, and we're going to answer for our misdeeds if we're doing bad shit. We can't betray that trust. I get goosebumps, believe it or not, when I talk about it.' And he sounds so heartfelt when he says this that I do believe him.

This feels like a chink of vulnerability amid all of Garland's confidence and bluster, a recognition, perhaps, that even with all his openness to scrutiny, his safeguards, and his drive to be better than the 'bad actors' that have besmirched his industry's reputation, he has chosen to be in a business rife for exploitation.

'Perhaps you're motivated by wanting to have a clear conscience,' I suggest.

Garland bursts out laughing. 'I sleep soundly at night, *even though* I make money,' he shoots back. 'How's that?'

Epilogue

Gone are the days when I'd gasp as the effective altruists mulled over the worst age for a child to die. From the Home Office *Research Report 99* to Annex E of *The Criminal Injuries Compensation Scheme 2012* to Garland Shreves' consent form, the tariffs, tallies, spreadsheets and contracts that determine the value of a human being have lost their power to shock me. My quest to find the price of life has changed me, though I'm still not sure whether I'd call it moral progress.

Without flinching or celebrating, I now know that, as a British woman in my forties, my life is neither worth saving by the world's richest philanthropists nor enslaving by human traffickers. The NHS is prepared to spend at least a million pounds on treatments that will keep me alive for the rest of my life, given the average female life expectancy. For the next few years at least, my eggs and womb will make my body far more valuable than a man's, but my cadaver will be worth the same as any other after I'm dead. I will spend around £600,000 raising my two children, but, as a straight person with no fertility problems, I got them for free anyway. They would get the same £11,000 compensation for my murder as anyone else's family, unless I'd been killed by a car or shot from the grounds of a chain of luxury hotels in the US. If I was in the wrong place at the wrong time and stabbed by someone I hardly knew, the

Home Office would view my murder as costing society the same as any other. But, because I'm a white woman, it would no doubt spark far more outrage than the murder of Shaquan Sammy-Plummer.

Great misery seems to come from having either the lowest or the highest price put on your life. Pain, trauma, enslavement and violence exist most acutely at either end of the scale. But there are some uncomfortable truths in the middle of the range too. In the UK it costs almost the same to create a life through IVF treatment as it does to hire the average hitman to end it. We are prepared to spend more on conceiving an unborn person than compensating for a life taken, or paying for a life sold into slavery. The fact that a cadaver is cheaper than almost every human life would be comforting, were it not the case that slaves are sold in Libya for less than 10 per cent of what their dead bodies could be bought for in the USA. The full absurdity of human existence is revealed within the twelve prices I've investigated in these pages: the life of an Afghan girl might be worth $500 to her starving parents, but the life of an Afghan fighter is worth hundreds of millions – if not billions – to the US Marine Corp prepared to drop a bomb on him from an F-35B.

Sometimes prices depend on the going rate for a service that varies widely according to market forces: the cost of providing a body part, or fertility treatment, or a child bride, or keeping a hostage. Sometimes the price might reflect the political will to fight violent crime or wage war, or the desperation of a hitman or kidnapper. But often these prices are simply tokens that bear little relation to the market value of anything. The cost of saving a life demonstrated in the NHS's willingness to pay for drugs falls into this category; and so does the cost of a murder, even though the Home Office added up a lot of numbers to reach its absurdly precise final figure. When it's a token, it's supposed to allow for comparisons to be made and resources more wisely allocated; its function is to get politicians to sit up and listen, or billionaires to put their hands into their pockets. But it's a blunt instrument, used to make decisions and distinctions that deserve nuanced consideration.

The danger comes, perhaps, when people treat tokens as if they truly represent the real price of a human life. The effective altruists wanted me to see that numbers can help us do more good in the world than feelings can, but they run the risk of treating the price of life as if it were a fact, not a token. We shouldn't let the clarity of numbers beguile us. They are only useful if we know and accept what they *don't* tell us. They can be dangerous: putting a price on human life requires acceptance of the idea that human beings have different values depending on who, when and where they are born, and accepting that inequality makes it easier to both help and to exploit those who are cheapest. Numbers can also flatten differences in human experience. They can both reveal and blind us to the truth that some lives – and deaths – matter more than others in our societies.

Sometimes we get to set the price of our own lives – like when we take out life insurance. Often, it's us that set the price of other people: through our taxes, our purchasing choices, our willingness to exploit those whose lives are valued as cheaper than ours and our eagerness to look away are fundamental parts of the equation. Investigating the price of life gives us the ability to reveal great injustices, and an opportunity to put things right.

The price of life tells us something about ourselves: not our value, but *what* we value in a given place and time. It reveals what we think matters in a world of finite resources, and it can show us if we're saying something that we don't intend to say – that the lives of African children are worth less than homeless adults, perhaps, or that only the rich should be helped to become parents. We need the price of life as a tool to help us get closer to justice and fairness. It can show us where injustice is, but it can't tell us what we should be doing to address it. For that, we need a bigger toolbox. Empathy and humanity have to be part of it.

We need to be brave enough to ask what the price is, even if the question makes us uncomfortable, because our reluctance to discuss it openly can perpetuate enormous unfairness. The inequality in criminal injury compensation would be hard to justify if the differences in payments were better known, but it's not in the interests of those who win big civil payouts – or their lawyers – to be forthcoming about it. The same goes for traffickers, the 'experts' that help determine ransom payments and the companies that set the almost inconceivable price of the world's most expensive weapons system. The people who benefit from negotiating these arrangements would rather we had no idea what was involved. We need to get better at talking about all of this.

And if we are prepared to put prices on lives, we need the courage to listen and act when the numbers are telling us something, no matter how awkward or challenging. If they show that nations are spending hundreds of billions on a weapons system that will not be able to defend us from the greatest threat to human existence, we need to ask what we're truly getting for our money. If they show that genetic parenthood is only an option for the biologically fortunate or the wealthy, then we need to ask whether that's a society we want to be part of.

But we also have to get better at talking about what matters, without first converting it into a bill. It's only possible to put a price on human life if we can reduce the people we're pricing up to a series of indices; if we can ignore the humanity of them. This is a dangerous exercise, and not one that we want to become good at.

I have changed since I began researching the price of life. So have you. You've survived a pandemic, endured a cost-of-living crisis, and now you've entered the age of the AI revolution. We're shedding increasingly useable data every moment that we live, providing an exponential number of metrics that ever more clever algorithms can use to value our lives. The more data we reveal about ourselves, the more that the numbers will become personalized and better reflect our true worth as individuals. The blunt instrument of the price of life will sharpen up, becoming more specific, more accurate, more reflective of our true market value, and more available to those who seek to use it.

Should certain data points be off limits? Our genetic code, how likely we are to be able to conceive a child, where we go and who we talk to, the kinds of conversations we have on- and offline? Are we happy for the numbers on our heads to be a product of these kinds of metrics if it makes governments pour the right resources in our direction, and gives us cheaper insurance premiums?

The price of life is going to become an even more powerful tool. We will need to make sure we use it wisely.

Acknowledgements

The book you hold in your hands exists only because a huge number of people agreed to share their experiences with me and give me their time. I am so grateful to everyone who did.

In particular, I'd like to thank Jessica Plummer and Julie and Mark Wallace, for their incredible courage and willingness to tell their children's stories. You can support Julie and Mark's work at sarzsanctuary.com, and Jessica's work through the Shaquan Sammy-Plummer Foundation at shaqsworld.co.uk.

Stephen and Chris Collett – thank you for trusting me after so many other journalists have let you down. Megan Willis – Edward is so lucky to have you.

This book also wouldn't exist without the support and ideas of my agent, Zoe Ross; Olivia Davies, who stepped into Zoe's shoes; and my editor, Andrea Henry, who immediately understood what I wanted to do and encouraged me to do it my way.

I'd also like to thank:

Duncan Gardham, Afsaneh Knight, Casimir Knight, Marsha Lowe at ATLEU, and Marissa Begonia at the Voice of Domestic Workers, who helped me find the right people.

Susan Bewley, Alec Nacamuli, Sir Brian Pommeroy and Annie Kelly, whose ideas were so useful in framing my approach.

My editors at *The Guardian* and Tortoise Media: some of the stories I've covered in these pages began as articles that they worked on with me. I'm eternally grateful to Melissa Denes at *Weekend*, and Ruth Lewy, Rob Fearn and Merope Mills at *Saturday*, for the expert eyes they cast over my pieces, and to David Taylor at Tortoise who helped me make sense of the effective altruists.

Manou Kleeman, for her translation services. Olly Owen, for the Nigeria expertise. Anne Cori, for idiot-proofing the lock-down chapter. Naser Turabi, for his wise insight into some early drafts. Nina Raingold for the photo and all the WhatsApps.

A special thank you to Nicole Kleeman, who let me pick her brain a little too often when I was feeling alone at my desk.

My parents, David and Manou, and my sisters, Julie, Nicole and Susanna.

Corrie and Keith Bramley, for their kindness and generosity, and Rebecca Burke, for her excellent child distraction skills. This book certainly wouldn't exist were it not for you three.

Ben and Bella, my eternal inspiration. Thank you for understanding that sometimes I need to take time away from you – even on Boxing Day, because that's the only time the person whose dad faked his own death can speak to me.

And to Scot, who makes everything that matters in my life possible. I love you.

Notes and Sources

Chapter 1

p. 17 **Orsini said at the time** Frignani, Rinaldo, 'Confessioni di un killer a pagamento "Mi vestivo da ufficiale guidiziario"', *Corriere della Sera* (23 March 2015). https://roma.corriere.it/notizie/cronaca/15_marzo_23/confessioni-un-killer-pagamento-mi-vestivo-ufficiale-giudiziario-e7770342-d12b-11e4-8608-3dead25e131d.shtml

p. 18 ***The British Hitman 1974–2013*** MacIntyre, Donal; Wilson, David; Yardley, Elizabeth; and Brolan, Liam, 'The British Hitman: 1974–2013', *The Howard Journal of Crime and Justice*, Vol. 53, Issue 4, pp. 325–40 (2014). http://dx.doi.org/10.1111/hojo.12063

p. 19 **an analysis of 163 contract killings** Mouzos, Jenny and Venditto, John, 'Contract Killings in Australia', *Australian Institute of Criminology* (2003). https://www.aic.gov.au/sites/default/files/2020-05/rpp053.pdf

p. 20 **'When we saw the CCTV'** Summers, Chris, 'How schoolboy hitman Santre Gayle murdered for £200', *BBC News* (24 May 2011). https://www.bbc.co.uk/news/uk-13443358

Chapter 2

p. 24 **the world's largest defence contractor** 'Top 100 for 2023', *Defense News* (2023). https://people.defensenews.com/top-100/

p. 27 **an average of $110 million** 'Department of Defense Fiscal Year 2021 Budget Estimates', *Air Force Justification Book*, Vol. 1, p. 53 (2020). https://www.documentcloud.org/documents/7221495-FY21-Air-Force-Aircraft-Procurement-Vol-I-1.html#document/p53/a584115

p. 27 **the US Government Accountability Office found** 'F-35 Sustainment: Enhanced Attention to and Oversight of F-35 Affordability Are Needed', *GAO* (22 April 2021). https://www.gao.gov/products/gao-21-505t

p. 28 **British taxpayers are spending £2.2 billion** 'UK to purchase at least 74 F-35 jets', *Navy Lookout* (27 April 2022). https://www.navylookout.com/uk-to-purchase-at-least-74-f-35-jets/

p. 28 **a further twenty-six in the pipeline** Allison, George, 'Britain confirms plans to purchase 74 F-35B jets', *UK Defence Journal* (1 May 2022). https://ukdefencejournal.org.uk/britain-confirms-plans-to-purchase-74-f-35b-jets/

p. 29 **just over $80 billion apiece** Ciralsky, Adam, 'Will It Fly?', *Vanity Fair* (16 September 2013). https://www.vanityfair.com/news/2013/09/joint-strike-fighter-lockheed-martin

p. 29 **By the time the F-35 was ready** 'Israel says it is the first country to use U.S.-made F-35 in combat', *Reuters* (22 May 2018). https://www.reuters.com/article/us-lockheed-f35-israel/israel-says-it-is-the-first-country-to-use-u-s-made-f-35-in-combat-idUSKCN1IN0ON

p. 30 **the UK alone** Urban, Mark, 'UK to spend £2.5bn on F-35 fighters', *BBC News* (11 February 2014). https://www.bbc.co.uk/news/uk-26124894

p. 37 **the Mitchell Institute report** Deptula, Lt Gen David A. and Birkey, Douglas A., 'Resolving America's Defense Strategy-

Resource Mismatch: The Case for Cost-Per-Effect Analysis', *Mitchell Institute for Aerospace Studies* (8 July 2020). https://mitchellaerospacepower.org/resolving-americas-defense-strategy-resource-mismatch-the-case-for-cost-per-effect-analysis/

p. 38 **the Pentagon's testing and evaluation office** Capaccio, Anthony, 'F-35 Flies With 871 Flaws, Only Two Fewer Than Year Earlier' *Bloomberg* (12 January 2021). https://www.bloomberg.com/news/articles/2021-01-12/f-35-flies-with-871-flaws-only-two-fewer-than-a-year-earlier

p. 38 **a risk to pilot safety** Insinna, Valerie, 'The Pentagon is battling the clock to fix serious, unreported F-35 problems', *Defense News* (12 June 2019). https://www.defensenews.com/air/2019/06/12/the-pentagon-is-battling-the-clock-to-fix-serious-unreported-f-35-problems/

p. 39 **a Pentagon press release** 'Marine Corps F-35B Conducts Combat Strikes in Afghanistan', *U.S. Department of Defense* (28 September 2018). https://www.defense.gov/News/News-Stories/Article/Article/1647694/marine-corps-f-35b-conducts-combat-strikes-in-afghanistan/

p. 39 **a network of ISIS tunnels** 'U.S. Air Force F-35As conduct first combat mission', *U.S. Central Command* (30 April 2019). https://www.centcom.mil/MEDIA/NEWS-ARTICLES/News-Article-View/Article/1831452/us-air-force-f-35as-conduct-first-combat-mission/

p. 39 **two Iranian drones** Egozi, Arie, 'Israeli F-35s shot down two drones; first confirmed air-to-air kills for JSF', *Breaking Defense* (7 March 2022). https://breakingdefense.com/2022/03/israeli-f-35s-shot-down-two-drones-first-confirmed-air-to-air-kills-for-jsf/; and https://twitter.com/IAFsite/status/1500851354557898760?ref_src=twsrc%5Etfw%7Ctwcamp%5Etweetembed%7Ctwterm%5E1500851354557898760%7Ctwgr%5E4239a5f1d32037d0caf646e6886cd543e6d3daa0%7Ctwcon%5Es1_&ref_url=https%3A%2F%

2Fbreakingdefense.com%2F2022%2F03%2Fisraeli-f-35s-shot-down-two-drones-first-confirmed-air-to-air-kills-for-jsf%2F

p. 39 **OIR released an aerial video** 'Video shows explosives being dropped on IS occupied territory in Iraq', *BBC News* (11 September 2019). https://www.bbc.co.uk/news/av/world-us-canada-49669610

p. 39 **had lost their lives** Ioanes, Ellen, 'US jets smashed an island ISIS was using "like a hotel" and troops found rockets and bombs stashed in caves', *Business Insider* (11 September 2019). https://www.businessinsider.com/us-jets-smashed-island-isis-was-using-like-a-hotel-2019-9?r=US&IR=T

p. 40 **690 miles per hour** Yeo, Mike, 'Japan blames spatial disorientation for F-35 crash', *Defense News* (10 June 2019). https://www.defensenews.com/global/asia-pacific/2019/06/10/japan-blames-spatial-disorientation-for-f-35-crash/

p. 43 **once in 2002** In Oruzgan, leading to at least 30 civilian casualties: Harding, Luke and Engel, Matthew, 'US bomb blunder kills 30 at Afghan wedding', *The Guardian* (2 July 2002). https://www.theguardian.com/world/2002/jul/02/afghanistan.lukeharding

p. 43 **and twice in 2008** In Wech Baghtu, leading to 40 civilian deaths: 'Karzai says air strike kills 40 in Afghanistan', *Reuters* (5 November 2008). https://www.reuters.com/article/idUSTRE4A44EW20081105; and Haska Menya, leading to 47: 'Afghan official: U.S. strike hit wedding party', *NBC News* (11 July 2008). https://www.nbcnews.com/id/wbna25635571

p. 46 **for an entire year** Rajaeifar, Mohammad Ali; Belcher, Oliver; Parkinson, Stuart; Neimark, Benjamin; Weir, Doug; Ashworth, Kirsti; Larbi, Reuben; and Heidrich, Oliver, 'Decarbonize the military — mandate emissions reporting', *Nature* (2 November 2022). https://www.nature.com/articles/d41586-022-03444-7#ref-CR2. It produces the same emissions as the average UK passenger car when it flies 100 nautical miles;

flown at the supersonic speed of 1,200mph, this would take five minutes.

Chapter 3

p. 51 ***Research Report 99*** Heeks, Matthew; Reed, Sasha; Tafsiri, Mariam; and Prince, Stuart, *Research Report 99*, 'The Economic and Social Costs of Crime', *Home Office* (July 2018). https://assets.publishing.service.gov.uk/government/uploads/system/uploads/attachment_data/file/732110/the-economic-and-social-costs-of-crime-horr99.pdf

p. 51 **It was the fourth time** The first Home Office paper estimating the economic and social costs of crime was published in 2000 (Brand and Price, 2000), updated in 2005 (Dubourg, Hamed and Thorns, 2005), and then a minor update was published in 2011 based on the latest crime data (*Home Office*, 2011).

p. 53 ***Home Office Research Study 217*** Brand, Sam and Price, Richard, *Home Office Research Study 217*, 'The Economic and Social Costs of Crime', *Home Office* (December 2000). https://www.researchgate.net/publication/247849478_The_Economic_and_Social_Costs_of_Crime_-_Home_Office_Research_Study_217

p. 54 **costs America $8,649,216** Heaton, Paul, 'Hidden in Plain Sight: What Cost-of-Crime Research Can Tell Us About Investing in Police', *RAND Corporation* (2010). https://www.rand.org/pubs/occasional_papers/OP279.html

p. 54 **The European Institute for Gender Equality** 'Gender-based violence costs the EU €366 billion a year', *EIGE* (7 July 2021). https://eige.europa.eu/news/gender-based-violence-costs-eu-eu366-billion-year

p. 54 **20.8 percent of Mexico's GDP** 'Mexico Peace Index 2022: Identifying and Measuring the Factors that Drive Peace', *Institute for Economics and Peace* (2022). https://www.

economicsandpeace.org/wp-content/uploads/2022/05/ENG-MPI-2022-web.pdf

p. 58 **what was said in court** De La Mare, Tess, 'Man who stabbed teenager to death after he gatecrashed house party faces life in jail', *Mirror* (25 April 2016). https://www.mirror.co.uk/news/uk-news/man-who-stabbed-teenager-death-7831123

p. 59 **At 9.33 p.m.** A lot of the details about the sequence of events in this chapter are taken from Piscopo, Jamie, 'Operation Lamesley: The investigation into the murder of Shaquan Sammy-Plummer', *The Journal of Homicide and Major Incident Investigation*, Vol. 11, Issue 2 (November 2016). https://library.college.police.uk/docs/appref/Homicide%20Journal%2011.2%20November%202016.pdf

p. 59 **30 per cent of his workload** The details about Rock and Konig come from Lydall, Ross, 'Mother of knife victim Shaquan Sammy-Plummer: killer took my boy's life for nothing', *Evening Standard* (20 September 2016). https://www.standard.co.uk/news/london/mother-of-knife-victim-shaquan-sammyplummer-killer-took-my-boy-s-life-for-nothing-a3349186.html

p. 59 **Konig wrote the day after the murder** Lydall, Ross, '"We held the heart of a young boy in our hands and willed it to beat and to survive. We could not save him": London surgeon pleads for knife crime to halt after yet another killing', *Evening Standard* (2 February 2015). https://www.standard.co.uk/news/london/surgeon-plea-knife-crime-end-boy-17-stabbed-in-heart-house-party-enfield-london-ambulance-knife-deaths-10017828.html

p. 64 **he admitted it was normal** Morley, Nicole, 'Party host "stabbed gatecrasher to death to limit number of guests so his mum wouldn't be mad"', *Metro* (19 April 2016). https://metro.co.uk/2016/04/19/party-host-stabbed-gatecrasher-to-death-to-limit-number-of-guests-so-his-mum-wouldnt-be-mad-5827931/

p. 64 **a fairly average sentence for murder** See average sentencing guidelines here: https://www.sentencingcouncil.org.uk/wp-content/uploads/FINAL-Murder-sentencing-leaflet-for-web1.pdf

p. 67 **long form magazine features** 'Knife Crime: Cherrie Ives, sister of murdered Alan Cartwright, finds out how the Met Police are fighting knife crime', *I Was There* podcast. https://www.bbc.co.uk/programmes/p034jbmd; Millard, Rosie, 'A Stabbing on My Doorstep', *Sunday Times* (8 May 2016). https://www.thetimes.co.uk/article/a-stabbing-on-my-doorstep-85xl9n9hj; Butter, Susannah, 'Alan Cartwright's sister Cherrie Smith on her family's tragic loss', *Evening Standard* (4 June 2015). https://www.standard.co.uk/lifestyle/london-life/alan-cartwright-s-sister-cherrie-smith-on-her-family-s-tragic-loss-10296606.html

p. 67 **made national television news bulletins** 'Woman Who Killed Teen Over Pasta Gets Life', *Sky News* (27 April 2016). https://news.sky.com/story/woman-who-killed-teen-over-pasta-gets-life-10260336

p. 70 **the most recent set of figures** 'Costs per place and costs per prisoner by individual prison', *Ministry of Justice* (27 January 2022). https://assets.publishing.service.gov.uk/government/uploads/system/uploads/attachment_data/file/1050046/costs-per-place-costs-per-prisoner-2020_-2021.pdf

Chapter 4

p. 86 **A recent study by Coalition Against Insurance Fraud** 'The Impact of Insurance Fraud on the U.S. Economy', *Coalition Against Insurance Fraud* (26 August 2022). https://insurancefraud.org/wp-content/uploads/The-Impact-of-Insurance-Fraud-on-the-U.S.-Economy-Report-2022-8.26.2022.pdf

p. 86 **every policy holder** 'The Impact of Insurance Fraud',

Insurance Europe (2013). https://insuranceeurope.eu/publications/492/the-impact-of-insurance-fraud/

p. 86 **In the UK alone** 'UK Insurance & Long-Term Savings Key Facts', *Association of British Insurers* (February 2021). https://www.abi.org.uk/globalassets/files/publications/public/key-facts/abi_key_facts_2021.pdf

p. 86 **the German supermodel Heidi Klum** *The Ellen Show* (18 January 2022). https://www.youtube.com/watch?v=RaJs6FejT_c

p. 87 **insured for ridiculous sums** Like I say, these are rumours, all quoted in *Elle*, and are very likely to be entirely made up. Makan, Sunil, '13 Celebrities With Insured Body Parts That Are Worth More Than Your House', *Elle* (11 February 2019). https://www.elle.com/uk/life-and-culture/articles/a30167/mariah-carey-jennifer-lopez-doly-parton-celebrities-insured-body-parts/

p. 87 **Cadbury owner Mondelez announced** 'Chocolate scientist has taste buds insured for £1m', *BBC News* (6 September 2016). https://www.bbc.co.uk/news/av/uk-england-birmingham-37287937

p. 87 **insured for £10 million** Sayid, Ruki, 'Coffee taster Gennaro Pelliccia insures tongue for £10m', *Mirror* (9 March 2009). https://www.mirror.co.uk/news/uk-news/coffee-taster-gennaro-pelliccia-insures-381336

p. 87 **£80,485 in 2021** 'Payouts for bereavement, illness, and injury claims top £18.6 million a day' *Association of British Insurers* (21 May 2022). https://www.abi.org.uk/news/news-articles/2022/05/payouts-for-bereavement-illness-and-injury-claims/

p. 88 **that figure is £116,414** 'Employees Benefit as Group Risk Industry Pays Out Record Amount in Claims During 2021' *Group Risk Development* (12 May 2022). https://grouprisk.org.uk/2022/05/12/employees-benefit-as-group-risk-industry-pays-out-record-amount-in-claims-during-2021

p. 88 **€291,162 for men** 'Men in Ireland Value Themselves 64% More than Women', *Royal London* (June 2021). https://www.royallondon.ie/siteassets/site-docs/press/2021/why_are_men_in_ireland_valued_more_than_women.pdf

p. 89 **have their first child** Francis-Devine, Brigid, 'The gender pay gap', *House of Commons Library* (1 December 2022). https://commonslibrary.parliament.uk/research-briefings/sn07068/

p. 91 **reviewed every year** 'Code on Genetic Testing and Insurance', *Department of Health and Social Care* (23 October 2018). https://www.gov.uk/government/publications/code-on-genetic-testing-and-insurance

Chapter 5

p. 94 **on 3 June 2017** The timings in this chapter all come from the inquest into the London Bridge attacks of 2017, reported here: Siddique, Haroon, 'London Bridge attacks: how atrocity unfolded', *The Guardian* (28 June 2019). https://www.theguardian.com/uk-news/2019/jun/28/london-bridge-attacks-how-atrocity-unfolded

p. 94 **at the northern end of London Bridge** Anderson Q.C., David, 'Attacks in London and Manchester March–June 2017: Independent Assessment of MI5 and Police Internal Reviews', *Home Office* (December 2017). https://assets.publishing.service.gov.uk/government/uploads/system/uploads/attachment_data/file/664682/Attacks_in_London_and_Manchester_Open_Report.pdf

p. 96 **a few hours earlier** Dodd, Vikram, 'Family had reported London Bridge attacker to police, inquest hears', *The Guardian* (28 May 2019). https://www.theguardian.com/uk-news/2019/may/28/london-bridge-attacker-job-carrying-out-security-checks-london-underground

p. 96 **weighed down with bags of gravel** Jackson, Marie, 'Chaos and killings: 10 minutes at London Bridge', *BBC News* (28 June 2019). https://www.bbc.co.uk/news/uk-48619714

p. 96 **Molotov cocktails and blowtorches** Dodd, Vikram, 'London Bridge: more arrests as police tell how terrorists wanted to use truck', *Guardian* (10 June 2017). https://www.theguardian.com/uk-news/2017/jun/10/worse-terror-attack-on-london-bridge-foiled-by-chance-police-say

p. 96 **she told the inquest** From the inquest and reported here: Gibbons, Katie, 'Survivor tells of premonition of London Bridge terror attack', *The Times* (10 May 2019). https://www.thetimes.co.uk/article/survivor-tells-of-premonition-of-london-bridge-terror-attack-3h3ns7npq

p. 96 **before their rampage** Weaver, Matthew, 'London Bridge attack trio "had taken large quantities of steroids"', *The Guardian* (9 February 2018). https://www.theguardian.com/uk-news/2018/feb/09/london-bridge-attack-trio-had-taken-large-quantities-of-steroids-inquest

p. 96 **two miles downstream** Jackson, Marie, 'Chaos and killings: 10 minutes at London Bridge', *BBC News* (28 June 2019). https://www.bbc.co.uk/news/uk-48619714

p. 96 **the bridge's central reservation** From the inquest and reported here: Siddique, Haroon, 'London Bridge attacks: how atrocity unfolded', *The Guardian* (28 June 2019). https://www.theguardian.com/uk-news/2019/jun/28/london-bridge-attacks-how-atrocity-unfolded

p. 96 **in Tyler's arms** 'London Bridge attack inquest: Court hears of victims' final moments', *BBC News* (7 May 2019). https://www.bbc.co.uk/news/uk-48185656

p. 97 **away from the crash site** 'London Bridge attack inquest: Sara Zelenak "slipped" before attack', *BBC News* (13 May 2019). https://www.bbc.co.uk/news/uk-48252390

p. 97 **tried to find her** From the inquest and reported here: McLaughlin, Chelsea, '"I didn't know where she was." Sara Zelenak's last moments before she was killed in the London

Bridge terror attack', *Mamamia* (13 May 2019). https://www.mamamia.com.au/sara-zelenak/

p. 98 **a witness told the inquest** From the inquest and reported here: 'London Bridge attack inquest: Sara Zelenak "slipped" before attack', *BBC News* (13 May 2019). https://www.bbc.co.uk/news/uk-48252390

p. 98 **A shower of rubble** Topping, Alexandra; Malkin, Bonnie; and Doherty, Ben, '"It was a rampage": witnesses describe horror of London terrorist attacks', *The Guardian* (4 June 2017). https://www.theguardian.com/uk-news/2017/jun/04/it-was-a-rampage-witnesses-describe-horror-of-london-terrorist-attacks

p. 98 **to save Alexandre's life** Chief Coroner, 'Inquests Arising from the Deaths in the London Bridge and Borough Market Terror Attack: Regulation 28 Report on Action to Prevent Future Deaths', *Courts and Tribunals Judiciary* (2019). https://www.judiciary.uk/wp-content/uploads/2019/11/London-Bridge-Borough-Market-Terror-Attack-2019-0332.pdf

p. 98 **joined in the assault** From the inquest and reported here: De Miguel, Rafa, 'Inquest reveals how Spain's "skateboard hero" rushed to protect victims', *El País* (22 May 2019). https://english.elpais.com/elpais/2019/05/22/inenglish/1558518214_666396.html

p. 98 **eye, leg and hand** Siddique, Haroon and agency, 'Policeman tells how he fought London Bridge attackers with baton', *The Guardian* (28 June 2017). https://www.theguardian.com/uk-news/2017/jun/28/policeman-fought-london-bridge-attackers-baton-wayne-marques

p. 99 **twenty people in his bakery** 'London Bridge terror attack heroes on Civilian Gallantry List', *BBC News* (19 July 2018). https://www.bbc.co.uk/news/uk-england-44872988

p. 99 **but survived** Mann, Tanveer, '"They're not alive, I am" says Lion of London Bridge who fought off attacker', *Metro* (7 June 2017). https://metro.co.uk/2017/06/07/theyre-not-alive-i-am-says-lion-of-london-bridge-who-fought-off-attackers-6691048/

p. 99 **on Stoney Street** From the inquest and reported here: Dodd, Vikram, 'London Bridge attack: police lawfully killed terrorists, inquest finds', *The Guardian* (16 July 2019). https://www.theguardian.com/uk-news/2019/jul/16/london-bridge-attack-police-lawfully-killed-terrorists-inquest-finds

p. 99 **the first emergency call was made** Chief Coroner, 'Inquests Arising from the Deaths in the London Bridge and Borough Market Terror Attack: Regulation 28 Report on Action to Prevent Future Deaths', *Courts and Tribunals Judiciary* (2019). https://www.judiciary.uk/wp-content/uploads/2019/11/London-Bridge-Borough-Market-Terror-Attack-2019-0332.pdf

p. 100 **injuring over a thousand** 'Manchester Arena Inquiry, Day 44, December 7, 2020', *Opus 2* (7 December 2020). https://files.manchesterarenainquiry.org.uk/live/uploads/2020/12/07182655/MAI-Day-44.pdf

p. 102 **the CICA guidelines** 'Criminal injuries compensation: a guide', *Criminal Injuries Compensation Authority* and *Ministry of Justice* (26 March 2014). https://www.gov.uk/guidance/criminal-injuries-compensation-a-guide

p. 102 ***Criminal Injuries Compensation Scheme 2012*** 'The Criminal Injuries Compensation Scheme 2012', *Ministry of Justice* (2012). https://assets.publishing.service.gov.uk/government/uploads/system/uploads/attachment_data/file/808343/criminal-injuries-compensation-scheme-2012.pdf

p. 103 **their ten-year-old son** Jones, Murray, 'Life Values: How the British Military Calculated the Cost of an Afghan Life', *Byline Times* (24 September 2021). https://bylinetimes.com/2021/09/24/life-values-how-the-british-military-calculated-the-cost-of-an-afghan-life/

p. 104 **his eighty-year-old mother** Gadher, Dipesh, 'London Bridge attack: stabbed Millwall fan Roy Larner is different kind of hero', *The Times* (12 May 2019). https://www.thetimes.co.uk/article/london-bridge-attack-stabbed-millwall-fan-roy-larner-is-different-kind-of-hero-86b0r2bjc

p. 104 **entitled to CA$10,000** Teich, Sarah, 'Developing a modernized federal response plan for Canadians victimized abroad in acts of mass violence: How Canada can address the needs of cross-border victims based on international best practices', *Government of Canada* (March 2021). https://www.victimsfirst.gc.ca/res/cor/CCAT-CCAT/indexCCAT1.html#_Toc67662020

p. 104 **a quarter of a million euros** 'Ley 29/2011, de 22 de septiembre, de Reconocimiento y Protección Integral a las Víctimas del Terrorismo', *Gobierno de España* (23 September 2011). https://www.boe.es/eli/es/l/2011/09/22/29/con – Annex 1 – 250,000 euros

p. 104 **siblings up to €15,000** 'Guide de L'Indemnisation des Victimes d'actes de Terrorisme', *Fonds de Garantie des Victimes des Actes de Terrorisme et d'autres Infractions* (September 2020). https://www.fondsdegarantie.fr/wp-content/uploads/2017/07/Guide-pour-lindemnisation-des-victimes-des-actes-terrorisme_SEPT2020.pdf

p. 104 **which is AU$75,000** 'Australian Victim of Terrorism Overseas Payment Scheme', *Australian Government Department of Home Affairs*. https://www.disasterassist.gov.au/disaster-arrangements/australian-victim-of-terrorism-overseas-payment

p. 105 **for the Insurance Day website** Muir-Wood, Robert, 'Viewpoint: Crossing the terrorism casualty protection gap', *Insurance Day* (29 October 2019). https://insuranceday.maritimeintelligence.informa.com/ID1129467/Viewpoint-Crossing-the-terrorism-casualty-protection-gap? But it can be read without a paywall on the RMS site: https://www.rms.com/blog/2019/11/19/crossing-the-terrorism-casualty-protection-gap

p. 106 **agreed in 2020** 'Cash payouts for victims of London Bridge attack ahead of third anniversary', *ITV News* (24 May 2020).

https://www.itv.com/news/2020-05-24/cash-payouts-for-victims-of-london-bridge-attack-ahead-of-third-anniversary

p. 106 **in excess of £150 million** 'Use of hire vans in terror attacks may result in rental price increase', *Fleet News* (20 January 2018). https://www.fleetnews.co.uk/news/fleet-industry-news/2018/01/30/use-of-hire-vans-in-terror-attacks-may-result-in-rental-price-increase

p. 107 **killing fifty-eight people** 'FBI finds no motive for Las Vegas shooting, closes probe', *Reuters* (29 January 2019). https://www.reuters.com/article/us-lasvegas-shooting-idUSKCN1PN31N

p. 107 **was independently owned** 'onePULSE Foundation Founder Barbara Poma', *onePULSE Foundation*. https://onepulse foundation.org/task-members/barbara-poma/

p. 108 **albeit in the British press** Miller, Shari, 'London Bridge terror attack survivors and victims' families secure insurance payouts after killers hired van to commit atrocity', *Daily Mail* (24 May 2020). https://www.dailymail.co.uk/news/article-8352567/London-Bridge-terror-attack-survivors-victims-families-secure-insurance-payouts.html

p. 110 **his method of payment failed** Symonds, Tom, 'London attack: Men "planned to use 7.5 tonne lorry"', *BBC News* (10 June 2017). https://www.bbc.co.uk/news/uk-40228756

p. 111 **largely on his own** 'London Bridge attack: Who were the victims?', *BBC News* (22 May 2019). https://www.bbc.co.uk/news/uk-40153090

p. 115 **five separate JustGiving pages** https://www.justgiving.com/crowdfunding/chloe-long-2; https://www.justgiving.com/crowdfunding/chris-gardner-2; https://www.justgiving.com/crowdfunding/alexklis; https://www.justgiving.com/crowdfunding/tescocliftonmoor; https://www.justgiving.com/crowdfunding/angelikamarcin

p. 115 **an additional half a million pounds** Pidd, Helen, 'Manchester Arena attack: families of 22 people killed to get

£250,000 each', *The Guardian* (15 August 2017). https://www.theguardian.com/uk-news/2017/aug/15/manchester-arena-victims-we-love-families-receive-250000-killed

p. 115 **£75,000 to the next of kin** 'London Bridge/Borough Market Attack', *London Emergncies Trust.* https://londonemergenciestrust.org.uk/how-we-helped/london-bridgeborough-market-attack

p. 115 **a GoFundMe that raised nearly AU$24,000** https://www.gofundme.com/f/wpgbg-london-terror-affects-local-family

p. 116 **$4.4 million in charitable donations** 'Fund raises $6.3 million for victims and survivors of Pittsburgh synagogue shooting', *CBS News* (5 March 2019). https://www.cbsnews.com/news/pittsburgh-synagogue-shooting-tree-of-life-victims-survivors-families-fund/

p. 116 **following the massacre** Associated Press in Charleston, South Carolina, 'Emanuel AME church to give half of donations to Charleston victims', *The Guardian* (26 November 2015). https://www.theguardian.com/us-news/2015/nov/26/charleston-shooting-emanuel-ame-church-donations

p. 116 **a review of criminal injury compensation** 'New compensation scheme for victims of terrorism', *WiredGov* (17 July 2020). https://www.wired-gov.net/wg/news.nsf/articles/New+compensation+scheme+for+victims+of+terrorism+17072020101500?open

p. 117 **where Sara was killed** 'London Bridge attack: Sara Zelenak's parents begin charity bike ride', *BBC News* (23 June 2019). https://www.bbc.co.uk/news/uk-england-london-48736087

Chapter 6

p. 121 **announced in the *New York Times*** Merians, Sarah, 'Corey Briskin and Nicholas Maggipinto' (27 March 2016). https://www.nytimes.com/2016/03/27/fashion/weddings/corey-briskin-and-nicholas-maggipinto.html

p. 122 **on human eggs** 'Financial Compensation of Oocyte Donors: An Ethics Committee Opinion (2021)', *American Society for Reproductive Medicine* (2021). https://www.asrm.org/practice-guidance/ethics-opinions/financial-compensation-of-oocyte-donors-an-ethics-committee-opinion/?_t_tags=siteid%3A01216f06-3dc9-4ac9-96da-555740dd020c%2Clanguage%3Aen&_t_hit.id=ASRM_Models_Pages_ContentPage/_98baa829-2977-4c81-8781-b1845d7511a1_en&_t_hit.pos=9

p. 122 **are not appropriate** 'Financial compensation of oocyte donors', *American Society for Reproductive Medicine* (20 April 2007). https://www.fertstert.org/article/S0015-0282(07)00235-X/fulltext

p. 125 **quadrupled from 2011 to 2020** Deahl, Jo, '"Surrogacy is absolutely what I want to do"', *BBC News* (22 September 2021). https://www.bbc.co.uk/news/uk-58639955

p. 125 **passed by parliament in 2013** 'Same sex marriage becomes law', *Department for Digital, Culture, Media & Sport, Government Equalities Office, and The Rt Hon Maria Miller MP* (17 July 2013). https://www.gov.uk/government/news/same-sex-marriage-becomes-law

p. 125 **thousands of women** Kale, Sirin, '"Will the babies be left in a war zone?" The terrified Ukrainian surrogates – and the parents waiting for their children', *The Guardian* (10 March 2022). https://www.theguardian.com/lifeandstyle/2022/mar/10/will-the-babies-be-left-in-a-war-zone-the-terrified-ukrainian-surrogates-and-the-parents-waiting-for-their-children

p. 130 **a maximum of $207,500** 'Your Guide to Fertility Costs for Dads-to-Be' *Gay Parents To Be*, https://www.gayparentstobe.com/for-gay-men/financial-packages/

p. 130 **around $194,100** 'Surrogacy Budgeting Guide', *Men Having Babies* (2020). https://menhavingbabies.org/cms-data/depot/docs/Budgeting-Guide-USA_2020_MHB-Handout.pdf

p. 130 **over a million dollars a year** 'The Gay Parenting Assistance

Program (GPAP) of Men Having Babies', *Men Having Babies*. https://www.menhavingbabies.org/assistance/

p. 130 **One in six people worldwide** 'Infertility Prevalence Estimates, 1990–2021', *World Health Organisation* (3 April 2023). https://www.who.int/publications/i/item/9789200 68315

p. 130 **sperm counts have declined** Levine, Hagai; Jørgensen, Niels; Martino-Andrade, Anderson; Mendiola, Jaime; Weksler-Derri, Dan; Mindlis, Irina; Pinotti, Rachel; and Swan, Shanna H, 'Temporal trends in sperm count: a systematic review and meta-regression analysis', *OUP Academic*, Vol. 23, Issue 6 (November–December 2017). https://academic.oup.com/humupd/article/23/6/646/4035689?login=false

p. 131 **their mothers' generation** 'Childbearing for women born in different years, England and Wales: 2020', *Office for National Statistics* (27 January 2022). https://www.ons.gov.uk/peoplepopulationandcommunity/birthsdeathsandmarriages/conceptionandfertilityrates/bulletins/childbearingforwomen bornindifferentyearsenglandandwales/2020

p. 131 **by 2029** 'Global Fertility Services Market – Industry Trends and Forecast to 2029', *Data Bridge Market Research* (September 2022). https://www.databridgemarketresearch.com/reports/global-fertility-services-market

p. 131 **on the NHS** 'Fertility problems: assessment and treatment', *National Institute for Health and Care Excellence* (20 February 2013). https://www.nice.org.uk/guidance/cg156/ifp/chapter/in-vitro-fertilisation

p. 131 **one cycle of IVF** 'Availability: IVF', *NHS*. https://www.nhs.uk/conditions/ivf/availability/

p. 131 **a 2022 survey** 'The far-reaching trauma of infertility: Fertility Network UK survey' *Fertility Network UK* (2022). https://fertilitynetworkuk.org/the-far-reaching-trauma-of-infertility-fertility-network-uk-survey/

p. 135 **£20,000 for a cycle** 'Older women exploited by IVF clinics, says fertility watchdog', *BBC News* (22 April 2019). https://www.bbc.co.uk/news/uk-48008635

p. 137 **fertilizing an egg** Richter M.D., Michael A.; Haning Jr M.D., Ray V.; and Shapiro M.D., Sander S., 'Artificial donor insemination: fresh versus frozen semen; the patient as her own control', *Fertility and Sterility*, Vol. 41, Issue 2 (February 1984), pp. 277–280. https://www.sciencedirect.com/science/article/pii/S0015028216476041?via%3Dihub

p. 138 **barely studied** Robinson, K.; Galloway, K.; Bewley, S.; and Meads, C., 'Lesbian and bisexual women's gynaecological conditions: a systematic review and exploratory meta-analysis', *BJOG: An International Journal of Obstetrics and Gynaecology* (2017). https://obgyn.onlinelibrary.wiley.com/doi/full/10.1111/1471-0528.14414

p. 138 **the Gaia promotional video** Gaia + London Women's Clinic (12 August 2022). https://www.youtube.com/watch?v=0iEclgB7hIU

p. 138 **across the board** Meads, Catherine; Thorogood, Laura-Rose; Lindemann, Katy; and Bewley, Susan, 'Why Are the Proportions of In-Vitro Fertilisation Interventions for Same Sex Female Couples Increasing?', *National Library of Medicine* (30 November 2021). https://pubmed.ncbi.nlm.nih.gov/34946383/ Table 1

p. 139 **'fertility equality'** 'New Federal Bill Could Allow Tax Deduction for Surrogacy Expenses, Remove Discrimination Against LGBTQ Tax Payers', *Men Having Babies*. https://menhavingbabies.org/news/user-view/post.php?permalink=bill-surrogacy-expense-tax-dedication-legislation-tax-deduction-for-reproductive-treatments-in-lgbtq-community

p. 140 **£160,000–200,000 in the UK** 'The Cost of a Child in 2022: Summary and Recommendations', *Child Poverty Action Group* (November 2022). https://cpag.org.uk/sites/default/files/files/policypost/COAC_summary_recommendations.pdf

p. 140 **$310,00 in the US** Sawhill, Isabel V.; Welch, Morgan; and

Miller, Chris, 'It's getting more expensive to raise children. And government isn't doing much to help', *Brookings* (30 August 2022). https://www.brookings.edu/blog/up-front/2022/08/30/its-getting-more-expensive-to-raise-children-and-government-isnt-doing-much-to-help/

p. 140 **just under £70 million** *NHS* (January 2023). https://resolution.nhs.uk/wp-content/uploads/2023/01/FOI_5735_Obstetrics-and-wrongful-birth.pdf

p. 140 **high court claim** Associated Press, 'Father loses damages claim over forged IVF signature', *The Guardian* (17 December 2018). https://www.theguardian.com/law/2018/dec/17/father-loses-damages-claim-over-forged-ivf-signature

p. 141 **the consent form** ARB v. IVF Hammersmith, *Royal Courts of Justice* (17 December 2018). https://www.judiciary.uk/wp-content/uploads/2018/12/arb-v-ivf-hammersmith-final.pdf

p. 141 **over £1 million** 'Schrödinger's consent: ARB v IVF Hammersmith Limited & R', *Hempsons* (13 November 2017). https://www.hempsons.co.uk/news-articles/schrodingers-consent-arb-v-ivf-hammersmith-limited-r/

p. 141 **couldn't be awarded anything** Associated Press, 'Father loses damages claim over forged IVF signature', *The Guardian* (17 December 2018). https://www.theguardian.com/law/2018/dec/17/father-loses-damages-claim-over-forged-ivf-signature

p. 141 **£19.5 million** Urwin, Jenny, '£19.5m for wrongful birth of boy with spina bifida and chromosome 9 abnormality', *Fieldfisher*. https://www.fieldfisher.com/en/injury-claims/case-studies/19m-for-wrongful-birth-of-boy-with-spina-bifida

p. 141 **a six-figure sum** 'Mother wins ruling over Royal Berkshire NHS Down's syndrome test failure', *BBC News* (8 October 2019). https://www.bbc.co.uk/news/uk-england-berkshire-49980157

p. 141 **Down's syndrome** Bagot, Martin, 'Mum who would have aborted baby with Down's syndrome gets NHS payout', *Mirror*

(8 October 2019). https://www.mirror.co.uk/news/uk-news/mum-who-would-aborted-baby-20541139

p. 141 **Edyta's medical notes** As reported in the judgement Edyta Ewelina Mordel v Royal Berkshire NHS Foundation Trust (8 October 2019). https://vlex.co.uk/vid/edyta-ewelina-mordel-v-818736401

p. 142 **similar failings** 'Mother wins ruling over Royal Berkshire NHS Down's syndrome test failure', *BBC News* (8 October 2019). https://www.bbc.co.uk/news/uk-england-berkshire-49980157

Chapter 7

p. 146 **the richest person** McEvoy, Jemima, 'Where The Richest Live: The Cities With The Most Billionaires 2022', *Forbes* (5 April 2022). https://www.forbes.com/sites/jemimamcevoy/2022/04/05/where-the-richest-live-the-cities-with-the-most-billionaires-2022/?sh=1e557ffb4e09

p. 150 **around $10 billion a year** The Chronicle of Philanthropy, 'A list of America's top 50 donors of 2020', *AP News* (10 February 2021). https://apnews.com/article/technology-amazoncom-inc-michael-bloomberg-jeff-bezos-philanthropy-43ff7817a0c8b7babfd2ab9bb67d3b5e

p. 154 **$1 billion a year** 'We aim to cost-effectively direct around $1 billion annually by 2025', *GiveWell* (22 November 2021). https://blog.givewell.org/2021/11/22/we-aim-to-cost-effectively-direct-around-1-billion-annually-by-2025/

p. 156 **$2,000–3,000 per life saved** You can see their working for this here: https://docs.google.com/spreadsheets/d/1CuIwrlmOchJMRojhKLiuitDXTnT0XJQVs0qAdX6Hi4E/edit#gid=1350747058

p. 158 **anywhere else in the US** Fortson, Danny, 'American nightmare: the homelessness crisis in San Francisco', *The*

Times (29 August 2021). https://www.thetimes.co.uk/article/san-francisco-homelessness-crisis-tent-cities-bclgk20s5

p. 159 **chronic medical conditions** Hepler, Lauren and Knight, Heather, 'S.F. homeless deaths more than doubled during the pandemic's first year – but not because of COVID', *San Francisco Chronicle* (10 March 2022). https://www.sfchronicle.com/sf/article/San-Francisco-homeless-deaths-more-than-doubled-16990683.php

p. 159 **'More permissive policy'** 'We seek to reduce the harms caused by excessively restrictive local land use regulations', *Open Philanthropy*. https://www.openphilanthropy.org/focus/land-use-reform/

p. 165 **$26.5 billion** 'Sam Bankman-Fried', *Forbes*. https://www.forbes.com/profile/sam-bankman-fried/?sh=455ed2984449

p. 165 **effective causes** Lewis-Kraus, Gideon, 'The Reluctant Prophet of Effective Altruism', *The New Yorker* (8 August 2022). https://www.newyorker.com/magazine/2022/08/15/the-reluctant-prophet-of-effective-altruism

p. 167 **a blog post** 'Why Is It So Expensive to Save Lives?', *GiveWell* (December 2021). https://www.givewell.org/cost-to-save-a-life

p. 168 **'Sam Bankman-Fried perpetrated** 'Sam Bankman-Fried found guilty on all seven criminal fraud counts', CNBC, 2 November 2023. https://www.cnbc.com/2023/11/02/sam-bankman-fried-found-guilty-on-all-seven-criminal-fraud-counts.html

p. 168 **from Bankman-Fried** As explained in this Twitter thread: https://twitter.com/willmacaskill/status/1591218014707671040?s=43&t=PojMJra02nB-2Ax9Lg5tHA

Chapter 8

p. 170 **£1.798 million** 'NHS treats first patient with the "world's most expensive drug"', *NHS England* (1 June 2021). https://

www.england.nhs.uk/2021/06/nhs-treats-first-patient-with-the-worlds-most-expensive-drug/

p. 171 **genetic cause of death** Tisdale, Sarah and Pellizzoni, Livio, 'Disease Mechanisms and Therapeutic Approaches in Spinal Muscular Atrophy', *National Library of Medicine* (10 June 2015). https://www.ncbi.nlm.nih.gov/pmc/articles/PMC4461682/

p. 171 **1.67 million** 'Spinal Muscular Atrophy – A Brief Summary', *Spinal Muscular Atrophy UK*. https://smauk.org.uk/sma-summary-info

p. 172 **Type 1** Verhaart, Ingrid E. C.; Robertson, Agata; Wilson, Ian J.; Aartsma-Rus, Annemieke; Cameron, Shona; Jones, Cynthia C.; Cook, Suzanne F.; and Lochmüller, Hans, 'Prevalence, incidence and carrier frequency of 5q-linked spinal muscular atrophy – a literature review', *National Library of Medicine* (4 July 2017). https://pubmed.ncbi.nlm.nih.gov/28676062/

p. 172 **Spinraza** Grant, Charley, 'Surprise Drug Approval is Holiday Gift for Biogen', *Wall Street Journal* (27 December 2016). https://www.wsj.com/articles/surprise-drug-approval-is-holiday-gift-for-biogen-1482856447

p. 172 **babies with SMA1** 'EPAR summary for the public: Spinraza (Nusinersen)', *European Medicines Agency* (2017). https://www.ema.europa.eu/en/documents/overview/spinraza-epar-summary-public_en.pdf

p. 172 **every year that follows** Erman, Michael, 'NHS England, Biogen reach deal on pricey drug for deadly disorder', *Reuters* (15 May 2019). https://www.reuters.com/article/uk-biogen-england-idUKKCN1SK2QH

p. 173 **NICE approval** 'NHS England to fund first ever treatment for children with rare muscle-wasting condition', *NHS England* (15 May 2019). https://www.england.nhs.uk/2019/05/nhs-england-to-fund-first-ever-treatment-for-children-with-rare-muscle-wasting-condition/

p. 174 **significant cost savings** Kuchler, Hannah, 'Novartis wins approval for world's most expensive drug', *Financial Times* (24 May 2019). https://www.ft.com/content/10086870-7e50-11e9-81d2-f785092ab560

p. 174 **forever confidential** 'NHS England strikes deal on life-saving gene-therapy drug that can help babies with rare genetic disease move and walk', *NHS England* (8 March 2021). https://www.england.nhs.uk/2021/03/nhs-england-strikes-deal-on-life-saving-gene-therapy-drug-that-can-help-babies-with-rare-genetic-disease-move-and-walk/

p. 175 **ITV News** Frost, Charlie, 'Essex family's desperate plea for life-saving treatment for 8-month-old Edward', *ITV News* (3 June 2021). https://www.itv.com/news/anglia/2021-06-01/essex-familys-desperate-plea-for-life-saving-treatment-for-8-month-old-edward

p. 175 **This is really cruel** Jones, Charlie, 'Colchester baby's parents feel "abandoned" over £1.7m drug', *BBC News* (24 May 2021). https://www.bbc.co.uk/news/uk-england-essex-57171722

p. 178 **NICE's first official act** Rawlins, Michael D., 'National Institute for Clinical Excellence: NICE works', *Journal of the Royal Society of Medicine*, Vol. 108, Issue 6 (2015). https://journals.sagepub.com/doi/10.1177/0141076815587658

p. 178 **By March 2020** 'Technology appraisal data: appraisal recommendations', *National Institute for Health and Care Excellence*. https://www.nice.org.uk/about/what-we-do/our-programmes/nice-guidance/nice-technology-appraisal-guidance/data/appraisal-recommendations

p. 179 **QALYs are calculated** Glossary, *National Institute for Health and Care Excellence*. https://www.nice.org.uk/glossary?letter=q

p. 181 **$77,000 in Taiwan** McDougall, Jean A.; Furnback, Wesley E., Wang, Bruce C. M.; and Mahlich, Jörg, 'Understanding the global measurement of willingness to pay in health', *National Library of Medicine* (2020). https://www.ncbi.nlm.nih.gov/pmc/articles/PMC7048225/

p. 181 **Obamacare** 'Public Law 111–148: The Patient Protection and Affordable Care Act', 111th Congress (23 March 2010). https://www.congress.gov/111/plaws/publ148/PLAW-111publ148.pdf

p. 181 **$50,000 to $200,000** '2020–2023 Value Assessment Framework', *Institute for Clinical and Economic Review* (31 January 2020). https://icer.org/wp-content/uploads/2020/10/ICER_2020_2023_VAF_102220.pdf

p. 184 **'One way or another** Whipple, Tom, 'Lifesaving drug Spinraza, rejected for NHS, wins $3m prize', *The Times* (18 October 2018). https://www.thetimes.co.uk/article/lifesaving-drug-spinraza-rejected-for-nhs-wins-3m-prize-qlflw5h6t

p. 186 **February 2022** 'NHS to roll out life-saving gene therapy for rare disease affecting babies', *NHS England* (4 February 2022). https://www.england.nhs.uk/2022/02/nhs-to-roll-out-life-saving-gene-therapy-for-rare-disease-affecting-babies/

p. 186 **European regulator** 'Orchard Therapeutics Receives EC Approval for Libmeldy™ for the Treatment of Early-Onset Metachromatic Leukodystrophy (MLD)', *Orchard Therapeutics*. https://ir.orchard-tx.com/news-releases/news-release-details/orchard-therapeutics-receives-ec-approval-libmeldytm-treatment

p. 186 **Over 3,000 babies a year** 'Abortion statistics, England and Wales: 2020', *Department of Health and Social Care* (2020). https://www.gov.uk/government/statistics/abortion-statistics-for-england-and-wales-2020/abortion-statistics-england-and-wales-2020#key-points-in-2020

p. 188 **£8,000** 'NHS deal on spinal muscular atrophy at home treatment', *NHS England* (19 November 2021). https://www.england.nhs.uk/2021/11/nhs-deal-on-spinal-muscular-atrophy-at-home-treatment/

p. 189 **Novartis gives away** 'When a lottery "wins" sick babies life-saving drugs', BBC News, 30 January 2020. https://www.bbc.co.uk/news/world-us-canada-51181840

p. 189 **'real-life hunger games'** Jani-Friend, Isabelle, 'Zolgensma Lottery: A Real Life Hunger Games', *Just Treatment* (3 February 2020). https://justtreatment.org/news/2020/1/29/zolgensma-lottery-a-real-life-hunger-games

Chapter 9

p. 190 **16,975 people** 'Number of COVID-19 patients in hospital', *Our World in Data*. https://ourworldindata.org/grapher/current-covid-patients-hospital?country=GBR

p. 191 **451 people** https://github.com/CSSEGISandData/COVID-19

p. 193 **more than 150 protesters** Gayle, Damien and Busby, Mattha, 'Police arrest 155 anti-lockdown protesters in London', *The Guardian* (28 November 2020). https://www.theguardian.com/world/2020/nov/28/met-police-anti-lockdown-protest-london

p. 194 ***The Argus*** Doherty-Cove, Jody, 'Lockdown protest leader was on Labour's Executive Committee', *The Argus* (22 May 2020). https://www.theargus.co.uk/news/18467876.lockdown-protest-leader-labours-executive-committee/

p. 196 **Covid death figures** 'The pandemic's true death toll', *Economist* (25 October 2022). https://www.economist.com/graphic-detail/coronavirus-excess-deaths-estimates?fsrc=core-app-economist?utm_medium=social-media.content.np&utm_source=twitter&utm_campaign=editorial-social&utm_content=discovery.content

p. 197 **stay at home** Sandford, Alasdair, 'Coronavirus: Half of humanity now on lockdown as 90 countries call for confinement', *Euronews* (2 April 2020). https://www.euronews.com/2020/04/02/coronavirus-in-europe-spain-s-death-toll-hits-10-000-after-record-950-new-deaths-in-24-hou

p. 197 **World Bank** 'COVID-19 to Add as Many as 150 Million Extreme Poor by 2021', *World Bank* (7 October 2020). https://www.worldbank.org/en/news/press-release/2020/10/07/covid-19-to-add-as-many-as-150-million-extreme-poor-by-2021

p. 197 **shutting the economy down** Yakusheva, Olga; van den Broek-Altenburg, Eline; Brekke, Gayle; and Atherly, Adam, 'Lives saved and lost in the first six month of the US COVID-19 pandemic: A retrospective cost-benefit analysis', *Plos One* (21 January 2022). https://journals.plos.org/plosone/article?id=10.1371/journal.pone.0261759

p. 198 **compared with 2019** 'Alcohol-specific deaths in the UK: registered in 2020', *Office for National Statistics* (7 December 2021). https://www.ons.gov.uk/peoplepopulationandcommunity/healthandsocialcare/causesofdeath/bulletins/alcoholrelateddeathsintheunitedkingdom/registeredin2020

p. 198 **during lockdown** 'Shifts in alcohol consumption during the pandemic could lead to thousands of extra deaths in England', *University of Sheffield* (26 July 2022). https://www.sheffield.ac.uk/news/shifts-alcohol-consumption-during-pandemic-could-lead-thousands-extra-deaths-england

p. 198 **calls and contacts** 'A year of lockdown: Refuge releases new figures showing dramatic increase in activity', *Refuge* (23 March 2021). https://www.refuge.org.uk/a-year-of-lockdown/

p. 198 **same calendar period** Smith, Karen Ingala, 'Coronavirus Doesn't Cause Men's Violence Against Women' (15 April 2020). https://kareningalasmith.com/2020/04/15/coronavirus-doesnt-cause-mens-violence-against-women/

p. 198 **same period in 2019** 'Serious incident notifications', *Gov.uk* (15 January 2021). https://explore-education-statistics.service.gov.uk/find-statistics/serious-incident-notifications/2020-21-part-1-apr-to-sep

p. 198 **a televised address** The televised address where Cuomo says this can be viewed at '"How much is a human life worth?" Cuomo questions the costs of reopening', *ABC7 New York* (5 May 2020). https://www.yahoo.com/entertainment/much-human-life-worth-cuomo-175254762.html

p. 198 **'whatever it takes'** 'Speech: Chancellor of the Exchequer, Rishi Sunak on COVID19 response', *HM Treasury and The Rt*

Hon Rishi Sunak MP (17 March 2020). https://www.gov.uk/government/speeches/chancellor-of-the-exchequer-rishi-sunak-on-covid19-response

p. 199 ***The Spectator*** Wood, Simon, 'Covid, lockdown and the economics of valuing lives', *The Spectator* (3 October 2020). https://www.spectator.co.uk/article/how-much-does-it-cost-to-save-lives-from-covid

p. 199 **£550 billion** https://obr.uk//docs/dlm_uploads/CCS1021486854-001_OBR-EFO-October-2021_CS_Web-Accessible_v2.pdf – Table 3.30

p. 199 **three million** 'Direct and Indirect Impacts of COVID-19 on Excess Deaths and Morbidity: Executive Summary', Table 5, *Department of Health and Social Care, Office for National Statistics, Government Actuary's Department* and *Home Office* (15 July 2020). https://assets.publishing.service.gov.uk/government/uploads/system/uploads/attachment_data/file/907616/s0650-direct-indirect-impacts-covid-19-excess-deaths-morbidity-sage-48.pdf

p. 200 **landmark report** Marmot, Professor Sir Michael; Allen, Jessica; Boyce, Tammy; Goldblatt, Peter; and Morrison, Joana, 'Health Equity in England: The Marmot Review 10 Years On', *Health Foundation* (February 2020). https://www.health.org.uk/publications/reports/the-marmot-review-10-years-on

p. 201 **1 in 19 chance** Spiegelhalter, David and Masters, Anthony, *Covid by Numbers: Making Sense of the Pandemic with Data* (London: Pelican Books, 2021)

p. 202 **still rising** Wood, Simon N. and Wit, Ernst C., 'Was R < 1 before the English lockdowns? On modelling mechanistic detail, causality and inference about Covid-19', *Plos One* (22 September 2021). https://www.maths.ed.ac.uk/~swood34/rep41-plos.pdf

Chapter 10

p. 215 **kidnapped every year** 'Kidnapping', *United Nations Office on Drugs and Crime* (2017). https://dataunodc.un.org/data/crime/kidnapping

p. 215 **foreign nationals** 'Kidnap for Ransom in 2022', *Control Risks* (19 April 2022). https://www.controlrisks.com/our-thinking/insights/kidnap-for-ransom-in-2022

p. 216 **No demands were made** There is a transcript of this conversation, and all the conversations Paul and Rachel had with Stephen, in the Chandlers' memoir of their time in captivity: Chandler, Paul and Chandler, Rachel with Edworthy, Sarah, *Hostage: A Year at Gunpoint with Somali Gangsters* (Edinburgh: Mainstream, 2012)

p. 217 **164 kidnappings** 'Piracy around the world: all the attacks by pirates in 2009', *The Guardian DataBlog*. https://www.theguardian.com/news/datablog/2009/oct/27/piracy-attacks-somalia-2009

p. 217 **$3 million in cash** Ibrahim, Mohamed and Bowley, Graham, 'Pirates Say They Freed Saudi Tanker for $3 Million', *New York Times* (9 January 2009). https://www.nytimes.com/2009/01/10/world/africa/10somalia.html#:~:text=MOGADISHU%2C%20Somalia%20%E2%80%94%20A%20Saudi%2D,the%20tanker%20was%20being%20held.

p. 220 **'I have no doubt'** 'Footage of Couple Kidnapped by Somali Pirates', On Demand News (20 November 2009). https://www.youtube.com/watch?v=Rbfl9yjTWjI

p. 224 **£12,000 a month** Estimate taken from Chandler, Paul and Chandler, Rachel with Edworthy, Sarah, *Hostage: A Year at Gunpoint with Somali Gangsters* (Edinburgh: Mainstream, 2012)

p. 224 **a contribution** 'Former cabbie who helped to broker ransom deal is a hero, says his family', *Evening Standard* (12 April 2012). https://www.standard.co.uk/hp/front/former-cabbie-who-helped-to-broker-ransom-deal-is-a-hero-says-his-family-6536054.html

p. 225 **attempts at escape** Shortland, Anja, 'Inside the ransom business – why kidnapping rarely pays', *The Conversation* (8 February 2019). https://theconversation.com/inside-the-ransom-business-why-kidnapping-rarely-pays-110678

p. 225 **$77.3 million** 'Kidnap for Ransom in 2022', *Control Risks* (19 April 2022). https://www.controlrisks.com/our-thinking/insights/kidnap-for-ransom-in-2022

p. 226 **K&R insurance** Simon, Joel, 'The business of kidnapping: inside the secret world of hostage negotiation', *The Guardian* (25 January 2019). https://www.theguardian.com/news/2019/jan/25/business-of-kidnapping-inside-the-secret-world-of-hostage-negotiation-ransom-insurance

p. 227 **stock in trade** Shortland, Anja, *Kidnap: Inside the Ransom Business* (Oxford: Oxford University Press, 2019) is a very readable but also brainy primer on the economics of the kidnap for ransom market.

p. 230 **piracy in Somalia** 'Vingt ans pour Afweyne, le "roi des pirates somaliens"', *La Libre* (15 March 2016). https://www.lalibre.be/belgique/2016/03/15/vingt-ans-pour-afweyne-le-roi-des-pirates-somaliens-RGWZWBGCRBHMFFISNQ 6UPLYDPQ/

p. 234 ***Daily Mail*** Johnson, Angella, 'Kidnapped by pirates: Tortured and held hostage in a desert hell for 388 days, so why IS this couple setting sail again?', *Daily Mail* (28 October 2012). https://www.dailymail.co.uk/news/article-2223979/Paul-Rachel-Chandler-Kidnapped-pirates-Tortured-held-hostage-desert-hell-388-days-IS-couple-setting-sail-again.html

p. 234 **on their blog** http://blog.mailasail.com/lynnrival/posts/2010/11/15/117-free

p. 234 **twenty years in jail** Johnson, Angella, 'Kidnapped by pirates: Tortured and held hostage in a desert hell for 388 days, so why IS this couple setting sail again?', *Daily Mail* (28 October 2012). https://www.dailymail.co.uk/news/article-2223979/Paul-

Rachel-Chandler-Kidnapped-pirates-Tortured-held-hostage-desert-hell-388-days-IS-couple-setting-sail-again.html

p. 234 **'experimental vaccines'** http://blog.mailasail.com/lynnrival/posts/2021/12/26/443-a-time-for-new-thinking

Chapter 11

p. 236 **in the video** https://www.facebook.com/watch/?ref=search&v=324967686058553&external_log_id=284a9b9b-288d-4f1a-aae9-19657819731a&q=aliyu%20na%20idris

p. 236 **$48,000, at the time** https://www.exchangerates.org.uk/NGN-GBP-02_10_2021-exchange-rate-history.html

p. 236 **sandwich board** '"Dangote, Bua Can Buy Me", Man Who Put Self For Sale Speaks', *Trust TV News* (26 October 2021). https://www.youtube.com/watch?v=sBEk4c9Hdrs

p. 237 **forbidden in Islam** Abubakar, Mansur, 'Man in Nigeria who put himself up for sale arrested', *BBC News* (27 October 2021). https://www.bbc.co.uk/news/live/world-africa-47639452?ns_mchannel=social&ns_source=twitter&ns_campaign=bbc_live&ns_linkname=617920ac17cef931bb3d2a59%26Man+in+Nigeria+who+put+himself+up+for+sale+arrested%262021-10-27T10%3A53%3A10.861Z&ns_fee=0&pinned_post_locator=urn%3Aasset%3A05c4a963-08c8-4907-9ef4-9dd4e7733324&pinned_post_asset_id=617920ac17cef931bb3d2a59&pinned_post_type=share&at_medium=custom7&at_custom1=%5Bpost+type%5D&at_custom2=twitter&at_campaign=64&at_custom3=BBC+Africa&at_custom4=F9CE943C-372D-11EC-9C8C-4F7F96E8478F OR 'Aliyu Na Idris put himself up for sale for N20M, Kano Hisbah arrest am – See why', *BBC News* (27 October 2021). https://www.bbc.com/pidgin/world-59034461 but this is in Pidgin

p. 238 **£1,600** https://humancost.carlo.im/. This is a beautiful infographic provided by the Kantar Information is Beautiful awards. It is based on data detailed in this spreadsheet:

https://docs.google.com/spreadsheets/d/1Wekpe3ZY1l qKHgTbmEdJlv5Y9IUWeUK9bUbwGAPm2sM/edit#gid=1

p. 238 **£31,000** Evans, Robert Jr., 'The Economics of American Negro Slavery 1830–1860', *Aspects of Labor Economics* (Princeton: Princeton University Press, 1962), pp. 185–256. Out of print. https://www.nber.org/system/files/chapters/c0606/c0606.pdf: $1,100, which is $40,000 in today's money, as cited here: https://www.in2013dollars.com/us/inflation/1860?endYear=2024&amount=1100&future_pct=0.03, and converted into GBP in August 2023

p. 238 **in all their forms** 'Universal Declaration of Human Rights', *United Nations*. https://www.un.org/en/about-us/universal-declaration-of-human-rights

p. 238 **$400 apiece** Elbagir, Nima; Razek, Raja; Platt, Alex; and Jones, Bryony, 'People for sale: Where lives are auctioned for $400', *CNN* (15 November 2017). https://edition.cnn.com/2017/11/14/africa/libya-migrant-auctions/index.html

p. 239 **$500 each** Anderson, Imogen, 'Afghan baby girl sold for $500 by starving family', *BBC News* (25 October 2021). https://www.bbc.co.uk/news/av/world-asia-59034650

p. 239 **enough to eat** 'In the grip of hunger: only 5 percent of Afghan families have enough to eat', *World Food Programme* (23 September 2021). https://www.wfp.org/stories/grip-hunger-only-5-percent-afghan-families-have-enough-eat

p. 239 **one of their daughters** 'Afghanistan: Poor families sell underage daughters into marriage', Sky News (3 February 2022). https://www.youtube.com/watch?v=27tK0XQooXY

p. 239 **16,938 potential victims** 'Modern Slavery: National Referral Mechanism and Duty to Notify statistics UK, end of year summary 2022', *Home Office* (2 March 2023). https://www.gov.uk/government/statistics/modern-slavery-national-referral-mechanism-and-duty-to-notify-statistics-uk-end-of-year-summary-2022/modern-slavery-national-referral-mechanism-and-duty-to-notify-statistics-uk-end-of-year-summary-2022

p. 239 **50 million people** 'Global Estimates of Modern Slavery: Forced Labour and Forced Marriage', *International Labour Organization, Walk Free* and *International Organization for Migration* (September 2022). https://www.ilo.org/wcmsp5/groups/public/---ed_norm/---ipec/documents/publication/wcms_854733.pdf

p. 239 **72 per cent in 2016** 'Global Report on Trafficking in Persons 2022', *United Nations Office on Drugs and Crime* (2022). https://www.unodc.org/documents/data-and-analysis/glotip/2022/GLOTiP_2022_web.pdf

p. 240 **£3,000–£4,000** Webb, Sarah and Burrows, John, 'Research Report 15: Organised immigration crime: a post-conviction study', *Home Office* (July 2009). https://webarchive.nationalarchives.gov.uk/ukgwa/20110314171826/http://rds.homeoffice.gov.uk/rds/pdfs09/horr15c.pdf

p. 241 **each other's arms** Boffey, Daniel, 'Vietnamese people smuggler jailed for 15 years over deaths of 39 people', *The Guardian* (19 January 2022). https://www.theguardian.com/uk-news/2022/jan/19/vietnamese-people-smuggler-jailed-for-15-years-over-deaths-of-39-people

p. 241 **Vietnamese biscuits** Waterfield, Bruno, 'Couple suffocated in each other's arms, trial over Vietnamese migrant lorry deaths told', *The Times* (16 December 2021). https://www.thetimes.co.uk/article/couple-suffocated-in-each-others-arms-trial-over-vietnamese-migrant-lorry-deaths-told-rn8772r6s

p. 241 **Pham Thi Tra My** 'Essex lorry deaths: Vietnamese families fear relatives among dead', *BBC News* (25 October 2019). https://www.bbc.co.uk/news/uk-england-50185788

p. 241 **Sky News** 'The Perilous Journey That Left 39 Dead', *Sky News*. https://news.sky.com/story/essex-lorry-deaths-the-perilous-journey-that-left-39-people-dead-12169421

p. 241 **in a nail bar** Thompson, Paul, '"What sort of people can put others into a container and let them die?": Family of "youngest death truck victim', 19, beg for her body to be returned home after they clubbed together to pay smugglers £8,000 for her new life in Britain', *Daily Mail* (28 October 2019). https://www.dailymail.co.uk/news/article-7618377/Family-youngest-death-truck-victim-19-beg-body-returned-home.html

p. 241 **victims of trafficking** 'Modern Slavery: National Referral Mechanism and Duty to Notify statistics UK, end of year summary 2022', *Home Office* (2 March 2023). https://www.gov.uk/government/statistics/modern-slavery-national-referral-mechanism-and-duty-to-notify-statistics-uk-end-of-year-summary-2022/modern-slavery-national-referral-mechanism-and-duty-to-notify-statistics-uk-end-of-year-summary-2022#annex; 'Combating modern slavery experienced by Vietnamese nationals en route to, and within, the UK', *Independent Anti-Slavery Commissioner* (2017). https://www.antislaverycommissioner.co.uk/media/1159/iasc-report-combating-modern-slavery-experience-by-vietname-nationals-en-route-to-and-within-the-uk.pdf

p. 241 **nail salons** 'Precarious Journeys: Mapping Vulnerabilities of Victims of Trafficking from Vietnam to Europe', *Anti-Slavery International, Every Child Protected Against Trafficking (ECPAT) UK, Pacific Links Foundation* and *Home Office* (2019). https://www.antislavery.org/wp-content/uploads/2019/03/Precarious-Journeys-full-report.pdf

p. 242 **previous five years** 'The newly National Hair & Beauty Federation releases key industry statistics for 2019', *ProHair* (26 November 2019). https://professionalhairdresser.co.uk/news/the-newly-national-hair-beauty-federation-releases-key-industry-statistics-for-2019/

p. 242 **tragic incident** https://twitter.com/pritipatel/status/1186931323514097665

p. 242 **Gangmasters and Labour Abuse Authority** 'Industry Profiles – Nail Bars – 2020', *Gangmasters and Labour Abuse*

Authority (2020). https://www.gla.gov.uk/who-we-are/modern-slavery/industry-profiles-nail-bars-2020/

p. 242 **anti-trafficking charities** 'Spot the Signs: Nail Salons', *Stop the Traffik*. https://www.stopthetraffik.org/what-is-human-trafficking/spot-the-signs/nail-salons/

p. 242 **British Beauty Council** Beauty Editor, 'The dark side of nail bars', *British Beauty Council* (27 January 2020). https://britishbeautycouncil.com/the-dark-side-of-nail-bars/

p. 242 ***Stylist* magazine** Qureshi, Sophie, 'Nail salons are used for modern slavery. Here's how to spot an ethical one', *Stylist* (2019). https://www.stylist.co.uk/beauty/ethical-nail-salons-issues-exploitation-workers/201334

p. 242 **popular as ever** 'Nails: United Kingdom', *Statista* (2023). https://www.statista.com/outlook/cmo/beauty-personal-care/cosmetics/nails/united-kingdom

p. 248 **10 per cent of GDP** 'Philippines: Remittances, percent of GDP', *The Gobal Economy* (2021). https://www.theglobaleconomy.com/Philippines/remittances_percent_GDP/

Chapter 12

p. 261 **promotional video** Shreves, Garland, 'Research For Life Tour', Research for Life (12 August 2020). https://www.youtube.com/watch?v=1Kiuc3KNnxk

p. 262 **10,000 families** https://www.researchforlife.org/about-us/

p. 264 **in Arizona** https://www.aatb.org/accredited-bank-search?title=&sort_by=title&sort_order=ASC&field_geo%5Bvalue%5D=arizona&field_geo%5Bdistance%5D%5Bfrom%5D=40000&q=https%3A//www.aatb.org/accredited-bank-search%3Ftitle%3D%26sort_by%3Dtitle%26sort_order%3DASC%26field_geo%255Bvalue%255D%3Darizona%26field_vvfgeo%255Bdistance%255D%255Bfrom%255D%3D40000&f%5B0%5D=tissue%3ANon-Transplant%20Anatomical%20Material%20%28NAM%29

p. 264 **7 per cent** Innes, Stephanie, 'Arizona is a hotbed for the cadaver industry, and potential donors have plenty of options', *AZ Central* (10 June 2019). https://eu.azcentral.com/in-depth/news/local/arizona-health/2019/06/10/arizona-has-thriving-business-based-whole-body-donations-donate-body-to-science/3579828002/

p. 264 **Reuters investigation** Grow, Brian and Shiffman, John, 'The Body Trade: Cashing in on the donated dead: A Reuters Series', Part 1, *Reuters Investigates* (24 October 2017). https://www.reuters.com/investigates/special-report/usa-bodies-brokers/

p. 265 **he told reporters** Innes, Stephanie, 'For-profit body donation executive wants to be an Arizona legislator', *AZ Central* (2020). https://eu.azcentral.com/story/news/politics/elections/2020/08/21/phoenix-body-donation-executive-garland-shreves-seeking-seat-arizona-legislature-district-27/5610068002/

p. 268 **for profit** 'Colorado funeral home owner accused of selling body parts and giving clients fake ashes is sentenced to 20 years in prison', *CBS News* (4 January 2023). https://www.cbsnews.com/news/megan-hess-sentenced-colorado-funeral-home-owner-accused-selling-body-parts/

p. 268 **hazardous shipping laws** 'U.S. v. Rathburn et al: Court Docket #16-CR-20043', United States Attorney's Office: Eastern District of Michigan (updated 1 April 2022). https://www.justice.gov/usao-edmi/us-v-rathburn-et-al-court-docket-16-cr-20043

p. 268 **HIV and hepatitis** Grow, Brian and Shiffman, John, 'The Body Trade: Cashing in on the donated dead: A Reuters Series', Part 4, *Reuters Investigates* (31 October 2017). https://www.reuters.com/investigates/special-report/usa-bodies-rathburn/

p. 269 **pollution charge** Grow, Brian and Shiffman, John, 'The Body Trade: Cashing in on the donated dead: A Reuters Series', Part 1, *Reuters Investigates* (24 October 2017). https://www.reuters.com/investigates/special-report/usa-bodies-brokers/

p. 269 **he said at the time** Innes, Stephanie, '"Cooler filled with male genitalia" found in raid of Phoenix body-donation company', *AZ Central* (2019). https://eu.azcentral.com/story/news/local/arizona-health/2019/07/19/cooler-penises-frankenstein-head-found-phoenix-body-donation-company/1720254001/

p. 269 **national market** 'Protect the Dignity of Those Who Donate Their Bodies for Medical Research and Give Peace of Mind to Families', *National Funeral Directors Association*. https://nfda.org/advocacy/current-legislation/body-broker-bill

p. 270 **since 2011** Osborne, John, 'Sullivan County ends pauper burial service', *Chattanooga Times Free Press* (27 November 2011). https://www.timesfreepress.com/news/2011/nov/27/sullivan-ends-pauper-burial-service/

p. 271 **anyone he likes** https://d27322ujth7jn8.cloudfront.net/wp-content/uploads/Arizona-Donor-Self-Registration-Packet-rev-102422.pdf

p. 272 **Pizza Express** https://global-uploads.webflow.com/5df3d56e20b6d37f8de5e660/62e84f25c4483c6f11b63bb9_science-care-self-consent-form-packet-2022v2.pdf

p. 274 **radio reporters** 'The Resurrection Men', BBC World Service (9 June 2015). https://www.bbc.co.uk/programmes/p02sr293

p. 275 **$1,100** Reported in Innes, Stephanie, '"Cooler filled with male genitalia" found in raid of Phoenix body-donation company', *AZ Central* (2019). https://eu.azcentral.com/story/news/local/arizona-health/2019/07/19/cooler-penises-frankenstein-head-found-phoenix-body-donation-company/1720254001/

p. 275 **$5,000** Grow, Brian and Shiffman, John, 'The Body Trade: Cashing in on the donated dead: A Reuters Series', Part 3, *Reuters Investigates* (26 October 2017). https://www.reuters.com/investigates/special-report/usa-bodies-science/#slideshow-slideshow-pricelist

p. 275 **$4,600 per organ** Bengali, Shashank and Mostaghim, Ramin, '"Kidney for sale": Iran has a legal market for the organs, but the system doesn't always work', *LA Times* (15 October 2017).

https://www.latimes.com/world/middleeast/la-fg-iran-kidney-20171015-story.html

p. 275 **$3,800** Salehi, Nasir Ahmad, 'Poor and Displaced Fall Victim to Herat's Illegal Kidney Trade', *Tolo News* (7 February 2021). https://tolonews.com/afghanistan-169833

p. 275 **$1.7 billion a year** Mavrellis, Channing, 'Transnational Crime and the Developing World', *Global Financial Integrity* (27 March 2017). https://gfintegrity.org/report/transnational-crime-and-the-developing-world/

p. 276 **United Nations Office on Drugs and Crime** 'High-Level Launch Event: UNODC Toolkit on the Investigation and Prosecution of Trafficking in Persons for Organ Removal', *United Nations Office on Drugs and Crime* (25 October 2022). https://media.un.org/en/asset/k1p/k1p9jd6kx5

p. 276 **$3,000 a time** Williams, Carol J., 'Pay ban on donor organs doesn't include bone marrow, court says', *LA Times* (2 December 2011). https://www.latimes.com/local/la-xpm-2011-dec-02-la-me-bone-marrow-20111202-story.html

p. 276 **a dollar an ounce** https://www.onlythebreast.com/

p. 276 **$30 to $50 in the US** Greenberg, Zoe, 'What Is the Blood of a Poor Person Worth?' *New York Times* (1 February 2019). https://www.nytimes.com/2019/02/01/sunday-review/blood-plasma-industry.html

p. 276 **imported from the US** 'The contaminated blood scandal', *The Haemophilia Society*. https://haemophilia.org.uk/public-inquiry/the-infected-blood-inquiry/the-contaminated-blood-scandal/

p. 276 **fifty countries worldwide** 'FAQ: Medical researchers & educators', *Science Care*. https://www.sciencecare.com/resources/faq-medical-researchers-educators

Epilogue

p. 283 **female life expectancy** 'National life tables – life expectancy in the UK: 2018 to 2020', *Office for National Statistics* (23 September 2021). https://www.ons.gov.uk/peoplepopulationandcommunity/birthsdeathsandmarriages/lifeexpectancies/bulletins/nationallifetablesunitedkingdom/2018to2020

Index

References in *italics* indicate images.